The

Saucy Sisters'

GUIDE TO WINE

Barbara Nowak & Beverly Wichman

NEW AMERICAN LIBRARY

The
Saucy Sisters'

GUIDE TO WINE

New American Library
Published by New American Library, a division of Penguin Group (USA) Inc.,
375 Hudson Street, New York, New York 10014, U.S.A.
Penguin Books Ltd, 80 Strand, London WC2R 0RL, England
Penguin Books Australia Ltd, 250 Camberwell Road,
Camberwell, Victoria 3124, Australia
Penguin Books Canada Ltd, 10 Alcorn Avenue, Toronto, Ontario, Canada M4V 3B2
Penguin Books (N.Z.) Ltd, Cnr Rosedale and Airborne Roads,
Albany, Auckland 1310, New Zealand

Penguin Books Ltd, Registered Offices: 80 Strand, London WC2R 0RL, England

First published by New American Library, a division of Penguin Group (USA) Inc.

First Printing, March 2004
10   9   8   7   6   5   4

REGISTERED TRADEMARK—MARCA REGISTRADA

LIBRARY OF CONGRESS CATALOGING-IN-PUBLICATION DATA:

Nowak, Barbara.
The Saucy Sisters' guide to wine / Barbara Nowak and Beverly Wichman.
p.   cm.
Includes index.
ISBN 0-451-20989-3
1. Wine and wine making—Handbooks, manuals, etc.   I. Wichman, Beverly.
II. Title.
TP548.N68 2004   641.2'2—dc22   2003019340

Set in Minion
Designed by Katy Riegel

Printed in the United States of America

To Mom and Dad

Acknowledgments

One beautiful April evening we were dining at Bayard's in New York's Wall Street area with our good friend and frequent radio guest Nancy Dunnan (author of *Dunnan's Guide to Your Invest-ment$, Never Call Your Broker on Monday, The Amy Vanderbilt Complete Book of Etiquette* and scores of other financial and travel books) and engaging in some serious bad-girl chitchat. As we sipped what we all considered to be a quite lusty Châteauneuf-du-Pape (Château de Beaucastel), Nancy turned to us and said, "The Saucy Sisters should write a girl's guide to wine." "Brilliant idea!" we said. And that was the beginning.

Turning concept into reality, of course, was something else. All we had to do was find an agent, get a publisher . . . and figure out how to write a book on wine without putting our readers to sleep. The stars must have been aligned when we sent our book proposal to agents because the goddesses sent us June Clark. Before work-ing with June, we never understood why authors and actors were always publicly thanking their agents. Now we know. June has not only been our most fervent advocate, she's become our soul sister. From our first meeting in New York at Artisanal over wine (125 to choose from) to lunch at Barolo (Batasiolo Barolo) to dinner at Amarone (Arano Amarone) to a reunion at Nashville's F. Scott's (Saintsbury Reserve Pinot Noir), we've shared countless fun hours talking about books, food, wine—and, naturally, men.

Through June's representation we landed a book deal with the Penguin Group. Our first meeting with Claire Zion, NAL's editorial director, just about blew us away. Claire's enthusiasm for our project was so unexpected and so contagious that we paid almost no attention to the lively Vietti Roero Arneis that we were drinking.

Now we had to get down to writing the book. Our previous collaborations on books and radio shows had been easy. After all, we're sisters. And for years we've lived only a few miles apart. But this venture was going to be more of a challenge. During the events leading up to signing our book contract, Beverly moved eight hundred miles away, which meant that our primary research (i.e., wine tasting) would have to be shared by e-mail and over the phone. This took drinking and dialing to new dimensions.

Not all of our research came from personal experience. Because we hosted a radio show for five years, we had the good fortune to interview lots of wine experts and connoisseurs whose professional advice we treasured. Dorothy Gaiter and John Brecher—whose *Wall Street Journal* "Tastings" column and books (*The Wall Street Journal Guide to Wine* and *Love by the Glass*) have, deservedly, made them celebrities—taught us that wine is part of life. Their lifelong enjoyment and chronicling of their wine experiences convinced us that the story of wine could be told from a girl's perspective.

Joe Davis, winemaker and owner of Arcadian Winery (Arcadian Pinot Noir Sleepy Hollow Vineyard and Arcadian Pinot Noir Bien Nacido Vineyard), shared with us his extraordinary passion for wine and grape growing. Joe took us to his Santa Ynez vineyards in California to touch the vines and feel the beauty of the hills, to do some first-time barrel tasting of his finest Pinot Noirs and to spend a languorous lunch together at the Los Olivos Café while savoring some Brewer Clifton Blanc de Blanc and a bottle of Verdad Albariño.

Korbel president Gary Heck and director of public relations Margie Healy have joined us as captivating radio guests and occasional promotional partners since we first became the Saucy Sisters. They have eloquently expressed our shared belief that everything in life is improved with a little bit of bubbly. Our family has celebrated almost every life event with a bottle (or case) of Korbel Brut.

Vickie Turner, wine broker, noted Nashville wine personality and friend, brought many winemakers to our show and helped introduce us to some stunning wines like Mitch Cosentino's The Novelist and The Zin, Jean-Noël Fourmeaux's Château Potelle Cabernet Sauvignon VGS, Jeff Gordon's Gordon Brothers Merlot, and Tom Huggins's Eola Hills (Oregon) Cabernet Sauvignon.

Carolyn Wente, president of Wente Vineyards, shared her personal stories of growing up on the country's oldest family-owned vineyard and her first tastes of wine. She took us on a tour of the beautiful Livermore Valley and had us sample, among other memorable wines, Wente Chardonnay and Murrieta's Well Zinfandel.

Contrary to what most of our friends think, our wine research was more than a series of bacchanalia. We relied heavily on experts in the field. Notable among them is Ralph Whiteway, who, as a wine professional, stand-up comedian and creative writer, reviewed all of our drafts. We wish we had the nerve to include all of his delicious, irreverent and outrageous suggestions. Ralph offered us much more than literary advice. He brought a different wine (or two) to each of our review sessions. Because of Ralph, we were introduced to Gundlach Bundschu Chardonnay, Domaine Laroche Chablis, Adelsheim Vineyard Chardonnay, Verdillac White

Bordeaux, Delbeck Champagne, Dark Star Cabernet Sauvignon, Estancia Pinot Noir, Rodney Strong Symmetry, Sanford Vin Gris... Oh well, maybe *bacchanalia* does apply in this case.

Tommy Bernard, owner of Horizon Wine & Spirits, opened up his wine library to us and allowed us free rein. All the while we were hoping he'd turn us loose in his vast wine warehouse. While that didn't happen, Nancy Wempe (the *real* power at Horizon) packed samples for us to take home. Trefethen Dry Riesling and St. Francis Old Vines Zinfandel made particularly memorable doggie bags.

Two prominent physicians helped guide us through the maze of information regarding wine and women's health. Dr. Fred Freitag, physician with the Diamond Headache Clinic in Chicago and wine enthusiast and winemaker, provided clarity for the mystery of wine and the wine headache. And Dr. Michael Talbot, Nashville physician specializing in women's health and weight management, gave us insight into the medical realities of wine's effects on our bodies.

For a couple of the less-familiar wine-producing countries—namely Austria and South Africa—we relied on two experts: Judy Collins of Austrian Specialty Wine Company and Lisa Hough, president of Cape Wineland Tours. They're such advocates of their respective countries that we were ready to pack our bags even before drinking their wines.

Organizing all the material for this book would have driven both of us back to drinking Boone's Farm had it not been for Beverly's Six Sigma training at Atlantic Envelope Company. Its methodology was indispensable for outlining our stories, facts and data.

Before we dared submit our manuscript to the publisher, we wanted some experts to review what we'd written. But who would have both the knowledge and the patience to do the job? David Gay, operations manager and wine specialist at Cool Springs Wines and Spirits in Franklin, Tennessee, not only read every word but gave us valuable advice on every chapter. He also steered us to

Velletri Rosso Reserva and Alamos Bonarda, just two of his many delicious, well-priced, out-of-the-mainstream wine suggestions.

With all the i's dotted and all the t's crossed, we sent in our manuscript. Our work was done at last . . . or so we thought. We had a new editor, Laura Cifelli (whom we had not yet met), who would undoubtedly have some ideas of her own to add. With some trepidation, we decided it was time for a face-to-face meeting with her. We introduced ourselves over lunch and wine (Les Jalets, Crozes-Hermitage) at the Cub Room in SoHo. Laura had just the right offbeat sense of humor to appreciate our book and more than enough experience in the business to give us practical and positive feedback. Her input made our book even better. Whew!

There might not even be a book without the encouragement of family and friends. Paul Nowak, Barbara's husband, has—for years—demonstrated his good nature by putting up with *two* Saucy Sisters and has guided us in important legal and business matters. His taste in wine, however, tends toward Corona. Our brother, Jeff Wichman, is the quintessential Cab guy (see Chapter 2): big heart and lots of character. Thanks to his generosity and good taste, we've had the opportunity to drink some of his Silver Oak Napa Valley Cabernet Sauvignon.

When it comes to sharing a bottle or two of wine, our friends are the best. It doesn't take much Santa Margarita Pinot Grigio for Joseph Collins to launch us into riotous laughter with his stories of the stage. And then there are certain men who seem to be born wine snobs. A few we love and most we love to hate. Jim Zawick mastered the wine snob title long before its time, but we love him for it. He's the only guy we know who will willingly open a bottle of 1995 Château Lafite-Rothschild after the group has already emptied four bottles of a lesser name.

Writing can be a lonely endeavor, but we both had companions to keep us going when the going got tough. Our everyday liquid companions (Banrock Station Sparkling Chardonnay for Barbara and Pine Ridge Chenin Blanc–Viognier for Beverly) kept us happy and under budget. But, certainly, our most loyal companions were our four-legged *children*—Sheba, Duke, Slasher, Sneaky, Daisy, Rocky and Azucena. Their gratuitous kisses, their demands for attention, their lying on our feet and sitting on our papers provided us with necessary diversions and helped us maintain our sense of humor.

We've drunk fine wines and we've drunk some not-so-fine. For us, it's really the pleasure of the company. There could be no better company than our mom and dad. We've shared stories, jokes, tears, songs, memories and expressions of love—all over a glass of wine. Our parents are like all fine wines. While they improve with age, they're meant to be enjoyed every day.

Our sincere thanks to all of you! *Nunc est bibendum!*

Contents

Chapter 1

∼∼∼

The Way to Wine...

AN INTRODUCTION

ATTENTION, GIRLFRIEND: You're about to become a wine diva. Being a diva means drinking what you like—with apologies to no one. It means boldly exploring new wine-tasting frontiers. It means savoring every wine experience regardless of the wine's superiority or mediocrity—but recognizing the difference.

THE BENEFITS OF WINE KNOWLEDGE

So you don't know what wine to order and don't know where to start? Believe us, gaining wine smarts isn't as intimidating as you think. It's easier than interpreting your daily horoscope. And it could be your entrée to a world of greater popularity, love, sex, health and beauty. No, we're not kidding.

There was a time, we're not ashamed to say, when we couldn't have told you the difference between a Meursault and a Merlot. We were just siblings with a shared genetic passion for the fermented juice of the grape. We weren't particularly discriminating. But these days we have a much better appreciation for what we're actually tasting.

We grew up in a household where wine was the norm as an accompaniment to meals. As such, the wine played second fiddle to the food. Years later when we became restaurant writers and radio show hosts, food was again our main focus. We don't recall the exact moment of the epiphany. It may have been during the interview of a winemaker who brought samples of his wares for an on-air tasting. But what we discovered was that wine could stand on its own and deliver previously unimaginable nuances of taste. It was the beginning of an exhilarating—and never-ending—educational journey.

We're not saying you have to become a connoisseur. You don't have to be an expert to enjoy drinking wine, but a little bit of knowledge can be a good thing. It's like watching football. Some of us couldn't tell a draw play from a screen pass from a clip. And what's more, we don't care. It's enough for us that we recognize which team is which, which direction the ball is headed, and which cheerleaders are sporting breast implants. Even without knowing much about the game, when our team wins, we celebrate just as hard.

We apply the same attitude to wine: You don't have to know about *terroir*, appellations or vintages to appreciate the taste of a good wine. You just need to know what you like. You need to know what tastes good to you and what doesn't. If you like the way it tastes, it's a good wine. Winemakers will tell you, as they've told us, they can only lay claim to what's in the bottle. When it comes to taste, you're the judge.

But learning something about wine does have advantages. Here's what it's done for us:

- *It freed us to be adventurous.* It opened up a whole new world of wines to try. Now, it's not that we haven't always had adventurous spirits. It's just that we're also thrifty. Who wants to go out on an expensive limb by trying new wines that could possibly be *horrible*? Not us. We want some degree of certainty that we'll actually *like* what we're spending our hard-earned money on. Once we learned, for example, that most white wines from France's Burgundy region are made from Chardonnay grapes, we had an expectation of what they'd taste like. Sometimes we were surprised when we tried them . . . but surprised in a positive way.

- *It gave us confidence in the face of snooty waiters and insufferable wine snobs* (Mostly men, by the way. Have you noticed?). We found that the intimidation we were feeling was really self-imposed. Like a lot of women, we hate to look foolish or uninformed. Armed with a little knowledge, we suddenly had respect from so-called experts. Far from being a dangerous thing, a little knowledge gave us the self-assurance to talk about what we know, ask questions and learn more.

- *It showed us that wine intimidation isn't solely a female phenomenon.* We've witnessed the beads of sweat slowly trickle down the faces of successful businessmen when confronted with the responsibility of ordering wine. But, hey, they're big boys. They can go get their own book.

- *It made dining out much more fun.* We learned about the "three-to-four" rule from our friends Dorothy Gaiter and John Brecher, authors of *The Wall Street Journal* "Tastings" column. When faced with the momentous task of selecting a bottle of wine from a restaurant's massive list, Dottie and John suggest choosing three or four in your price range and asking your server to describe them. Then watch him closely. (Of course, that's the fun!) No matter what he says, his body language will alert you to which one is best.

- *And,* most important, *it made us much more sought after at cocktail parties than all the model-thin waifs combined.*

So, stick with us and we'll show you the way to wine.

DO YOU HAVE WHAT IT TAKES TO JOIN
THE SAUCY SISTERHOOD OF WINE DIVAS?

1. The president of the company has assigned you the task of selecting the wines for an upcoming reception. Do you:

    a. Go home and cry.

    b. Call the wine manager at the liquor store for advice.

    c. Spend two weeks researching on the Internet.

    d. Buy some bottles, call up your friends and try them for yourselves.

2. You're hosting a dinner at a restaurant for clients. Do you:

    a. Order the most expensive bottle on the wine list. After all, it's on the expense account.

    b. Take a chance and order a wine that's had good word of mouth but that you've never tasted.

    c. Order a nationally advertised brand because you know your guests will recognize it.

    d. Order the wine that you'd like to drink.

3. A female associate with some wine-tasting experience asks you for a wine recommendation. Do you:

    a. Ask her what kinds of wines she usually enjoys.

    b. Give her the titles of some good wine books and tell her to do her own research.

    c. Give her the names of wines she'll never be able to afford.

    d. Tell her about some of your favorites.

4. At parties where wine is served, what do others say to you—or about you?

a. I want what she's having.

b. What's your expert opinion of this wine?

c. Give her a little wine, and she's the life of the party!

d. You'd never serve this swill, would you?

SCORING YOUR ANSWERS:

1. a = 0, b = 3, c = 2, d = 4

While a true wine diva welcomes the opinions of others, she trusts her own palate above all. She likes to experience the wines for herself, but would just as soon make a party out of it rather than taste in solitude.

2. a = 0, b = 4, c = 1, d = 3

A real diva is gutsy. She's never boring with her wine choices. She's willing to take calculated risks. What's the worst that can happen? The wine will be terrible, and she'll go to her fallback position of ordering a personal favorite.

3. a = 3, b = 0, c = 0, d = 4

A wine diva plays well with others. She isn't threatened by other wine divas. She seeks them out and learns from them. She nurtures divas in the making and generously shares her knowledge.

4. a = 4, b = 2, c = 4, d = 1

A wine diva radiates excitement. Her enthusiasm about wine attracts others to her. She is never pretentious and only hopes others will behave in a similar fashion.

INTERPRETING YOUR SCORE:

11–12 points	Your membership in the sisterhood is a foregone conclusion. You've got the confidence, compassion and innate party-girl temperament to make the grade.
8–10 points	Your adventurous spirit, sensitivity and personal charm are all-important attributes for being a true diva. You've got great potential!
1–7 points	Your willingness to learn will take you far. Not all divas test well.

THE PHYSIOLOGY OF TASTE

One of your girlfriends dresses in pleated pants, a cashmere turtleneck and a single-breasted blazer from Talbots. Conservative, classic, preppy. Another friend wears a black bomber jacket with fur sleeves over a tight skirt by Prada. Avant-garde, nonconformist, sexy. They couldn't be more different, but both of them have good taste.

Wine is very much like fashion. There's no absolute right or wrong. It's all about discovering tastes you love. When it comes to wine, however, there are physiological differences that affect our choices. No two people experience flavor exactly the same way. We have unequal abilities to taste and, consequently, unique flavor preferences.

Not only are there differences *among* individuals, there are differences *within* individuals over time. Have you ever just flipped over a fabulous wine while you were out with friends, then been acutely disappointed when you tried the same wine at home alone? How good something tastes is affected by our moods, by how hungry or tired we are and by our health. It's affected by our outside environment—like the temperature and humidity—and by our internal environment. What else we eat at the same time—whether a spicy bowl of chili or a sugary Krispy Kreme—will alter our taste perceptions. It's no wonder you won't find consensus in a crowd of wine tasters.

WINE BAR:
Looking for a drinking partner?

Foods have an unmistakable influence on the way a wine tastes. Wine accompanied with a salty snack will taste different than with a spicy entrée or sweet dessert. To experiment on your individual tastes and wine's effect on foods, try our fun popcorn game. Divide some plain popcorn into five separate batches, then add one of the following ingredients to each batch:

butter
salt
garlic powder
brown sugar
cayenne powder

Open a bottle of wine—any wine. Take a sip before you start eating and note how the wine tastes. Now sample the butter-flavored popcorn, take another sip of wine, and observe how different the wine tastes. Move on to the other popcorn batches and you'll experience even more taste changes. Only you can decide which is the best drinking partner.

Let's Get Physical

Your attraction to a wine involves the four physical sensations of sight, smell, taste and touch. Each element will give you part of the picture, but using all the senses in combination will help you identify what it is about a particular wine that you like.

Come to think of it, we use these same senses when we determine whether we're attracted to a man: sight to check out the way he looks, smell to get an idea of his unique fragrance, taste of his lips with that first kiss, and touch when you feel his body next to yours. One sense alone isn't enough to decide if there's a romantic attraction. Likewise, we need all those senses to adequately assess a wine.

Use these four basic physical perceptions to see if a wine—or a man—is worthy of you.

You See:

The man you see across a crowded room is an excruciatingly handsome hunk right out of the pages of *GQ*. Your expectation is that his character will match his looks. Ditto for wine. If the wine you're looking at is visually appealing, you expect it's going to taste as good as it looks.

You Smell:

Just a whiff of Aramis can bring back vivid memories of a long-ago romance and steamy weekends together at the beach. The sense of smell is the most acute of all the senses and the most easily stimulated. It's a thousand times more sensitive than the sense of taste. Consequently, what's called *flavor* is really 75 percent smell and only 25 percent taste. That's why when your nose is stuffed up from a cold you can't taste—or really even enjoy—food.

Of the seventeen thousand aromas that have been catalogued, humans can recognize about ten thousand. We smell aromas either directly by inhaling through the nose or indirectly by inhaling through the interior nasal passage at the back of the mouth. Wine consists of over two hundred different chemical compounds, many of them identical or similar to ones found in fruits, vegetables, herbs, spices and other substances. So, when we sniff wine, we can often smell these other things.

You Taste:

Your tongue may be an indispensable instrument of passion in French kissing, but its role in tasting is more limited. In comparison to the huge number of aromas you can identify, only four primary tastes are generally recognized: sweetness, saltiness, acidity and bitterness. (Sounds like the stages of a relationship gone bad. . . .) The tip of your tongue registers sweetness first. Salt is detected just behind that, in an area comprising about a third of the tongue. Acidity registers next as a sour taste along the tongue's side edges. Bitterness is sensed at the back of the tongue near the throat. The center of the tongue has a mixture of all these different receptors, but in lower concentrations.

You'll rarely encounter a wine that tastes salty. But sweetness and acidity are two of the most important measurements of a wine. The two tastes actually balance each other. Think of lemonade. Without any sugar, straight lemon juice and water would make us pucker up big time. The more sugar we add to the mixture, the less noticeable the acidity becomes.

A fifth taste, called *umami*, has been isolated and is the subject of much debate among food scientists. It appears to act as a flavor enhancer and deserves mention in a discussion of wine because it shows up during processes like ripening, aging and fermentation. It gives food a "completeness" of flavor or "delicious" quality.

Monosodium glutamate (MSG) is an example of umami. Forget the headaches for a moment; never consumed alone but used in combination with other foods, MSG brings out the flavorful qualities of those foods.

You Feel:

Through the sense of touch, you can tell whether your man is hot or cold, rough or smooth, heavy or light, dry or wet. The same holds true for evaluating wine. The way wine feels in your mouth will tell you a lot about its nature.

If you experience a mouth-drying, astringent sensation on your gums and inside your cheeks—like you just drank some oversteeped tea—you're sensing the wine's tannins. Tannins come mainly from grape skins and oak barrels and are often cited in relation to red wine. Tannins are key to the graceful aging of red wines. In young red wines tannins can be obvious and "in your face," but they mellow over time. If a wine tastes too tannic, you may be drinking it before it has had time to mature.

If you feel a burning sensation in your nose and a hot feeling at your throat and on the roof of your mouth, you're experiencing a high alcohol level. Wine is all about balance. If you're subjected to too much alcohol, you won't notice or be able to appreciate the wine's other qualities. Our advice is: When you're looking for that high-octane experience, a tequila shooter is the drink of choice.

Much ado is made about a wine's *body*, the impression of its weight or fullness in your mouth. Now, a full-bodied wine doesn't actually weigh any more than a light-bodied one, but it feels heavier in your mouth. Think of the difference in how cream and skim milk feel. Not all wines strive to be full-bodied—nor should they. Some lighter styles are just meant to be thinner.

HOW TO TALK ABOUT WINE

People who get excited about wine like to talk about it. Trouble is, words fail utterly to communicate taste. Worse yet, there's a snob element in wine circles that likes to make wine descriptions mysterious and pretentious. The famous James Thurber *New Yorker* cartoon perfectly captured this phenomenon, with a character at the dinner table remarking, "It's a naive domestic burgundy, but I think you'll be amused by its presumption." Here's our advice when you're put in a position of having to comment on a wine: *Do not use words at all unless absolutely necessary.*

Facial expressions can be very effective: a smile, nod or raised eyebrows for affirmative responses, a frown or shake of the head for negative responses. An enthusiastic "Mmmmm" will indicate that you're impressed, and, conversely, a disapproving "Hmmmm" will imply just the opposite. If you're absolutely compelled to respond in a complete sentence but you don't know what to say, commenting on the wine's color is always safe: "This Pinot Noir is the same beautiful color as Dorothy's ruby slippers."

There are times, however, when words—as inadequate as they may be—are essential. Like when a waiter or wine-store owner asks about your preferences. Telling him to show you something "as blond as Cher's new wig" just won't cut it—or get you a wine that you're likely to enjoy. We need ways to describe the features we appreciate in a wine, and language is all we have.

No official wine-tasting language exists. There are no tasting terms unique to wine. The best we can do is compare wine to other tastes and smells that are familiar to us.

Become a Sniffing Detective!

Now's your time to start sniffing around. Smelling a wine's aromas is an essential part of enjoying and discussing the qualities of a wine. But our society doesn't make it easy to discern true aromas. We're advised to disguise the odors on our bodies, in our homes and cars and even of our pets. Manufactured perfumed fragrances are everywhere. But let's be real. Do any of these soaps, shampoos, candles or air fresheners *really* smell like a freshly squeezed orange, a rose right out of your garden or the ocean breeze that you remember? It's no wonder our sense of smell of all things natural has been numbed.

When is the last time you picked up a bunch of asparagus and smelled it, or stood in a park and breathed in the aromas of the woods around you, or enjoyed the intoxicating smell of a fine chocolate before popping it into your mouth? Just these simple acts of recognizing and appreciating everyday smells will help you become a better wine sniffer.

Wine's aromas are similar to those smells that surround you in your yard and garden, your neighborhood park, your local fruit and vegetable stand, your spice cabinet, and yes, even Fido's favorite wool rug. When you stick your nose in a wineglass, think of these smells. Your yard and garden: grass, mint, rose, geranium. Your neighborhood park: pine, oak, musk. Your local fruit and vegetable stand: apple, grapefruit, raspberry, asparagus. Your spice cabinet: pepper, nutmeg, cinnamon. Fido's favorite wool rug: yes, wine too has some pungent odors.

All of these and many more are possible wine aromas. One thing we know for certain is the more we sniff around, the more discerning and knowledgeable we become in detecting the smells of a particular wine. And every once in a while we uncover a new wine smell—which proves that anyone can develop her smelling capabilities.

Taste Is Touchy-Feely

The descriptive words for tastes are not as precise as they are for aromas. Take "dry," for example. Technically, dryness in a wine is simply the absence of sugar. Therefore, the opposite of a dry wine is a sweet wine. For the most part, red wines are dry. By contrast, white wines range from bone dry to dry to medium dry to medium sweet to sweet. Too many categories? Use these three instead: dry, off dry (just a hint of sweetness), and sweet.

You probably think that having grown up in a sugar-saturated culture where Twinkies and Cokes are part of a normal everyday diet, you'd recognize sweetness when you tasted it. But many wine drinkers—especially beginners—confuse sweetness with fruitiness. Test your ability to spot sweetness by holding your nose the next time you sip a white wine. If the wine truly is sweet, you'll taste the sweetness on your tongue, instead of sensing the aroma of the fruit.

Then there are the tactile terms. What do *body, big, full, hard, hot* and *finish* remind you of? Hey, get your mind out of the bedroom! The answer's "wine." How about *flabby, heavy* and *soft*? (We'll ignore any unkind remarks about our thighs.) Yes . . . "wine" again. The impression wine leaves in the mouth makes for some really touchy-feely descriptions that can only be understood— if at all—through experience.

TOP 9 WINE-TASTING TERMS THAT YOU SHOULD KNOW

Sure, there are lots of words and phrases wine tasters use to try to explain what they're experiencing. But if you know these few words, you can talk to absolutely anyone about absolutely any wine.

Balance . . . in wine means that it has all its components—acid, alcohol, fruit, tannins—working together so that none of the elements overpowers the others.

Body . . . is a description of a wine's style rather than a comment on its quality. It's the perception of fullness or texture in the mouth due primarily to the wine's alcohol. The more potent the wine, the more full-bodied it will be. At the other end of the spectrum, a wine that lacks sufficient body is described as *watery* or *thin.*

Complex . . . wine has layers and nuances of flavors. Like an interesting man, a complex wine is not one-dimensional and often achieves complexity with aging. A complex wine is also said to have *depth.*

Crisp . . . is a term that describes good acidity and taste without excessive sweetness—kind of like an apple. The relatively high acidity, while noticeable, doesn't overwhelm the wine's other components.

Dry . . . is the opposite of sweet. In a wine that's completely dry, all the sugar from the grapes has been converted to alcohol during fermentation. There are degrees of dryness, and a wine can still be dry with some unfermented sugar left over. If you taste just a hint of sweetness in the wine, it's said to be *off dry. Dry* is in vogue, and some people don't want to admit their fondness for sweet wines. We figure that's why the term "off dry" is used instead of "a little sweet."

Finish . . . is a wine's aftertaste. The flavor or aroma that lingers after you've swallowed the wine (or spit it out, heaven forbid) is supposed to be a sign of high quality. *Finish* is also referred to as *length*. A long finish is the ideal. A short—or nonexistent—finish is not good . . . unless, of course, you didn't like the taste of the wine in the first place.

Fruity . . . is used to describe the flavor or aroma of fruits in wine. The flavors aren't limited to grapes but encompass others such as lemons, blackberries, peaches, bananas and pineapples. *Fruity* has been used as a marketing euphemism for *sweet* for those wine drinkers who have been made to feel unsophisticated for liking sweetness in their wines. But *fruity* and *sweet* aren't really the same thing.

Oaky . . . is the flavor or aroma resulting from a wine's aging in oak barrels—sometimes described as *vanilla*. When the insides of the barrels have been charred, the consequent flavor has been called *smoky* or *toasty*. Because of the high cost of oak barrels, some winemakers use less expensive oak chips to add an oaky character to the wine.

Tannic . . . describes the mouth sensations—dry and puckery—attributable to tannins in the wine. Tannins are found mostly in red wines. They play an important part in helping wines age gracefully and will, in fact, mellow with age. So a young wine that tastes very tannic may be very pleasant after a few years. As a tannic youngster, the wine might also be called *hard*.

WHY WINES TASTE THE WAY THEY DO: WINEMAKING

Wine is just fermented grape juice. And fermentation is a natural process. So why don't all Chardonnays taste the same, or all Cabernets? That's like asking why all pizzas don't taste the same. First, it's the ingredients. Is your pizza made with fresh tomatoes

TOP 10 MOST MEANINGLESS AND IRRITATING WINE-TASTING TERMS

How do wine writers come up with these adjectives? The words may create impressions—but not about the wines they're supposed to describe. Read some reviews and just try to explain what various descriptors mean.

TERM	BETTER DESCRIBES . . .
Leathery	Overcooked meat at the Outback Steakhouse
Brawny	Paper towels
Sterile	Post-vasectomy condition
Taut	Janet Jackson's abs
Polished	Well-maintained shoes
Raw	Eddie Murphy uncensored
Lustrous	Four-carat diamond
Animated	Minnie Mouse
Mystical	Calling John Edwards
Finesse	Tiger Woods on the putting green

or canned tomato sauce? Is it plain or does it have mushrooms and Italian sausage? Then there's the role of the cook. Does she twirl and toss the dough and bake it on a pizza stone, or does she thaw a ready-made crust and put it into a toaster oven? Price, too, always comes into play. Is this a gourmet pizza at Spago or a pie delivered from Domino's? Depending on your objectives, your personal taste and your expectations, one is not necessarily "better" than the other. But they sure are different.

In winemaking you've got the same elements: the ingredients (the grapes), the cook (the winemaker who makes the grapes into wine), and the equipment (type of barrels, for example). Sometimes a winemaker—or wine company—will grow the grapes and make the wine. Other times growers will sell their grapes to others to make the wine.

Grape growing has a huge impact on what you eventually taste in the wine. The more grapes a particular grapevine produces, the less intense the flavors of the grapes will be, and the lower the quality of the end product. A "lower yield" (as growers refer to it) of grapes through pruning produces better grapes and, ultimately, better wines.

Grapes need to be picked at perfect ripeness. The difficulty is knowing just when that time has arrived. It is a brief stage and is a subjective judgment by the winemaker depending on the style of wine to be made. As grapes ripen, their acid levels decrease, while sugar, color and tannins increase. The wine's need for acidity has to be balanced with the advantages of further ripening.

There are two stages of winemaking, both of which have an effect on the taste of the wine: fermentation (when the juice turns into wine) and maturation (when the wine ages). Once the grapes have been crushed, fermentation can begin. Yeasts on the skin of the grapes convert the grape sugar into alcohol and carbon dioxide. Red wines are fermented with their skins, seeds and pulp to extract color and tannins. Whites are not. Fermentation can proceed until there is no residual sugar left (in which case the wine is bone dry), or it can be stopped at some point along the way to make wines at various levels of sweetness from off dry to extremely sweet. Fermentation temperature also has an effect. The lower the temperature, the longer fermentation takes and the more fruitiness in the resultant wine.

Oak barrels—used during fermentation or during maturation or both—influence a wine's flavor. The barrels leach tannins into the wine and impart the flavors specific to that wood. If the barrels have been charred on the inside, the flavor will be *smoky* or *toasty*. New barrels will pass on a stronger flavor than older ones because barrels lose their oakiness with age and with use. Not all wines are fermented or aged in oak barrels, of course. Today, most wineries use stainless-steel tanks, which are chemically neutral—neither adding nor diminishing flavors.

After fermentation, a coarse sediment called *lees* accumulates at the bottom of the barrel or fermentation vessel. This sludgelike material consists mainly of dead yeast cells and small grape particles. (Sounds appetizing, no?) The wine is usually separated from the lees after fermentation, but a winemaker can decide to extend the lees contact for further aging in order to produce a wine with a more complex flavor. This is done more so with whites than with reds.

A secondary fermentation, called *malolactic* fermentation, can take place, which changes the nature of the acids in the wine. A winemaker can encourage malolactic fermentation or can take steps to avoid it. Wines that undergo this process are softer and less acidic, but also less fruity. Most red wines go through this process, but it's definitely a matter of winemaker preference for whites.

Before bottling a wine, a winemaker can choose to create his own new wine recipe by blending barrels of wine. Winemakers producing a single varietal wine, like Merlot, will often mix different barrels of the same wine to achieve one homogeneous lot of wine. Other winemakers will blend different wines to produce a composite that's better than any of the wines individually. They may combine different varieties, different regions, different kinds of barrels or even different vintages. The result is a wine with its own unique personality.

Some wines are created to be drunk and enjoyed immediately. Others are made to age and develop their flavors over time. Once a wine has matured in the barrel and been bottled, it may require further aging in the bottle depending on the type of wine. Most whites, rosés and light reds are at their best soon after bottling. At the other end of the spectrum are long-lived reds that can improve over years—even decades. But all wines at some point begin to deteriorate. Drinking a wine before—or after—its time will have the ultimate effect on its taste.

WOMEN'S SPECIAL RELATIONSHIP TO WINE

Women have an affinity for wine that goes beyond just liking to drink it out of pretty glasses. Women, because of real anatomical differences from men, can experience a heightened taste of wine. And as she ages, drinking wine can actually help a woman be healthier and stronger.

Women approach wine on their own terms. We're more likely to learn through experimentation and personal experience and less likely to rely on experts. We want to buy what's good, but we also want to know where to find bargains. Wine savvy isn't a man's domain, and never has been. Wine divas have existed throughout the ages.

Women in Wine History

The way we look at it, there would be no wine at all without women—or at least one woman. According to an ancient Persian fable, a lady of the court was responsible for the discovery of wine. This princess had lost favor with the king. We don't know why, she just had—although we suspect the king, like lots of guys, had a roving eye. She tried to poison herself by eating some table grapes that had spoiled in a jar. Well, you can guess what happened. She became light-headed and giddy and then passed out. When she awoke, rather than a hangover she had a whole new positive outlook on life. The king was so taken by her new attitude that she was back in favor. And needless to say, the king personally sought out the source of her metamorphosis, which he then shared with the rest of his kingdom.

Fast-forward to the fourth century B.C. If you've reached a certain age, you'll remember the Italian Chianti bottles that were wrapped in straw, which, after you downed the wine, made really cool candlestick holders. The bottle is called a *fiasco*.

When the Etruscans were first developing glass production, they were elated to find out they could blow a bottle in the shape of a round bubble. The only trouble was, when the bubble cooled and they tried to stand it up, it fell over. To help them out of this *fiasco*, they called on their women to weave flat straw bases to hold the bottles. The women saved the day! Our only question is why men would continue to make bottles that wouldn't stand on their own.

According to local lore the great French white Burgundy, Corton-Charlemagne, owes its existence not to the powerful emperor Charlemagne but to his wife! It seems the vineyards were planted with red-wine grapes whose wines made a mess of the emperor's white beard. You can imagine how disgusted his wife must have become having to look at a perpetually stained beard. So she nagged and nagged until he ripped out the vines and replanted the vineyards with white-wine grapes. Voilà! Corton-Charlemagne.

Champagne—one of our favorite subjects—is another product of an inventive woman. The trick with making Champagne is removing the yeast sediment that forms in the bottle during secondary fermentation without losing all the bubbles at the same time. Madame Clicquot, a twenty-seven-year-old widow (*veuve* in French) who took over her husband's Champagne house at his death in 1805, came up with the solution that's still used today. She had her cellar carpenter cut a series of holes in her dining room table so that the bottles could be positioned upside down at a 45-degree angle. In this way, and after several weeks of turning and re-angling the bottles, all the sediment collected in the neck and could then be removed quickly.

Veuve Clicquot is one of the French Champagnes at the top of our wish lists. Another is Bollinger. Now, Lily Bollinger was a woman after our own hearts. Another Champagne widow, she took control of her husband's Champagne house in 1941 during the German occupation of France and doubled production. But her most endearing contribution was her response to an English reporter who asked her when she drank Champagne:

> I only drink Champagne when I'm happy and when I'm sad. Sometimes I drink it when I'm alone. When I have company I consider it obligatory. I trifle with it if I am not hungry and drink it when I am. Otherwise I never touch it—unless I'm thirsty.

Women Taste Better

We swear this story is true. We were standing in a group at a wine tasting sipping the wine that had just been poured when a

---

WINE BAR:
Let them drink Champagne with their cake!

Legend has it that the shallow Champagne glass was modeled after Marie Antoinette. It was first formed from wax molds made of her breasts. Given the popularity of breast implants, we have to wonder about the size of the glass if new glasses were made today. It might just make the drink menu at Hooters!

know-it-all on our left said, "It has an aura of smoked plums and an underlying resonance of barnacles." The men around us nodded. The rest of us knew this guy was full of . . . himself.

Even when you understand someone's description of a wine, you may not taste the same flavors. He says it tastes bitter. You say he's crazy. Who's right? Maybe you both are.

Scientists have discovered that anatomical differences in the tongue help explain why he could taste something bitter or sweet and you couldn't. The research says some people are just better tasters, and guess what? They're twice as likely to be women.

People can be classified as nontasters, regular tasters or supertasters. By applying a dye to the tongue, the taste buds become visible and can be counted. Supertasters have more taste buds than other people—as many as one hundred times more taste buds than nontasters. Supertasters perceive more intense tastes. And here's the kicker: Two-thirds of all supertasters are women.

Wine tasting involves more than just taste buds. We were weaned on Champagne, so we believe that, genetics aside, you can develop your taste through exposure and training.

Case in point: Carolyn Wente is president of Wente Vineyards, the oldest family-owned and -operated winery in the country. This fourth-generation Wente told us that her first taste of wine was as a teething infant. Her mother dipped a cork into wine and gave it to her to suck on to relieve her teething pain.

Eva Bertran, executive vice president at Gloria Ferrer Champagne Caves, has Carolyn Wente and the Saucy Sisters beat. She told us her first taste of the vine was when she was one hour old. Her father came to the hospital with a bottle of Champagne (*cava*, to be precise) and gave baby Eva her first drop. It's a tradition that Eva has carried on with her own children.

You can develop your own sense of taste through practice and plenty of drinking—but, please, not all at one time! When professional wine judges take a sip of wine, they don't just swallow it. In fact, sometimes they don't swallow it at all. They swish it around in their mouths to let it warm and to further develop the flavor. They then purse their lips and draw in a small amount of air across the wine. The professionals call this *slurping* ... because, well, that's how it sounds. Here's what actually happens: While in the mouth the bubbles aerate and oxidize the wine, and the saliva breaks down compounds and helps intensify secondary flavors. The aeration vaporizes the aromas so that they can be perceived by the nasal passage at the back of the mouth.

Paying attention to wines' flavors will help enhance your appreciation for the differences in wine styles and varieties. Unlike some professionals, though, we do not participate in spitting. While considered good form and an essential practice at professional tastings where dozens or even hundreds of wines are offered, we find the practice unladylike. And, besides, where's the buzz?

Women, Wine and Commerce

Here's something you may not know: Women are the leading purchasers of wine in the United States. It doesn't matter whether they're single or married, young or old. Women, by an overwhelming margin, are the ones who buy the wine for their households. Any wine retailer will tell you that Monday through Friday, it's women who cruise the aisles. And it's no accident that, in those states where laws permit, wine is available on grocery store shelves, making one-stop shopping that much easier. Now we can pick up dinner ingredients and a wine to match all under the same roof.

In restaurants, the best concept that's come down the pike in recent memory—and one that's been wholeheartedly adopted by women—is *good* wine by the glass. Let us repeat that: *good* wine by the glass. Sure, there may be drawbacks, like opened bottles sitting out for too long. But for the most part, wine by the glass offers us variety and value, and a great opportunity to sample different wines and further our wine knowledge.

In finer restaurants we can get a prix fixe menu that pairs a different wine with each course. That way, we can experiment with unfamiliar wines without spending a fortune. But even when we make our own wine selections, we can feel confident about them. Someone has put considerable time and thought into developing the wine list, and we can rest assured there's no real "dog" on it.

Many marketers think they have us pegged. We admit, in some cases they do. White Zinfandel is definitely a girl's wine—especially older, divorced girls. (We can't explain why. It's what the statistics tell us.) So coming up with so-called lighter and sweeter versions of traditional wine varieties is a trend targeted to females. First White Zin, now White Merlot and White Grenache.

Some winemakers have even created wines with catchy names— like Flirt, Envy and Lust—and colorful labels to attract women to them. Sure, they're gimmicky. And some have little substance, but others are indeed quality wines.

WINE BAR:
Never judge a wine by its label

During our radio show in Nashville, Jean-Noël Fourmeaux, owner of Château Potelle in Napa Valley and the most charming Frenchman we'd ever met, had just described his Zinfandel. Beverly looked at the bottle in front of her and asked what "VGS" on the label stood for. In his most enchanting French accent, he replied, "Very Good Shit."

Diet wine—yes, diet wine—is in aggressive development. It has about one-third the calories and one-half the alcohol of regular wine. Although we personally consider it on the same level as diet beer (no, thank you), it's coming. And we think our female compatriots will welcome it. And, perhaps, help perfect it.

The truth is, quality wines and unique wine products and packaging will continue to attract new wine drinkers. And we wholeheartedly believe most of those discerning wine drinkers will be women.

So let's brush up on our wine skills and drink a toast *to us*!

Chapter 2

~~~~~~

Varietals Are the Spice of Life...

LEARNING ABOUT WINE IS AS MUCH FUN AS LEARNING ABOUT MEN

GRAPES ARE THE STUFF that dreams are made of. If you're looking for the wine of your dreams, it'll help to define exactly what kind of experience you're in search of. Which of these scenarios best describes what you hope to find in the perfect wine?

- Something easy-drinking and uncomplicated that you can quaff at the end of a hectic day, with your feet up, the TV turned on and a glass of the familiar in hand.
- A multidimensional beverage that will challenge all your senses—something that requires thought and multiple tastings to fully appreciate.
- A relatively low alcohol drink that you can sip all night and still keep your wits about you.
- A beverage so big and powerful that it'll really ring your chimes.
- Something subtle and sophisticated that reveals itself slowly over time and whose taste lingers in memory.

• A dependable beverage that you can count on to deliver the same sense of satisfaction every time you drink it.

The saucy wine-drinking girl has all these dreams at one time or another—determined, perhaps, by the moment, the day, the season or the time of the month. She's not about to limit herself or be pigeonholed. She wants it all. And she gets it. She can find love in every glass.

POPULAR VARIETALS

Finding the right wine is like finding the right man: Having a strategy produces more immediate results than leaving it entirely to chance. Men come in all varieties, and so do wines—except that in the world of enology, they're called *varietals*. The strategy begins with determining which varietals are for you. Sampling is the key. You'll know, without anyone else having to tell you, when you've hit on a winner.

A varietal is a wine that's named after the grape variety it's made from, like Chardonnay from the Chardonnay grape or Merlot from the Merlot grape. Here are some popular varietals you're likely to see on a restaurant menu or on your retailer's shelves.

Red Varietals

Cabernet Sauvignon — Considered the king of red wine: dry, complex and long-lasting. Cabernets are definitely keepers. They can sometimes be a little harsh when young and need time to mature. But, boy, when they do, their age is an incredible advantage. They soften with time but retain their classic character.

Malbec — Think of a dark, lush, sleeping giant. Malbec was once relegated to the role of a blending grape, but it's come into its own as a varietal wine in Argentina. Its inky color and robust flavor make it a strong contender for future stardom.

Merlot — Merlot often plays second fiddle to Cabernet Sauvignon. What it lacks in respect, however, it makes up in versatility. It can be successfully blended with other grapes or can produce a high-quality wine all on its own. It's supple, fruity and soft and can be enjoyed when still young.

Pinot Noir — Pinot Noir is a real crowd pleaser. Some extol its adaptability because it's equally at home with a filet of beef or a filet of salmon. Others might say it's a chameleon because the flavor changes so dramatically according to its age or growing conditions. Pinot Noir can be temperamental and challenging to produce, but when it's on its best behavior there's nothing that can compare.

Shiraz/Syrah — Called Shiraz in Australia, this grape is known everywhere else as Syrah. It makes a dark, strong, full-bodied red wine with lots of potential for aging. The Syrah grape thrives in warm climates and is extremely adaptable. It has been grown in France's Rhone Valley since at least Roman times.

Zinfandel — Zins (as we devoted fans affectionately call them) are spicy and full of life. Some are produced in a light, Nouveau style that are ready to drink immediately. Others are more Cabernet-like and get better with age. They all share a mysterious past. Through DNA testing, scientists have found that Zinfandel is identical to Italy's Primitivo grape. They've both been traced back to a wild vine in Croatia.

White Varietals

Chardonnay — Chardonnay is the darling white wine of contemporary society. It's produced all over the world because of its popularity and because the grape is adaptable to many climates. Chardonnays that are aged in oak barrels have a distinctive toasty or smoky essence. But if oak isn't used, the wine will have the fruity flavor inherent in the grape itself. The Chardonnay grape is one of the three allowed to be used in the making of Champagne.

Pinot Gris/Pinot Grigio — With a name like Gris (translation, "gray"), you might think this wine would be boring. Far from it! It's crisp and flavorful with lots of substance. Pinot Gris—and its Italian version, Pinot Grigio—have found a trendy popularity among white-wine drinkers as an alternative to Chardonnay. Pinot Gris is a great match with food—especially seafood—but can easily stand on its own.

Riesling — Rieslings lack the enthusiastic audience of, say, Chardonnays. That may be because they're perceived as being too sweet. Some are sweet, for sure. But many are dry. The common denominator is that they're all light in body, low in alcohol, yet strongly flavored and very long lived.

Sauvignon Blanc — Sauvignon Blanc is friendly and gregarious. It mixes well with foods but is also content to be sipped all by itself. It has an instantly recognizable aroma that some people characterize as "grassy." It's definitely zesty and dry. When it's aged in oak—as is often the case in California—the wine becomes richer and more full-bodied than its unoaked counterparts.

Viognier — Viognier is fashionable and highly regarded, and not always easy to find. There are just not a lot of Viognier grapes around to produce large quantities of wine. Viognier is dry with a floral quality and vibrant flavor.

White Zinfandel — White Zinfandel is not white at all. It's pink. In the United States, it's called a blush wine. In France it would be called a rosé. White Zinfandels found a real niche in the 1980s, especially among women, as a sweet, easy-drinking alternative to other wines.

PLACE NAMES, OR
WHEN IS A VARIETAL *NOT* A VARIETAL?

Tired of solid colors? Bored with monochromatic? Feel like walking on the wild side with stripes and plaids and tie-dyed prints? Well, get out of your varietal-centric mindset. Check out a blend.

WINE BAR:
A rosé by any other name would smell as sweet

Call it blush wine. Call it rosé. Call it pretty in pink. Just don't call it sweet. Sure, lots of White Zinfandels have been sugared up for their fans. But many rosés are dry and off dry. Rosés get their color in one of two ways. One, from the skins of the red grapes they're made from. Just like red wines, the grape juice sits with the crushed grape skins to ferment, only not for very long. Just long enough to kiss the juice with color. Or two, a small amount of red wine is added to the clear juice of a white wine.

Treat rosés like they were white: chill them and drink them young.

Very often grape varieties are mixed together to produce a wine that the winemaker thinks will be better than its individual components. It's called a blend. Winemakers have been blending grapes for centuries and have produced some of the world's most famous wines. They couldn't be named after their grape variety. (Well, they could, but they'd be awfully *long* names.) So, for the most part, winemakers named them after the place where they were made.

In Europe, even single-grape wines are named after the town or region where they're produced. In the Burgundy region of France, for example, reds are usually from the Pinot Noir grape, and whites are from the Chardonnay grape. Yet you won't see the grape varieties listed on the label. Here are some of the more well known wines with place names.

Famous Place Reds

Beaujolais — Beaujolais, named after the important wine region in east central France, is made from the Gamay grape. It's made in a style that's light and fruity and ready to drink while young. Beaujolais Nouveau is ready even earlier. It's released each November after only seven to nine weeks of aging. Complexity is not an issue here.

Bordeaux — While white wines are produced in Bordeaux in southwest France, it's the reds that are responsible for most of the acclaim. They're made by blending particular grapes—primarily Cabernet Sauvignon, Cabernet Franc and Merlot—with occasional additions of Malbec and Petit Verdot. Bordeaux wines are meant for aging. Young ones—say, up to ten years old—can be very dry and tannic. But they mellow with age, developing a softer and more multifaceted flavor.

Châteauneuf-du-Pape — Translated, this means "new castle of the Pope." Why? It's named after the village in France where the summer palace of the Avignon popes was built. This wine is big, rich and full-bodied with a little bit of spiciness thrown in. Its high alcohol level contributes to its intoxicating allure. Long before California Cabernets, it was *the* accepted "steak" wine.

Chianti — Chianti comes from the region of the same name in Tuscany in central Italy. It's a blend of four grape varieties, Sangiovese being the dominant one. This sturdy, dry red wine was once instantly identifiable by its straw-covered bottle. While that bottle still exists, it usually indicates a cheaper, lower-quality Chianti. For the best-quality wine, look for a Chianti Classico, which is consistent from year to year and a great value too. Even better, try a Chianti Classico Riserva, which spends an extra two years in the barrel.

Rioja — For over twenty-five hundred years wine has been produced in Rioja, the major red-wine region in northern Spain. The main grape used in Rioja is Tempranillo, although a few others are allowed for blending. The outstanding characteristic of Rioja wines is their vanilla aroma and taste, which come from their long aging in oak barrels.

Famous Place Whites

Chablis — Don't for a moment think we're talking about big jugs of cheap white wine. Real Chablis comes from a district just a hundred miles from Paris. Real Chablis is made from Chardonnay grapes. Chablis producers rarely use oak—as American Chardonnay producers do—which explains, in part, why Chablis tastes different. You'll find it dry and crisp.

Champagne — It's only Champagne when it comes from the Champagne region of France. Every other effervescent competitor is sparkling wine. The common denominator, of course, is the bubbles. The three grapes used for Champagne are Chardonnay, Pinot Noir and Meunier. The taste can range from dry to sweet and from toasty and nutty to fruity.

Pouilly-Fuissé — Pouilly-Fuissé has a large international following that will pay impressive prices for this French Chardonnay. The soil where the grapes are grown is said to have been enriched by the remains of wild horses from the Stone Age driven from the top of the cliffs above.

Sauternes — Sauternes is a famous French sweet wine made primarily from the Semillon grape. Its sweetness comes from a beneficial mold called *Botrytis cinerea* which, under the right climatic conditions, causes the grapes to shrivel and concentrate their flavors. Because winemakers can't control the weather, botrytis doesn't appear every year, and neither do Sauternes.

Soave — You could call Soave a commoner. This dry white wine from northeast Italy is produced in high volume at low cost. It's also Italy's most popular white. The wines from the Classico area are usually of higher quality.

IS THIS MAN FOR YOU? JUDGING A MAN BY HIS WINE

Perhaps you've never thought about wine in relation to men (not likely, but perhaps). It's time to connect the dots between the two. One can help you learn about the other. The kind of wine a man drinks will shed some light on his nature and his personality.

Sure, you could judge a man by the car he drives, the size of his biceps or his astrological sign. But our love match profile reveals more about your man than you'll ever discover by a look at his bank account or daily horoscope. Here's how to judge your man by the wine he drinks.

- **Cabernet Sauvignon**
  As a young man, this guy might seem a bit abrasive. But don't let his immaturity overshadow his essential depth of character. As he ages, his true self is revealed. He's an asset in business and financial concerns. He'll make a loving husband and caring father. This is a man who's good for the long haul.

- **Champagne**
  This is a self-confident man who exudes power. He's all charm and calm on the outside. But kiss him once and you'll feel a force bubbling beneath the surface. Getting close to this man is not easy. But when you do, you're in for a thrill. As a partner, he'll urge you to greater career and personal successes. As your sexual mate, he'll be your "Screaming Orgasm!"

- **Chardonnay**
  The man's physical attributes and social skills are so well developed that he's referred to as the "Golden Boy." He has a way with words that you find fascinating and flattering—particularly because the subject is often you. This is a man who makes you dream of marriage. But be careful. He's not a one-woman man. You could be a one-night stand.

- **Merlot**
  This man is fun! He can be the life of the party. While bordering on verbose, his conversation is stimulating and his sense of humor is always evident. His passions are music and

food. But a word to the sexually adventurous: his passions don't necessarily extend to the bedroom.

• **Pinot Gris/Pinot Grigio**
Despite his sensitive personality and delicate physical constitution, the Pinot Gris man is really a survivor. His intuitions are reliable and should be trusted. He is likely to be an actor, writer or dreamer. Addicted to luxury and comfort, he has little to no inclination for physical exercise, unless it's in the bedroom. There he might be prone to play out his fantasies.

• **Pinot Noir**
This man is extremely strong-willed and demanding of himself. He is kind and generous with friends and lovers and easily establishes a rapport with strangers. The Pinot Noir man is creative and loves classical music and entertaining. He's an accomplished cook. His intense passion is underscored by his self-control. Find the key to unleash this passion and you'll experience unforgettable lovemaking.

• **White Zinfandel**
Here's your sweet, attentive, caring man. Have you ever desperately wanted a foot massage at the end of a stressful day? Well, this is your guy, sensitive almost to the point of gushiness. There's no pretense with him. He's not afraid to reveal his feminine side. He's honestly interested in everything you have to say. While you could fall head over heels in love with this guy, just make sure he's not trying on your panties while you're at work. In that case, perhaps he'd make a better girlfriend.

• **Zinfandel**
The Zin man is in constant pursuit of adventure and new ideas. His intellectual curiosity is ever-present and he can

get easily bored and restless when surrounded by dull people or activities. A world traveler, this man's adventurous spirit carries over into the bedroom, where he enjoys playful experimentation.

YOUR RELATIONSHIP PASSAGES AND THE WINES TO GO WITH THEM: FROM BLISS TO THE ABYSS

Every relationship has distinct stages—from the first exciting glance across a crowded room to "until death do us part." Each step along the way deserves its own special wine. We have some wine recommendations to help you celebrate the ups and survive the downs of your love-life passages.

It's your first date with Mr. Could-Be-Right. Big potential here. You're seduced—figuratively speaking. You're ready for some ac-

---

WINE BAR:
Remove those rosé-colored glasses before it's too late . . .

Scottish scientists have found proof of the so-called beer goggle effect—the phenomenon by which members of the opposite sex become more attractive as you consume more alcohol. The researchers found that drinking up to one liter of beer or four glasses of wine increased the perceived attractiveness of members of the opposite sex by about 25 percent. Alcohol, apparently, stimulates the nucleus accumbens, the part of the brain that judges facial attractiveness. The increase applied equally to ugly people and pretty people.

Now you know why you've kissed so many frogs in your quest for a prince.

tion, but only as a warm-up to something more serious later on. Our recommendation: Picpoul. It translates as "lip-stinger" and has just the right tangy tartness to get those lips puckered. It's a full-bodied white wine with lots of acidity. And it's affordable enough that you won't go broke when you buy a case of it for future dates.

You're engaged, and in love! You can't keep your eyes—or hands—off him. You constantly exchange sweet nothings with each other to the disgust of your friends. Our recommendation: Dolcetto. Meaning "little sweet one" in Italian, this soft and fruity red wine from Italy's Piedmont region is anything but sweet. You'll find it's definitely dry. Most Dolcettos are meant to be drunk within their first two or three years. So be sure to consume the wine young, before the fruit (or the romance) begins to fade.

The wedding! Of course, it's all about you . . . the Vera Wang dress, the Manolo Blahnik shoes, the Wonderbra. You're an illusion—uh, we mean vision—to behold! Our recommendation: Pouilly-Fumé, a crisp and tart white made from the Sauvignon Blanc grape. It's sometimes called Blanc Fumé (literally "white smoke," referring to its smoky taste).

Your first child . . . what a miracle! What overwhelming joy! Have you ever experienced anything so incredibly sweet? Our recommendation: An extraordinarily sweet and luscious ice wine. This precious dessert wine is a perfect match for motherhood. The grapes chosen for ice wine undergo tremendous physical stress in the production process, but the result is indescribably sublime. It's called ice wine because the grapes are allowed to freeze on the vine before they're picked, and then they're pressed before they thaw. Ice wines are good candidates for long aging, just like Junior.

Oh, jeez, a second mortgage. Sure, you're feeling strapped. You've borrowed to the max to pay for the new roof. Our recommendation: Sangria. Cheap wine and mixers will keep you under budget.

Our simple recipe is low-cost, yet with a high rate of interest. Mix together a *big* bottle of red, 1 cup each of orange juice and pineapple juice, and ½ cup of an orange liqueur (like orange Curaçao). Add some sliced fruit and serve over ice.

The big "D" . . . Divorce. You could be feeling bitter, but get over it. You're better off without that ungrateful you-know-what. Besides, sweet revenge is always more satisfying. Our recommendation: Port. This sweet fortified wine, usually served after a meal, can compensate for even the most distasteful repast that has preceded it. It's a pleasurably extravagant way to spend the alimony check, and the elevated alcohol content will help you forget the hell you went through. If it's any consolation, just remember that the Bastardo grape used in making Port is very boring all by itself.

The time has come for the reading of the will. After all the sacrifices you made for that man over the years, you're ready for a shopping spree. No one to answer to. No one to check the credit card statements. Our recommendation: 1986 Château Margaux. The Château Margaux wines of the 1980s are considered to be the best of any château in Bordeaux. They're rich and full-bodied with exquisite bouquets. The 1986 vintage could well last forty or fifty years. But who wants to wait? Of course, we're assuming that you're the major beneficiary named in the will. If not, you can drown your sorrows with a Chablis-in-a-box.

WINE FUNDAMENTALS . . .
DISTILLED IN A FEW SPARKLING PICK-UP LINES

Have you ever seen that gorgeous hunk of man—sitting all by himself, sipping a glass of wine—and not known what to say? You don't want to seem stupid. You don't want to appear easy. (Okay. Maybe you're willing to risk easy.) You want him to think you're sophisticated, intelligent and witty. So here's a primer on wine distilled into some (we hope) memorable pick-up lines. This really would have helped our studying for the SATs.

- To a man holding a glass of wine: "Go ahead, give me a swirl."
    Swirling wine in your glass isn't just some pretentious act of snobbery. It actually causes the wine's aromas to be released so you can smell them. That's why you see people stick their noses in the glass after they've swirled. One caution: If your glass is more than half full, don't even think about swirling unless you have an unlimited dry-cleaning budget.

- "If you think that wine has good legs, you should see mine."
    After you've swirled wine around in your glass, you may notice that the wine sometimes runs back down the side of the glass in little streams. These are called *legs* or *tears*. Some people will make a big deal out of them. Don't be fooled. A wine's legs won't tell you much about the quality of the wine—only that the better the legs, the higher the alcohol content.

- "Crush me, press me, make me wine."
    Crushing and pressing are two methods used to extract juice from grapes. The processes and machinery are different, but who—besides a winemaker or technogeek—really cares? Just make the wine.

- "I've got a soft, supple body, just like that Riesling you're drinking."
    Soft and *supple* are two related terms used often to describe a wine's taste and texture. Try thinking of these next time you sip a wine. Some wines will, quite literally, feel soft,

while others will seem rough or coarse. In white wines, low acidity is responsible for softness. In red wines, low levels of tannins are responsible.

- To a man at a wine tasting: "I swallow."

Why anyone would want to taste a wine and then spit it out is beyond us. But there are those purists (and professional wine tasters) who don't want a wine's alcohol to dull their senses for the next wine. For those of us who do swallow, we can predict that at any wine tasting the last wine on the menu will always taste better than the first.

- "Ooh, you're a nice vintage . . . mature but young enough to take advantage of right now."

Vintage refers to the year the grapes were harvested and turned into wine. For a wine to be labeled in the United States with a vintage year, 95 percent of the grapes have to have been harvested that year. Non-vintage wines are blends of wines whose grapes were harvested in two or more different years. Most people believe a vintage wine must be better than a non-vintage. That's just plain not the case.

- To a man with lots of wine in his shopping cart: "If your wine tasting is going to be horizontal, I hope you'll invite me."

A horizontal wine tasting is one where all the wines are of a similar type (for example, Cabernets from Napa Valley), all are from the same vintage, but all are from different wineries. A vertical tasting, on the other hand, features the same wine from the same winery but of different vintages.

- "I promise not to raise the subject of Meritage on our first date."

Meritage wines are American blended wines made from the traditional grape varieties of France's Bordeaux region. The term was coined by a group of winemakers in 1988 from the words "merit" and "heritage." A Meritage wine has to meet strict standards to carry the term on its label.

- To a man opening a bottle of Champagne: "How about you unmuzzle me that way!"

  A *muzzle* is the wire cage that surrounds the cork of a bottle of sparkling wine. Untwisting and removing the muzzle is potentially hazardous for anyone or anything in the bottle's line of fire.

- To a man opening a bottle of wine: "I bet you could keep my cork wet."

  A bottle of wine should be stored on its side so that its cork will remain moist and airtight. A cork that dries out and shrinks will let in air that can ruin the wine.

- "You're so Primitivo!"

  Primitivo is a grape variety grown primarily in southern Italy that produces wines with substantial body and high alcohol content. Recent DNA studies have concluded that Primitivo and Zinfandel are actually the same grape.

- "You're my kind of varietal."

  Varietal is wine named for the grape variety from which it's made, such as Chardonnay or Cabernet Sauvignon. By law in the United States, 75 percent of the wine has to come from the specified grape variety. This practice of naming wine after the grape is done primarily in North and South America and in Australia and New Zealand. In Europe the practice has been to name the wine after the region or village where the wine is produced.

- "I'm Sancerre-ly interested!"

    Sancerre is the winemaking region in the Loire Valley of France that is famous for its white wine called—you guessed it—Sancerre. It's made from the Sauvignon Blanc grape and has a crisp, refreshing taste.

- "Let me uncork your passion."

    Getting the cork out of a bottle should be simple enough. All you need is a good corkscrew. But what constitutes a good corkscrew is the subject of a lot of inane debate. Our advice is to try several and determine which is best for you. We think whatever gets us to the wine the fastest with as little cork in the wine as possible is the way to go.

- "You're such a Brut!"

    Brut means "dry" and applies to the relative level of sweetness in Champagne and sparkling wine. In order of driest to sweetest, look for these terms on a Champagne label: Extra Brut (or Brut Nature or Brut Sauvage), Brut, Extra Dry (which is actually not as dry as Brut), Sec, Demi-Sec and Doux.

- "How'd you like to come to my Private Reserve?"

    The term "reserve" on U.S. wine labels has no official meaning. It's put there to imply high quality. Sometimes it's true, and sometimes it's not. You may see "reserve" combined with such words as "private," "vintner's," "special" or "proprietor's." They don't make the implication any more true.

- "I'm just like that bottle of Cabernet. I like cool, dark places where I can work up a sweat."

For long-term storage, wines need a cool environment (around 55 degrees) that's away from the light (particularly direct sunlight) and with a good amount of humidity (but not enough to cause mold). Of course, there are those of us whose wines never make it beyond short-term storage.

HUDDLING WITH YOUR MAN . . .
SPORTS TALK FOR THE WINE-MINDED

TERM	WHAT HE MEANS	WHAT WE KNOW
Punt	What a football player does when his team has pissed away three downs.	The indentation at the bottom of some wine bottles— especially Champagne bottles. Back in the days of hand-blown glass, this served to strengthen the bottles.
Premier cru	Gold-medal racing team.	In French, "first growth," referring to the great old wine-making châteaus of France. On a label, it indicates an official class of wine that has achieved a certain status and high quality.
Sack	Quarterback crush.	The name for Sherry and other fortified wines imported to England during the time of Queen Elizabeth I.
Liqueur d'expedition	A beer run after the game.	A mixture of sugar and wine added to Champagne right before final bottling to increase its sweetness.

TERM	WHAT HE MEANS	WHAT WE KNOW
Fining agents	The guys who drained the bank accounts of John Rocker and Dennis Rodman.	Substances added to wine to eliminate cloudiness or bitterness.
Racking	The art form perfected by Minnesota Fats.	The process of separating clear juice from the sediment that has fallen to the bottom of the container.
Hang time	The eternity Michael Jordan spends in the air on his way to the basket.	The time the grapes are actually growing on the vine. The longer they stay on the vine, the riper they become. But too long, and you risk rot.
Split	A difficult spare.	A small bottle of wine about one-quarter the size of a standard bottle.
Starter	The person you bribe on a busy Saturday at the golf course.	The yeast added to the juice of freshly crushed grapes to start the fermentation process.
Press	What he does at the gym to impress girls.	To extract juice from grapes using one of several types of presses.
Skin Contact	What precedes a pin in wrestling.	The amount of time that the juice for white wine is in contact with the skins of the grapes. Too much exposure and the wine could absorb too much color and bitterness.

TERM	WHAT HE MEANS	WHAT WE KNOW
Disgorge	The result of too much tailgating.	In Champagne making, to remove sediment from the bottle.
Demijohn	Bathroom facilities at a marathon.	A large squat bottle with a short, narrow neck. It's usually covered with wicker and can hold from one to ten gallons.

BE A SAUCY SISTER, NOT A WINE SNOB

If anything has given wine a bad name, it's the overbearing snobs who either bore you to tears with tedious wine minutiae or—worse—pompously declare their opinions sacrosanct. No one in the world knows everything there is to know about wine. No one! Ask any true "expert." The more she learns, the more she realizes how much more there is to know.

The Saucy Sisterhood rejects wine snobs. A Saucy Sister, either by nature or conscious design, is the antithesis of a snob. She's an independent thinker and trusts her own judgment and taste. But she also respects the opinions of others and doesn't try to coerce them to her point of view. She's adventurous, always looking for another experience and the next new wine. Yet she appreciates and participates in age-old traditions. She can get down and dirty with the best of them, or rise to any occasion. Above all, a Saucy Sister maintains a sense of humor about herself and her wine. What fun is it if you can't laugh? Come to think of it, enough wine always makes her laugh.

If you're unsure about how to recognize a wine snob, here are some examples of their egregious behaviors.

- He insists that the alcohol in the wine has no bearing on the enjoyment he gets from drinking it.

  Liar, liar, pants on fire!

  If that were true, he could drink tea with his steak to taste the tannins or lemonade to savor some sweetness and acidity. Let's be honest here. The intoxicating element of wine is a central part of its charm.

- He brings his own specially designed wine stemware to a restaurant.

  While it may be true that the quality, shape and thickness of a glass all have an effect on the experience of wine tasting, this guy is just pretentious. He probably wears an ascot with his pajamas to protect himself from drafts.

  Very simply, a good wineglass should be clear to show off the wine's color, thin so you don't taste the glass, long-stemmed so your hand doesn't touch the bowl, slightly narrowed toward the rim so the bouquet doesn't evaporate, and big enough so you can swirl the wine without spilling it.

- He raises his eyebrow when you describe the riotous Beaujolais Nouveau party you went to last November.

  First of all, he'd never drink this "new" wine, which is just seven to nine weeks old when it's released each year. And, second, he's probably never even gatored. This is no party animal!

  Beaujolais Nouveau, from the Beaujolais region of France, is the first wine made from each year's grape harvest. This wine, which is quickly fermented and bottled after the harvest, was originally made for the enjoyment of the winery workers. It became increasingly popular at the bistros and cafés of Beaujolais and Lyons. Then word spread to Paris and beyond, and the onetime local tradition became an international phenomenon. The official release date of Beaujolais Nouveau is the third Thursday in November, and importers have to agree not to sell the wine before midnight on Wednesday. But come 12:01 A.M., let the festivals and parties begin!

• He refuses to drink any wine whose bottle has a synthetic cork.

If he's such a stickler about synthetics, what's with the boobs on his date? A growing number of prestigious wineries are using synthetic polymer corks, which duplicate both the elasticity and impermeable quality of natural cork, not to mention screwtops. Just like the bimbo, it's all marketing.

It's really very basic. The cork keeps air out and the wine in. Cork can be compressed to squeeze into the neck of the bottle, and then it expands again for a tight fit. Is cork the best material for the job? Probably not. A cork can be difficult to remove, and it can sometimes develop a mold that ruins the wine. But it was a good idea at the time, back in the seventeenth century. The jury is still out regarding the long-term effectiveness of synthetic corks and screwtops. One thing we know: cork still leads the pack when it comes to cachet.

• He refers to winemakers by their first names.

Sure, and he's close personal friends with Oprah, Britney and Madonna, too.

It's a sign of the times, we suppose, that some winemakers—like some chefs—have reached celebrity status. But let's make one thing very clear: The star of any great wine is the grape. The better the grape you start with, the less you have to do to turn it into a wonderful wine. Even the best winemaker in the world can't transform a mediocre grape into a spectacular wine.

- He demands that his bottle of wine be opened so it can "breathe."

  The idea of "breathing" is exposing the wine to air to enhance its flavor. But studies with experts whose palates are certainly more discriminating than his have shown that no one can really tell the difference between a wine that's been breathing in the bottle for minutes and one that's been breathing for hours. Wine can't breathe in a bottle; the neck is just too small to let enough air inside. If you really want to aerate your wine, pour it into your glass and let it sit for a while. (Of course, this never happens at our table. The temptation of a full wineglass sitting in front of us is just too overwhelming.) Actually, most wines don't even benefit from aeration. If a wine doesn't need further aging, it doesn't need to breathe. And that applies to almost all whites and many reds. The only wines that will really benefit from aeration are those reds that are very young and tannic.

- He scoffs at wine names like Fat Bastard and Faux Frog.

  Oh, lighten up! This humorless character will never know what he's missing.

  The only way to know for sure about whether or not you'll like a wine is to taste it. Just because a winemaker chooses a catchy marketing name doesn't mean she's camouflaging an inferior wine. A clever brand name helps make a wine stand out among the thousands of others in the marketplace. And, chances are, you'll remember the name next time you're in a wine shop.

- He commands the waiter to remove the flowers from the table because their fragrance will interfere with his appreciation of the wine.

Please! He should be more concerned about the aftershave he bathed in.

Smell and taste are interrelated, and strong aromas can interfere with what you taste. But under normal circumstances, environmental aromas won't affect your ability to taste the wine. It's interesting to note that most of a wine's flavors are actually aromas that are vaporized in the mouth and perceived through the interior nasal passage in the back of your mouth.

WINE PAIRINGS FOR SEXUAL APPETITES

Women's sexual desires can be diverse. What we want depends on what we're experiencing in life and the kind of mood we find ourselves in at any given moment. Sometimes we're looking for something slow and soothing—other times, something fast and rough. The same holds true with the wine that we choose to drink. We want it to fit our moods and fulfill our desires. Wine and sex are natural partners. Here are some wine and sex pairing ideas to share with your loved one. Try one or all and you'll experience lovemaking at its best.

Your Sexual Desire: The Quickie. You want immediate pleasure, and this guy is ready to satisfy you at a moment's notice. It'll be short, intense and fleeting. *Now get back to work!*

The Wine to Share: Heurige. This is the Austrian term for "new wine," referring to wine from the most recent vintage. Wine taverns by the same name serve these wines all across Austria.

Though *heurigen* are young and easy to drink, their memory will fade in a hurry.

Your Sexual Desire: Mr. Clean. Your Aquarian side craves lovemaking underwater. This will satisfy your lust and keep you squeaky clean. The bubbles will arouse you while he stimulates your passions.

The Wine to Share: Blanc de blanc. The bubbles in this version of champagne are intoxicatingly romantic. The name means "white wine from white grapes" and it's made entirely from Chardonnay grapes. This light and delicate sparkler pairs well with almost any edible partner and is the perfect accompaniment to amorous unions.

Your Sexual Desire: The Stripper. So you want to reveal yourself without actually baring your soul! The Stripper will slowly and methodically remove each piece of clothing from your longing body until you scream with ecstasy.

The Wine to Share: Grüner Veltliner. This mainly Austrian wine hasn't attracted much attention around the world until now. It has revealed itself to have light fruit and racy acidity and is reasonably affordable.

Your Sexual Desire: The Actor. You'd like to have sex as Cinderella with one glass slipper or as Madonna in a metallic bustier. Here's your chance to audition. Free yourself from the real world and climax with an Academy Award.

The Wine to Share: Grenache. Its chameleon-like properties allow it to blend well with other grapes. In fact, you'll rarely find 100 percent Grenache wines. But you'll discover it playing a role in Spain's Rioja wines and France's Châteauneuf-du-Pape.

Your Sexual Desire: The Gourmet. Your mother told you not to eat between meals, but she never said anything about eating between courses of sex. This is for the girl who finds food almost as sensual as lovemaking. Dig in to your favorite treats and discover the enrichment food gives to your erotic exploits.

The Wine to Share: Riesling. This could be the most versatile white wine with food. In fact, there are few dishes it doesn't enhance. There are many variations from bone dry to very sweet. If you prefer the dry version, look for *trocken* on German labels or *dry* on American labels.

Your Sexual Desire: The Sensualist. If aromas arouse you, the Sensualist knows how to please you. From vanilla-scented candles at bedside to his ultimate manly fragrance, scents are your essential aphrodisiac. Let him stimulate your body using his sensory perception.

The Wine to Share: Chenin Blanc. This French white wine has an intense and intriguing aroma. Some wine geeks refer to a wine's aroma as its *nose*. *Bouquet* seems much more romantic.

RECIPES FOR ROMANCE

Don't settle for a G rating. These aphrodisiacs of the wine kind are guaranteed to ignite a love inferno.

SEVENTH DEADLY ZIN

12 oz. Zinfandel
4 oz. 7-Up
2 maraschino cherries
ice cubes

Fill two 8-oz. glasses with ice. Pour half of Zinfandel into each glass. Top with 7-Up and stir. Garnish with cherries. Serves 2.

BUBBLING BARE NAVEL

8 oz. Champagne
½ oz. Chambord
4 oz. orange juice

Chill 2 Champagne glasses. Into each pour 4 oz. Champagne, ¼ oz. Chambord and 2 oz. orange juice. Serves 2.

BOTTOMS UP

4 oz. Gewürztraminer, chilled
2 wedges of lime
salt

Chill 2 shot glasses. Rub lime around rims of glasses. Pour 2 oz. Gewürztraminer in each glass. Pour salt to taste onto each lime wedge. Suck lime, and down the wine. Additional rounds are permitted. Serves 2.

KISS MERLOT AND KISS ME OFTEN

6 oz. Merlot
1 oz. Cherry Heering
2 Scoops vanilla ice cream
½ cup crushed ice

Put all ingredients into a blender, and blend until smooth. Pour into 2 large red wineglasses. Serves 2.

GRENACHE À TROIS

4 oz. Grenache
2 oz. Cognac
1 oz. passion fruit juice
ice cubes

Put all ingredients into a martini shaker. Shake vigorously for 15 to 20 seconds. Strain into 2 martini glasses. Serves 2.

SEX BY CHOCOLATE

8 oz. Beaujolais
½ oz. chocolate liqueur

Into each of 2 large red wineglasses pour 4 oz. Beaujolais and ¼ oz. chocolate liqueur. Swirl to mix. Serves 2.

DEEP THROAT DIABLO

6 oz. Cabernet Sauvignon
1 oz. Crème de Cassis
2 dashes tabasco (or to taste)

Mix all ingredients and stir well. Pour into 2 Port glasses. Serves 2.

ASK THE SAUCY SISTERS

Dear Sisters,
    On my third date with George, we were having a lovely dinner at a faboo restaurant. I was feeling confident and

free-spirited and drank quite a bit of wine. On my fourth (or whatever) glass, George looked me straight in the eye and called me an "eenafile." Was he saying I drink too much? I'm too embarrassed to talk to him again before I know what he meant.

Signed, Lying-Lo

Dear Lo,

Stand up straight, shoulders back, head high! Four glasses (or whatever) of wine is no sissy serving, but we think George was commenting more on your enthusiasm for the grape. An enophile (or oenophile, as traditionalists spell it) is a wine lover. It comes from "oenos," the Greek word for wine. If we were practitioners of the art of enomancy (fortune-telling through wine), we'd predict that you and George have a future together.

Dear Saucies,

I'm dating a self-described "wine geek." I appreciate the fact that he enjoys wine, but he always seems to buy the cheapest wine in every category. It's not that I don't like the wines he picks out. It's just that I'm afraid his cheapness will spill over into other areas I consider important—like jewelry. What do you think I should make of my Frugal McDougall?

Signed, Prospecting

Dear Prospecting,

As two women who consider diamonds a girl's best friend, we understand your concern. But there may be hope. Let's take the category of Merlot, for example. Price can be an indication of style. Expensive Merlots are more likely to be rich and tannic while less expensive ones are probably soft and fruit driven.

Or take Vouvrays. They're made from the Chenin Blanc grape and can range from dry to sweet. Generally speaking, the more expensive they get, the sweeter they are. So it could be that your friend isn't really cheap . . . just a man who knows how to get what he wants. And that certainly turns us on. . . .

Dear Saucy Sisters,

My friend Sarah recently lost sixty-five pounds and looks great. I'm going over to her house and wanted to take a special bottle of wine to say "congratulations" on her achievement. Do you have a recommendation?

Signed, Wish I Had Her Discipline

Dear Wish,

How about a bottle of Petite Sirah? It's a robust and peppery red that has lots of aging ability. But don't confuse it with Syrah. It's a different grape altogether. (To compound the confusion, Syrah and Shiraz are the same grape variety. Syrah was thought to have originated in the Middle East. What we know for sure is that it arrived in Australia in the 1830s by way of South Africa, but the Aussies call it Shiraz.)

Dear Saucy Sisters,

The last time I was at the wine store, I was looking for a Sauvignon Blanc. This really cute salesman tried to talk me into a Fumé Blanc. He said they were the same thing. Was he giving me the straight story, or was he just trying to make a sale? Or do you think he was making moves on me?

Signed, Puzzled

Dear Puzzled,

Without having seen him in action, it's hard to say whether his intentions were of a romantic nature. But wine is always a good starting point for flirting. Regarding your query about his truthfulness, yes, Sauvignon Blanc and Fumé Blanc are one and the same. You can hold Robert Mondavi responsible. Back in the '70s he used the name Fumé Blanc to market his Sauvignon Blanc. The name not only stuck, it was copied by wineries around the world. The term "Fumé Blanc" has no legal definition, but inside the bottle you'll find a wine made from the Sauvignon Blanc grape variety.

$\sim$

Grape Deals for the Home...
SHOPPING FOR WINE AND ACCESSORIES AND ENJOYING THEM AT HOME

OKAY, HOMEBODIES, let's get wined up. Put on your wine savvy and step into your sippin' boots. It's time to venture out into the world of commerce and bring back everything you need for total enjoyment of the grape. Will you be savoring a glass of Chianti and a chunk of Asiago alone in front of a *Sopranos* rerun? Or are you planning to serve your favorite bacon-wrapped trout to friends? Maybe you just want to stock up on wine assets for any eventuality. Whatever your motive, effective shopping benefits from a plan.

THE SAUCY SISTERS' $140 WINE CELLAR

Every week presents its own surprises, large and small—and lots of opportunities to accompany those moments with wine. But you've got to be prepared. Say a despondent friend appears at your door needing TLC. You can't just abandon her while you trek off to the wine store. No, you've got to have a suitable bottle within easy reach.

Each occasion, of course, demands its own special wine. Here's what to have on hand. Before the whining starts (*too much trouble, too much money, too little space*), let us reassure you: A minimal investment of dollars and space will produce a foolproof stash of wine for any and all occasions.

(When you get to our personal recommendations, note that we haven't mentioned vintage years. A particular vintage we bought may not be available when you get to the store. So, we've made our selections from wineries that produce consistently good quality from one year to the next. Also, remember that not all wines are available in all areas—and, because of varying state laws and taxes, certainly not all at the exact same prices.)

1 bottle	Champagne	$35

This is your all-purpose, mood-enhancing, celebratory beverage. It elevates every occasion. The bad times get better and the good times become orgasmic. And for $35 you can get an excellent non-vintage French Champagne. If French doesn't impress you, go for a sparkler from elsewhere and subtract $10 to $15.

Some of our favorite Champagnes:
Veuve Clicquot Yellow Label Brut NV—Rich and nutty
   for $35
Delbeck Champagne NV—A fresh treat for $24
Nicolas Feuillatte Brut Gold Label NV—Scrumptious
   for $23

Some of our favorite bargain sparklers:
Bouvet Signature Brut NV—Loire delicacy for $10
Banrock Station Sparkling Chardonnay—Good Aussie
   bubbles for $10

Cristalino Brut NV—Spanish crispness for $8
Gloria Ferrer Blanc de Noirs—Rich fruit and color for $13

2 bottles   "House" White $20
These are everyday wines under $10 that you
can enjoy after a day on the job or to celebrate
minor life events like the dog getting his bath
(in which case choose something with a flowery
fragrance, like a Riesling). Other good choices
are white Rioja and Sauvignon Blanc.

Some of our favorites:
Bonny Doon Pacific Rim Riesling—Vibrant flavor for $10
Coppola Bianco—Easy drinking for $9
RH Phillips Sauvignon Blanc—Clean and refreshing for $9

2 bottles   "House" Red $20
Same as house whites except maybe you're
just in the mood for red. Or the life events are a
touch more serious—like your dog was neutered.
Try a Malbec, Côtes du Rhone or Shiraz.

Some of our favorites:
A. Mano Primitivo Puglia—Dark and spicy for $10
Barwang Shiraz—Richness for $9
Bodega Norton Malbec—Argentinian pepper for $8

1 bottle   "Let's Boogie" White $25
You passed the Realtors/Bar/Series 7/History exam!
It's a night to celebrate. Reach for that exceptional
Chardonnay or Chablis you've been saving.

Some of our favorites:
Château Potelle Mount Veeder VGS Estate Chardonnay—

Subtle complexity for $25
Hugel Riesling—Alsace apples and spice for $18
King Estate Pinot Gris—Soft and citrus for $14

1 bottle   "Let's Boogie" Red   **$32**
This is the wine to celebrate love—first kiss,
first dance, first . . . Share a bottle of Cabernet,
Brunello or Hermitage with someone special over
a romantic dinner.

Some of our favorites:
Cosentino Napa Cabernet Sauvignon—Earthy and
    full-bodied for $30
Saintsbury Garnet Pinot Noir—Velvety and seductive
    for $19
Guigal Crozes Hermitage—Rhone intensity for $16

1 bottle   "Wacky" Wines   **$8**
This is the "it's-so-cheap-how-can-I-lose" wine.
Pick out something that you've never tasted
before—say, a Verdelho—and spring it on the
surprise guest who arrives unannounced.

Some of our favorite "finds":
Baron Herzog Chenin Blanc—Off-dry and kosher
    for $6
Staton Hills Cabernet Sauvignon—Character
    for $5
Duca Leonardo Montepulciano d'Abruzzo—
    Tart and fruity for $4

                                                                      ___

Total   **$140**

THE ART OF PURCHASING WINE

Wine shopping is no simple task. It's constant activity, physically and mentally. First there's the research. Hours of paging through *Wine Spectator* and *Food & Wine* (with Sauvignon Blanc in hand, naturally). Paying attention to the pros. Scouring newspaper ads to see where and when the best sales are. And then there are the scouting expeditions—store to store in search of quality inventory and informed sales staff. Checking labels . . . spotting trends. Whew! We're exhausted. Time for a wine break.

Scoring a Two-Thumbs-Up

Why is it that, as amateurs, we feel more confident in our selection of movies than in our selection of wines? Maybe it's that we haven't tried enough wines or enough diversity of wines to trust our instincts. So we turn to wine critics. Relying on the opinions of "experts" isn't a bad thing. But can we trust their judgments?

A recent study on the evaluation and appreciation of wine took that question to heart. It analyzed over 100,000 tasting notes—including those from the world's most famous wine critics—to produce a side-by-side chart of the rankings of eighteen wines. What was the consensus of the critics? None. Well, if no consensus, how about just some consistency? About as much as you'd get from a table of random numbers.

The same study assembled a group of expert tasters for a series of blind tastings and subjected them to a little underhanded—but revealing—trick. When served a particular white wine, the tasters gave the expected descriptions: *fresh, dry, honeyed, lively*. Later, they were served the same wine *dyed red*. The descriptions? *Intense, spicy, supple, deep*.

Enough said.

Vintage Charts

Not only wines get scores. Vintages, the years the grapes were harvested, get rated too, in the form of vintage charts. The charts are particularly useful for those wine-growing areas that have big weather fluctuations from year to year, where wine quality will vary as a result. The charts will point you to the best years.

Vintage charts range from basic to comprehensive, from one person's judgment to consensus opinion, from well-known wine experts to a local wine shop's own charts. Chart authors evaluate wine-growing regions each year and give the region and the year a numerical score. The ratings, usually mapped on a grid, indicate the promise for that area's wine for that year.

Wines that benefit from bottle aging will spend some time maturing at the winery before they're even released. No one, except the winemaker and her friends and family, get to taste them prior to release. (Remember "No wine before its time"?) Generally, you'll find that authors issue their evaluations two years after the vintage.

VINTAGE	1992	1993	1994	1995	1996	1997	1998	1999	2000	2001
California Red	93	91	94	95	92	96	86	90	88	95
California White	90	90	89	92	90	92	89	89	88	90
Burgundy Red	81	89	85	91	96	89	83	90	90	80
Burgundy White	92	76	88	92	94	89	86	88	88	85
Piedmont	76	87	80	88	96	97	93	90	94	89
Tuscany	75	88	85	91	78	95	86	94	92	88
Germany	91	88	90	87	93	88	86	87	87	91
Rioja	85	87	91	90	85	85	82	86	87	94

This chart is based on a 100-point scale. Others use a 5-point or 10-point scale. The more specific charts break down each country and region into subregions. After all, a state like California covers a lot of area. If you're buying a California Pinot Noir, there might be a difference that year between one from Napa and one from Santa Barbara. The more comprehensive charts also include symbols that tell you whether to hold the wine or drink it now—or whether it's past its prime. Vintage charts are at their most useful when you're buying older wines—at an auction, perhaps, or when you're trying to evaluate unfamiliar wines on a restaurant list.

Mediocre wine can be made in very good years. Conversely, talented winemakers manage to make very good wine even in average years. Probably more important than the vintage year is the winery that produces the wine and its track record over a period of years.

The Bargain Basement

Attention, Winemart shoppers! Today's special . . . a five-liter size PEE-NO-NOT from Antarctica on aisle six for $3.99. That's today only . . . $3.99.

Is this a good deal? If it were a handbag on sale, we could feel the material, check the workmanship. We'd *know!*

Wine is a different story. You never know exactly how good a deal it is until you take it home and drink it. And, by then, it's too late. Can you imagine returning your supersize PEE-NO-NOT to Winemart?

Clerk: And the reason you're returning it?
You: It didn't taste good.
Clerk: But was it defective in some way?

You: Yes, the taste was defective.

Clerk: No, I mean were there grape pits in the liquid or did it turn your teeth black?

You: It just tasted bad.

Clerk: But was anyone poisoned . . . hospitalized?

Whether the price was $3.99 or $39.99, no one wants to feel ripped off. We want value for whatever we spend. Wine doesn't have to be expensive to be good. On the other hand, cheap wine isn't always a bargain.

Let's look at what makes a wine cheap. Winemaking, while part art, is also a business. When an American winery produces a Cabernet Sauvignon, it's using one of the most popular and most expensive grapes around. In the United States a wine labeled "Cabernet" has to have at least 75 percent Cabernet grapes in the bottle. The remaining 25 percent can be an unspecified blending grape. In some cases the winemakers, because of the economics, will choose the cheapest grape available. Or, in an even more common cost-cutting measure, the winemaker will use press wine. (The first juice squeezed from the grapes is called "free run." Subsequent pressings yield more juice, but of lesser quality, "press wine.") With the press wine added in, the wine is still legally Cabernet, but without the quality usually identified with the varietal.

The flip side of this scenario is that "cheap" wine can be high in quality. The grape variety might simply be less in demand than a Cabernet and therefore less expensive for the winemaker to acquire (*ka-ching!*). The land where the grapevines are planted can be in parts of the world where real estate is inexpensive (*ka-ching!*). There are lots of factors that go into the mix, but the upshot is you can find some terrific wines with character at unbelievably low prices (*ka-ching, ka-ching!*).

Shopping Strategies

Smart girls are savvy shoppers. But we weren't born that way. It's taken years of cultivation and practice and shared insights from like-minded friends. Here are our strategies for those new to the wine-buying game.

1. **Buy lesser-known and underappreciated varietals.** Chardonnay and Cabernet continue to be the hot sellers, with price tags that reflect their popularity. Look instead for varietals not in such demand. Some may be totally unfamiliar to you, but when they're well priced, well, who can't afford to take a chance?

REDS	WHITES
Syrah/Shiraz	Sauvignon Blanc
Pinot Noir	Chenin Blanc
Zinfandel	Riesling
Mourvèdre	Gewürztraminer
Nebbiolo	Pinot Blanc
Malbec	Pinot Gris
Grenache	Viognier
Tempranillo	Blends
Blends	

2. **Buy by the case.** Most retailers and Internet sellers offer a 10 percent discount when you buy a case. And it doesn't always have to be a case of the same wine. Often retailers will let you mix and match any twelve bottles you want.
3. **Develop a relationship with your wine merchants.** Even if you only get on their e-mail lists, you'll be notified about special promotions and sales. And if they get to know your preferences, you could get a heads-up about special arrivals.

LABELS . . . TRUTH OR CONSEQUENCES?

Any girl who wears "Hilfiger" on her chest is obviously impressed by designer labels. And wineries have created some outrageous labels to get her attention. Rude Boy Chardonnay shows a muscular nude from shoulders to waist . . . until the bottle is chilled and Rude Boy reveals all. Then there's the buddies-on-the-run *Marge 'n Tina*—a takeoff on *Thelma & Louise*. But wine labels are serious business. If you doubt it, just consider that in the United States they're regulated by the Bureau of Alcohol, Tobacco and Firearms. The label provides guarantees that you're getting what you pay for. Here are some of the elements you'll find.

Name of the wine: In the United States and the rest of the "New World," wines are named for the grape—Chardonnay and Merlot, for example. In Europe they're named for places—Rioja and Chianti, for example.

Producer: In most cases the name of the producer is straightforward. In the United States and some other countries the producer name can be a trademark used by a winery with multiple lines of products. A winery may have second, third and fourth labels for wines it wants to sell to different market segments, usually expensive upscale wines and inexpensive everyday wines. Gallo, for example, uses E & J Gallo, Anapamu, Gallo of Sonoma, Bartles & James and others.

Vintage year: If a vintage year is stated on the label, 95 percent of the grapes must have been harvested that year. The vintage is particularly relevant for wines meant for long-term cellaring. A vintage date isn't required. Wineries often blend two or more vintages to achieve a uniform product from year to year.

Appellation (the place the grapes came from): The origin of the grapes helps predict the nature of the wine. Every country has it own rules governing appellations. In the United States, appellations start with "America" and are then identified by smaller and smaller areas ("California," "North Coast," "Mendocino County," "Anderson Valley") within the larger ones. "America," although not often used as an appellation, would suggest the wine was a blend of products from two or more states. The more narrowly defined an appellation is, the higher the price you can expect to pay.

Alcoholic content: Table wines in the United States are permitted alcohol levels between 7 and 14 percent. Wines below 12 percent are light-bodied, easy-drinking wines like Riesling and White Zinfandel. Most table wines will be between 12 and 14 percent. A wine that exceeds the 14 percent limit will be (1) very full-bodied and somewhat tannic, and (2) more expensive because it enters a higher tax bracket reserved for fortified wines.

The surgeon general's warning: It states that drinking alcoholic beverages can cause birth defects, impair your ability to drive a car or operate machinery, and cause health problems. Although wine producers have been lobbying to include a statement of the health *benefits* of wine based on scientific studies, they've so far been denied.

There are plenty of other label terms that can confuse an all-American Phi Beta Kappa. "Estate bottled" means that 100 percent of the grapes were grown in the winery's own vineyards (not by an independent farmer or another winery) and that the winery itself crushed the grapes, fermented the juice and put it into the bottles. "Estate bottled" is a sign of quality. How about "vinted and bottled by" and "cellared and bottled by"? While those

WINE BAR:
The Sulfite Story

We're warned every time we buy a bottle of wine. The notice right on the bottle's label tells us that this wine contains sulfites. Sulfites have been added to wines for hundreds of years as a preservative. Without them wines would only have a life of one to two years. So what's all the hoopla? The common belief that sulfites cause headaches is true for the approximately 1 percent of our population who have allergies to them, usually asthmatics. For the majority of us, they pose no problem. As a matter of fact, there are more sulfites in cookies, flour tortillas, canned and dried fruit, pizza crust, canned tuna and olives than in wine.

phrases don't necessarily indicate a lesser quality wine, they tell you that either the grapes or the already-fermented wine came from another source.

"Reserve" has no legal meaning on American wine labels. Some wineries use it to denote bottlings of their best wines. Others use the term just to make you think the wine is special. That goes for related terms like "private reserve" and "proprietor's reserve." However, "riserva" on Italian wine labels and "reserva" on Spanish labels have very specific meanings linked to the length of time a wine has been aged.

Pastiche, Rubicon, Elevage. No, these aren't grape varieties. They're in the same category—although expressed in a more genteel fashion—as Fat Bastard, Old Fart and Love My Goat. They're proprietary names given to wines to create market recognition. Occasionally, the same proprietary name is shared by more than one brand. Meritage, for example, is a trademark owned by the Meritage Association, whose member wineries may use the term for their wines that meet specified criteria. Also, in Alsace, a shared proprietary name is Gentil. Any producer there can use the term as long as at least 50 percent of the wine is made from the region's noble varieties—Riesling, Gewürztraminer, Muscat and Pinot Gris. Sometimes the label will tell you what grapes were used, although knowing the ingredients doesn't always tell you what the wine will taste like. It's kind of like reading garment labels: knowing the fabric content hasn't always kept us from shrinking our favorite blouses.

Sighting Your Target at Fifty Paces: The Bottles

A wine shopper on a tight schedule doesn't always have the time to read each label to find what she's looking for. She needs to home in quickly on her target and make her purchase without a lot of fanfare. The shape and color of a wine bottle offer her a way to identify the contents from across the room.

Over time, each region, such as Bordeaux, Burgundy, Champagne and Rhine, adopted a particular bottle shape and color, which have been pretty much adopted by winemakers everywhere. Bottle size, however, varied according to the appellation—each one having its own standard—until the 1970s, when the United States and the European Union adopted the 750-ml bottle as standard. Since then it's been accepted worldwide.

BOTTLE	DESCRIPTION AND TRADITIONAL CONTENTS
Bordeaux	High shoulders Dark green glass used for reds such as Cabernet Sauvignon, Merlot, Zinfandel, Chianti Clear and light green glass used for whites such as white Bordeaux, Sauvignon Blanc, Semillon
Burgundy	Slope shouldered Pale green, or occasionally clear glass used for both reds and whites such as Chardonnay, Pinot Noir, Syrah and Rhones
Champagne	Gently sloping shoulders Long neck Large indentation at the bottom Used for sparkling wines
Rhine	Tall and slender Brown glass in the Rhine region Green glass in the Alsace and Mosel region Used for Riesling, Gewürztraminer

Even though bottle size is mandated, American wineries don't have to adhere to any standards for bottle shape and color. With powerful marketing incentives to differentiate themselves on retail shelves, wineries have come up with imaginative variations— blue bottles, red bottles, bottles in the shape of half moons. Certainly bottle color has an impact on the wine inside (e.g., darker colors protect it from the light, which speeds spoilage), but the main factor in color choice is packaging appeal and easy identification.

SERVING SUGGESTIONS

Glass Is Class

On the road to the big homecoming game, you carefully close the curtains of your moderately priced motel room. You remove the cork from your well-traveled bottle of wine. You reach for the cup so thoughtfully provided by the motel management. You rip open the clear wrapping from what will be your precious drinking vessel. There it is, in all its glory—a curious amalgam of paper and plastic. And as you sip your Cardinal Zin, you remark to whomever how good the wine is. Don't lie! You've done this more than once. We all have.

The wine *did* taste good. But given the choice between a motel cup and a crystal glass with a stem, which one would you choose? The crystal, hands down. It's not just snobbishness and it's not just aesthetics. Wine really does taste better from a glass because glass is inert and doesn't affect the wine's flavor.

Now the conundrum (by the way, Caymus Conundrum is the name of a lovely California blend of Sauvignon Blanc, Semillon, Chardonnay, Viognier and Muscat): What kind of glass? Clean, clear, thin and stemmed. Clean goes without saying. Clear so that you can assess the wine's color and clarity. Thin so that as little foreign material as possible comes between your palate and the wine. And stemmed so that your hand doesn't touch—and warm—the bowl. Beyond those attributes the bowl ideally should narrow toward the rim so you don't spill the wine while swirling and so the bouquet will be captured and not evaporate before you get your nose to the glass. Sounds pretty basic, and it is.

For most households, one set of wineglasses will do. You don't necessarily need one glass for red and another for white. (As a practical matter, where do you store all those glasses?) But if you intend to grow your stemware collection as you develop your palate, here's what we think is a sensible purchasing plan.

- Start with a 12-ounce glass. Too big, you think? Not really. You're going to pour only about 4 ounces into the glass to leave plenty of room for swirling. You can use this all-purpose glass for red or white.
- A Champagne flute is next on the list. Champagne is the only wine that shouldn't be served in an all-purpose glass. The flute, which has a cone- or tulip-shaped bowl, retains the effervescence of champagne, which—after all—is the essence of the thrill. The sherbet-style Champagne glasses may be very cool looking, but they won't contain the bubbles. Use these glasses to serve something else—like sherbet.
- Purchase number three is another all-purpose glass, only a different size. Well, which is it: larger or smaller? Your choice. Whichever way you go (some girls favor really big ones), use the smaller set for white wines and the larger for reds.
- If you regularly serve Sherry or Port, a copita is called for. It looks almost like a little version of the flute. It's fine for all fortified wines, which are served in smaller quantities than table wines.
- Beyond the basics, what you'll find on your shopping sprees are minute variations in glass design. If you have the budget, the storage and the interest—then you go, girl!

Quit Corkscrewing Around

Now that you've prepared yourself for any wine-related contingency, how do you propose getting the cork out of the bottle? (This question may become moot in the years ahead because well-respected wineries around the world are turning to—gasp!—

screwtops instead.) We don't participate in discussions of how to open a bottle with the corkscrew-obsessed because we don't really care how the bottle gets opened as long as it's opened quickly.

There are hundreds of corkscrews to choose from. We've become enamored lately with an expensive mounted version that, with a single effortless pull of the handle, removes the cork—no fuss, no muss. Two drawbacks: It doesn't belong to us, and it's not very transportable. And did we mention expensive?

Our more frugal options include the butterfly corkscrew, which wine snobs hate because it can mangle the cork, but which we use often because, with the center screw (the "worm") and butterfly-wing handles for leverage, it does a perfectly fine job. And it's ubiquitous, so why fight City Hall? To keep broken pieces of cork from getting into the wine (which is the main criticism), just avoid screwing the worm through the bottom of the cork.

If you like to screw, you'll get some satisfaction from the screw-pull corkscrew. It looks like a giant plastic clothespin with a five-inch worm in the center. Once you've placed the plastic over the bottle top, you turn the lever at the top clockwise and keep turning until the cork emerges from the bottle.

The "waiter's friend" is cute and flexible and gets a lot of action. He performs nightly at a restaurant near you. You've seen him. He's got a worm, a lever and a little knife (handy for cutting the capsule—the wrapping that covers the cork and neck of the bottle) and folds up like a pocketknife. It works well with a little practice, and if you drink enough wine, you'll get plenty of practice.

It's Your Serve: How Cold Is Cold?

Ever notice how some women's personalities are affected by the temperature? When they're too cold, they clam up. Their chattering

WINE BAR:
Who drank my wine? The butler did it!

The corkscrew without a screw is known variously as a "butler's friend" or an "ah-so." It has two thin metal blades. You work them down into the tight space between the cork and the bottle, then twist and gently pull the cork out. This device was at one time referred to as "the thieving butler" because unscrupulous servers could remove the cork undamaged, replace the expensive wine with cheap stuff, and reinsert the cork so no one—including their employers—was the wiser.

teeth prevent them from showcasing the erudition and sophisticated manners they've cultivated from childhood. At the other extreme, the heat makes them sweaty and cranky. Their usually genteel dispositions turn harsh, and their natural sweetness becomes overbearing.

A wine's personality is influenced by temperature too. Too cold and much of the flavor and aroma are masked. Too hot and the sweetness and alcohol become unpleasantly dominant. So, what's the ideal temperature to serve wine? Just like all women are not created equal, not all wines are alike. White wines should be served cold, but just how cold is personal preference. Red wines are served somewhat warmer, but not as warm as the typical "room temperature" of American homes.

Sparkling wines and sweet young whites	40–50 degrees
Rich, full-bodied whites	50–55 degrees
Light-bodied young reds	55–60 degrees
Full-bodied mature reds	60–65 degrees

The Twenty-Minute Rule

Unless you keep your home at a cool 55 degrees, room temperature is just too warm to serve red wine. On the other hand, most white wines served right from the fridge are too cold to recognize any of their taste. Two problems . . . one solution. Twenty minutes before serving, take your white wine out of the refrigerator to warm up and put the red wine in to chill out.

Pouring Tips

Okay, fill the glasses! No . . . wait. We didn't mean that literally. We offer a couple of techniques for pouring without spillage for the benefit of the laundress later on. (From our experience the

---

WINE BAR:
Decant, if you can

As red wine ages, it develops a sediment ("throws" a sediment, in wine parlance), which you don't want to drink. Decanting, when done carefully, will separate the sediment from the wine. Begin by standing the bottle upright and leaving it for as long as possible. A couple of days is ideal, but even thirty minutes will help the sediment fall to the bottom of the bottle. Remove the cork without disturbing the sediment. Stand a candle or flashlight next to the decanter. Slowly pour the wine in a steady stream into the decanter with the light below the neck of the bottle. You'll be able to see the exact moment when the sediment appears mixed with the wine. Stop pouring.

hostess and laundress are often one and the same. As a result, the hostess has real compassion for the laundress and an incentive to keep the tablecloth clean.) Pour until a glass is one-third full, giving your guests ample room to swirl without creating a mess. As you finish pouring into a glass, give the bottle a little twist—only about 20 degrees—and return the bottle immediately to a vertical position. If you're completely inept, as some of our dear friends are, you can tie a napkin around the neck of the bottle to prevent spillage. Now you've done your part for the laundress.

STORING FOR THE FUTURE

Usual definition of wine cellar: an underground room that's temperature controlled at 55 degrees, humidity controlled, dark, well ventilated and vibration free. *Our* definition of wine cellar: display rack in the dining room, suitcase under the bed, box under the stairs, lineup in the hallway closet. Which best describes the conditions at your house? Just like we thought. Let's be real.

Our wine-storage philosophy is this: If you drink them as soon as you buy them, you don't have to worry about ideal conditions. Even so, there are certain special bottles that we're saving for the right occasion, and we want them to be at least as good when we drink them as they were when we bought them. The further away from ideal your storage conditions are, the faster the wine will age and the more likely the wine will deteriorate.

What hurts wine most is temperatures much over 75 degrees and rapid fluctuations in temperature. Wine stored in an area that has gradual temperature fluctuations with the seasons is better off than wines stored in a room that's hot during the day and cold at night. With a choice between an environment that's a little too hot and one that's a little too cold, err on the cooler side. If you've ever drunk wine that got lost in your refrigerator for weeks, you know it was none the worse for the wear.

A simple wood or metal wine rack is perfectly adequate for storing a few bottles of wine. It will fit into relatively small spaces, will keep the bottles well ventilated and provide easy access. If you're storing wine for just a few weeks, they'll be just fine standing upright. Any longer than that, bottles should be stored on their sides to keep the corks wet so they don't dry out and let in air that can damage the wines.

Some wines are better able to withstand punishment than others. Young wines hold up better than old ones. Wines with lots of tannin will last longer in the heat than those with less. So, a full-bodied Cabernet will likely outlast a lighter-bodied Pinot Noir. With little or no tannin, white wines are the most susceptible to oxidation. Fortified wines are the real champs. Port and Madeira can endure temperature fluctuations and even exposure to oxygen and still be at the top of their game.

MARRYING WINE AND FOOD

Wine and food can forge a terrific partnership. When the relationship works, it *really* works. On rare occasions their combination can produce an experience so sublime we're sure all the stars were perfectly aligned. On most occasions the combination falls short of sheer ecstasy but provides true pleasure nonetheless.

Some experts will tell you that good partnerships are predictable. To some extent, they are. But take the case of a restaurant that features wine and food pairings. The wine is not randomly selected from column A, the food from column B. No, a high-level tasting session is conducted involving the cooking staff, wait staff and, of course, the wine staff. Each course is tried with an array of different wines. Comparisons are made and discussed and, finally, a choice is made. If wine and food pairing was so simple and predictable, why would it take a roomful of professionals to make the decision?

Wine affects the food it's drunk with, and food alters the taste of the wine. Food can exaggerate or diminish the character of a wine. Wine can overwhelm a food. Or the combination can produce—for better or worse—a taste all its own. While there are general guidelines and some classic combinations that have proven themselves over time, there are no absolutes. And that's because we each bring our own palates and preferences with us.

Just think of all the variables that can affect a food and wine marriage. You've got thousands of basic foods that are cooked (baked, poached, sautéed, grilled, boiled, broiled) or processed (pasteurized, liquefied, tenderized) in combination with other foods that are cooked or processed (or not) and adorned with herbs, spices and sauces. Then you've got thousands of unique wines, each made with different grapes from different areas (possibly in combination with other grapes), processed in their own ways, aged or not, aged in oak or not, and with various levels of alcohol. Too many permutations for a girl to even want to contemplate!

Here's our advice: Don't sweat it. You're not going to "ruin" a meal by selecting the "wrong" wine. Choose a wine you enjoy. Period. It may not be a match made in heaven, but it certainly won't be a match from hell either. The success of food and wine combinations is always subjective. However, there are some basic guidelines, and a few pointers couldn't hurt for your next attempt at matchmaking. Our rules for a happy marriage:

- **Neither partner should dominate.** (Sure, he may have sought a dominatrix or two during his single days, but now he's looking for marriage material.) Can you imagine the poor Dover sole overwhelmed by that big brute of a Cabernet? Intensely flavored food requires intensely flavored wine. Heavy dishes need a full-bodied wine. And delicate foods deserve lighter wines.

- **Preparation should set the stage.** (If a woman takes a hot bath and douses herself with perfume, the man will know what she has in mind.) Pairing a wine and a food is not as straightforward as chicken=white wine or beef=red wine. You have to consider what the food is *prepared with*. Chicken piccata with its lemon and butter sauce needs a lighter wine than chicken cacciatore with tomatoes and Italian spices.

- **Natural attractions should be observed.** (If two people are hot for each other, why try to fix them up with someone else?) Foods with an underlying sweetness—like a teriyaki marinade or honey glaze—go well with slightly sweet (or should we say "off dry") wines such as Chenin Blanc and Riesling. Ditto with high-acid foods and wines. Lemon dressings are attracted to Sauvignon Blanc, Pinot Grigio and Pinot Noir. A big steak goes hand in hand with a big tannic red wine like a Zinfandel because the fat in the meat tones down the tannin in the wine.

We wanted to give you a food-and-wine pairing chart that would be of real help as you plan for parties and dinners. So we polled our fellow Saucy Sisters to find out what they like to eat—and, in some cases, what they eat most often. Here are their food selections and our choices for accompanying wines.

GIRLFRIENDS' FOOD AND WINE MATCHES

		Champagne	Chardonnay	Chenin Blanc	Gewürztraminer	Pinot Gris/Grigio	Riesling	Sauvignon Blanc	Viognier	Beaujolais	Cabernet Sauvignon	Chianti	Malbec	Merlot	Pinot Noir	Shiraz/Syrah	Zinfandel	Madeira	Port
Cheese	Brie	•	•	•			•	•	•			•			•		•	•	•
	Goat	•				•		•							•				
	Gorgonzola	•		•	•	•	•		•					•				•	•
Desserts	Apple Pie	•					•	•										•	•
	Cheesecake	•					•	•										•	•
	Chocolate Mousse Cake	•			•		•											•	•
	Crème Brûlée	•		•			•	•										•	•
Eggs	Cheddar Omelet	•	•	•		•				•		•			•				
	Eggs Benedict	•	•			•		•		•		•			•				
Fish & Seafood	Caviar	•																	
	Crab Cakes	•	•	•		•	•	•	•										
	Grilled Salmon	•	•	•			•	•			•			•	•				
	Lobster	•	•			•	•	•	•						•				
	Mussels in White Wine Sauce	•	•			•	•	•											
	Smoked Trout	•	•	•	•	•	•	•	•						•				
	Sole Amandine	•	•	•	•	•	•	•	•	•									
	Sushi	•				•		•											

		CHAMPAGNE	CHARDONNAY	CHENIN BLANC	GEWÜRZTRAMINER	PINOT GRIS/GRIGIO	RIESLING	SAUVIGNON BLANC	VIOGNIER	BEAUJOLAIS	CABERNET SAUVIGNON	CHIANTI	MALBEC	MERLOT	PINOT NOIR	SHIRAZ/SYRAH	ZINFANDEL	MADEIRA	PORT
Meats	Barbecued Ribs	•		•	•		•		•		•	•	•	•	•	•			
	Grilled Pork Chops	•	•	•	•	•			•		•			•	•	•			
	Lamb	•	•								•	•	•	•	•	•	•		
	Roast Beef	•	•								•	•	•	•	•	•	•		
	Steak au Poivre	•	•								•	•	•	•	•	•	•		
	Szechuan Beef	•			•	•	•			•									
	Veal Scallopini	•	•					•	•	•	•				•				
	Venison	•									•	•		•		•	•		
Pasta	Cheese Ravioli	•	•			•	•	•	•		•								
	Fettucini Alfredo	•	•	•		•	•	•											
	Lasagna	•				•	•			•	•	•				•			
	Spaghetti and Tomato Sauce	•				•	•				•			•	•	•			
Pizza	Pepperoni Pizza	•									•	•	•	•	•	•	•		
	Pesto Pizza	•	•		•		•	•	•			•		•					
Poultry	Lemon Chicken	•	•	•		•		•	•										
	Roast Turkey	•	•	•	•	•	•	•	•	•			•	•	•	•			
	Tandoori Chicken	•	•	•		•	•	•	•				•	•	•	•			
Salads	Arugula with Vinaigrette	•				•		•	•										
	Caesar	•	•			•	•	•	•										

		CHAMPAGNE	CHARDONNAY	CHENIN BLANC	GEWÜRZTRAMINER	PINOT GRIS/GRIGIO	RIESLING	SAUVIGNON BLANC	VIOGNIER	BEAUJOLAIS	CABERNET SAUVIGNON	CHIANTI	MALBEC	MERLOT	PINOT NOIR	SHIRAZ/SYRAH	ZINFANDEL	MADEIRA	PORT
Snacks	Goldfish	•				•	•	•	•	•									
	Hershey Kisses	•																•	•
	Popcorn	•				•	•	•	•										
Veggies	Bean Burrito	•				•		•	•	•				•	•				
	Corn on the Cob	•	•	•		•	•			•									
	Grilled Zucchini	•	•	•		•	•	•											
	Twice Baked Potato	•	•			•	•	•	•	•		•	•	•	•				

COOKING WITH WINE: SAUCY SISTERS IN THE KITCHEN

Create culinary masterpieces with a little help from an agreeable bottle of wine. Yes, a swig and a splash. The dual-purpose elixir—both magic ingredient and mood enhancer. (We figured if it worked for Julia Child, it can work for us too.)

Cooking with wine heightens the natural flavor of foods (reducing the need for salt) and adds moisture and aroma. But it can also curdle your cream. So, for our gastronomic goddesses of the vine, we issue these do's for divine results every time. (We hate to be told don't and presumed you would too.) Do:

- Use a wine you'd want to drink for cooking (almost goes without saying for the Wine Goddess). The flip side of this instruction is to avoid cooking wines from the supermarket. They contain salt (as a preservative) and are undrinkable. (This also exempts them from alcoholic beverage taxes . . . clever marketers.) Besides, we doubt the wine started out as anything approaching a *grand cru*.

- Use whatever wine you plan to serve with the meal as your cooking wine. (What more perfect food-and-wine match could you possibly come up with?)

- Unless otherwise instructed, use medium to dry wines for cooking.

- Use wine as part of a recipe's total liquid, not in addition.

- In general, use white wine for light-colored and mildly flavored dishes, such as poultry, pork and fish, and reds for darker-colored and more highly flavored red meats.

- To prevent curdling, add wine first to recipes that also call for milk, cream, eggs or butter.

- Be conservative with the salt shaker. Wine intensifies salty flavors.

- Use wine in marinades. It will tenderize as well as add flavor.

- Add table wines at the beginning of cooking to allow the alcohol to evaporate and produce a subtle taste. Add fortified wines—like Port or Sherry—at the end of cooking to retain their full-bodied taste.

- Reduce wine to intensify its flavors. One cup of wine will reduce to 1/4 cup when cooked uncovered for about 10 minutes.

The biggest mistake lesser goddesses make when cooking with wine is adding too much of it. Can you imagine? Remember to save some for sipping!

ASK THE SAUCY SISTERS

Are there any foods that just don't go with wine?

We don't reject any foods entirely. But some foods present quite a challenge: artichokes, asparagus, chocolate, olives, spinach, vinegar and yogurt, to name a few.

What if the cork breaks while I'm opening the wine?

First, try to remove the rest of the cork by attacking it from odd angles with your corkscrew. If that fails, push what's left of the cork into the bottle. You'll probably end up with cork in the wine, so strain the wine into a decanter.

I chilled several bottles of wine for a party but didn't use them all. Will it hurt to take the wines out of the refrigerator and store them back in the basement?

It won't hurt them at all. And we're sure you'll need the space in your refrigerator.

You always hear about wine and cheese going together. Does that mean all wines go with all cheeses?

There's an old wine merchant's saying, "Buy on an apple and sell on cheese"—meaning that a wine will taste thin and metallic when paired with a sweet, acidic fruit but taste fuller and softer when paired with cheese. Having said that, some wines go better with some cheeses. Hard cheeses like cheddar go well with full-bodied reds. Soft cheeses like Brie match well with mellow reds such as Pinot Noir. Blue cheeses work particularly well with sweet wines. Goat cheese is one of our favorites; we pair it with Sancerre and Pouilly-Fumé.

Why do wine bottles have two labels?

A back label isn't mandatory, but some wineries have found

that they can add fluffy verbiage on the back to encourage your purchase. Or they can expound on their winemaking philosophies, or give you a range of foods to serve with the wine. Other wineries have found that they can say all the boring stuff on the back and let the visual appeal of the front label draw you in. Technically, the required information on U.S. labels has to appear on the front label. So wineries just call the front the "back" and the back the "front."

What real power do wine critics have?

In some cases, minimal. In one particular case, lots. Robert J. Parker Jr. (maybe you've heard the name) is the single most influential wine critic in the world. He originated the much-imitated 100-point scale for rating wines. Wine merchants will tell you, "If Parker gives a wine a 90 or more, we have trouble getting the wine. If he gives it less than 90, we have trouble selling it." Not only availability but price is affected as well. Parker points have been instrumental in determining which wines become cult wines. The term "Parkerization" has emerged regarding wines that seem to have been made with the intention of garnering Parker points—that is, made in the rich, thick, ripe, oaky style that he appreciates. Whether to buy a wine based on Parker's (or anyone else's) points should depend on whether your taste in wine corresponds to that of the scorer.

I can't tell the difference between a $7 Chardonnay and one that costs $40. Why the big difference in price?

There are two elements at work here: One is the prestige and the track record of the producer. (Let's be honest, many of us pay top dollar for a Gucci bag even though a purse from Wal-Mart is perfectly adequate to hold all our stuff.) The other factor is that, up to a point, there can be differences in the cost of production. Your $7 Chardonnay could have been mass-produced from vines that yielded the maximum amount of grapes allowed, on land that was relatively cheap, and from juice that was acquired from several pressings. The higher-priced Chardonnay probably was planted on more expensive land, had lower grape yields through pruning, and was aged in expensive oak barrels.

What's the best age to drink a wine?

We assume by your question you're referring to the age of the wine, as opposed to the age of the drinker (who we think can enjoy wine throughout her life). We say, "Drink 'em young!" Contrary to popular perception, only a small group of wines benefit from extended bottle aging. Most wines sold today—reds as well as whites and pinks—are designed to be drunk within a year or two of bottling. And the finer wines that do need time to reach their full potential all mature at different rates. For the most part, if the wine is on the shelf, it's probably ready to drink.

Chapter 4

~~~

Wine Down Restaurant Row...

MASTERING THE ART OF
RESTAURANT WINE ETIQUETTE

CAN A WINE DRINKER find true value at a restaurant? That's like asking if a girl can get a good deal at Tiffany's. The answer is "sometimes," if you know what to look for and if you appreciate the Tiffany wrapping as much as you do the objet d'art.

Unlike shopping for wine in a retail setting, where your only concerns are price and selection, the restaurant experience has other fundamentals that can either delight or disappoint you. Is the wine list understandable? Is the server knowledgeable? Is the glassware suitable? Is the service attentive without being patronizing? You've got to be satisfied with all the elements to get real worth because—let's face it—you're paying a premium for it.

On average, wine sales comprise 20 percent of diners' total restaurant tabs. That jumps to 40 percent at expensive restaurants. Obviously, price is a consideration. Restaurants will cite labor, training and equipment costs as reasons for high prices. Whether justified or not, here's how restaurants determine their wine prices. They shoot for markups of three times the wholesale price (or two to two and a half times the retail price). So, a bottle they buy for $10 (which you could buy retail for $14), they'll sell to you for $30.

Of course, it's not always that cut-and-dried, especially when a bottle wholesales for $30 and the restaurant tries to charge $90 for it. Most wine drinkers we know aren't going to spring for a hundred-dollar bottle of wine. Restaurants realize this and make adjustments accordingly. The good news for us is that restaurants will usually sell higher-cost wines at less of a markup. The bad news is they'll mark up low-cost wines even higher than three times.

You may find it easy to determine how much you're prepared to spend on a bottle of wine, but deciding which wine to spend it on can be problematic, depending on the nature of the wine list you encounter. Wine lists are as different as the restaurants that produce them. But, like men, you can generally fit them into a category.

- A restaurant may offer no more than a house red, house white and house blush. Usually the wines will have a brand name, but sometimes they won't. This list is like the loser who keeps trying to impress you. No matter what he does, he'll never quite measure up. But on a dateless Saturday night, you're just grateful for the company.
- A restaurant may offer only common brands that everyone recognizes. This list is like the nice guy from high school you were so fond of. All the mothers loved him, too. When you want comfort and dependability, he's your pal.
- A (usually expensive) restaurant may offer thousands of wines from a list as thick as a phone book with prestigious names and vintages. This list is like the irresistible hunk in the Armani suit driving a red Carrera convertible. You could

spend days admiring him, but you know you'll never end up marrying him.

- A restaurant may offer a varied and thoughtful, but not exhaustive, selection of wines. You'll find some familiar names, but you'll see a bunch of unknowns thrown in as well. This list is like the smart, successful man who, while conscientious about planning ahead, will surprise you with a trip to Venice.

WHAT MAKES A RESTAURANT WINE-FRIENDLY

Wine List

How wines are presented on a list can help you with your wine selection—or not. The wines may be presented simply as red and white. They may be organized by country, region or grape variety. They may be arranged by wine style: fresh, crisp unoaked whites or full-bodied reds. Wines may be listed in a progressive sequence from lightest style to the richest or from cheapest to the most expensive. The most useful lists will provide brief descriptions of the wines and pairing suggestions . . . but don't hold your breath. You may have to call for help.

Your Server

Your server is the obvious first choice to answer your wine questions. If well trained, he'll be on a first-name basis with the wines on the list and will be able to describe how each one tastes. If his response, instead, is "Uh, well, they're all good," you'll know you're on your own. Or if his recommendations are limited to one wine and one wine only, you have a right to be suspicious of his motives. Sometimes servers are told to push certain wines because the restaurant makes more money on those.

The same profit-motivated restaurants train their servers to maximize wine sales in other ways. The energetic pourer will fill your group's glasses to capacity and keep topping off each glass until the bottle is prematurely empty—which can happen long before the first course has been cleared. The result? You order another bottle. Don't get us wrong. Second bottles are wonderful. We'd just like to drink the first bottle at our own pace. If you'd prefer to take charge of the pouring, it's perfectly okay to say so.

Glassware

No matter who pours, the glass should be filled about one-third full to facilitate swirling without splashing. A measly third may seem ridiculous, given the tiny little glasses that some restaurants provide. We think so and will ask for larger, stemmed water glasses instead.

You can tell a lot about a restaurant's attitude toward wine by the stemware it uses. If you're served in what amounts to a jelly glass on a stem, the restaurant doesn't give a hoot. It's amazing how many restaurants that spare no expense on their food will kiss off wine service with undersize, overweight glassware. Don't put up with it. Look at it this way: What restaurant would sell you a $30 entrée and then give you plastic utensils to eat it with?

A wine-friendly restaurant does more than just profit from wine. It offers us a diverse selection so we can stick with the familiar if we're feeling timid or jump on something novel if we're feeling adventurous. It offers us reasonable prices so we don't have to hock our grandmother's pearls to order another bottle. A wine-friendly restaurant gives us a clear and descriptive wine list so we have realistic expectations about what we're ordering. Through professional employee training, the restaurant provides knowledgeable and respectful service so we're comfortable asking questions. And it supplies appropriate wine accoutrements to heighten our dining and wine-tasting experience.

WINE BY THE GLASS

The women's rights movement may have had its roots in the suffrage movement of the nineteenth century and may have gained momentum from the feminists of the '60s, but it's wine by the glass that's granted us the license to experiment as we please. Some may call it reckless. We call it smart.

With wine by the glass, it's all about you. Never mind what others at your table want to drink. Who cares about matching a wine with someone else's meal! You can throw caution to the wind and order whatever your heart desires. This is your chance to discover true love. Tuned-in restaurants search for those out-of-the-ordinary wines for their lists and often get dazzlers that

---

WINE BAR:
"Would you care for a bottle of McWine, madam?"

If McDonald's served wine, a $10 bottle of Pinot Grigio would cost you $60. That's based on their average beverage markup of nearly 600 percent. That same $10 bottle will cost about $14 at a retail store and $30 to $40 at a fine restaurant.

aren't sold in any retail store. Sure, this may mean your true love will be a one-night stand. But who says you can't fall in love again tomorrow? Or even multiple times at one meal?

Expectations can be crucial during this period of experimentation. After all, if you're expecting Tom Cruise to knock at your door, you're bound to be disappointed when Ozzy Osbourne comes stumbling in. For a new wine experience to be enjoyable and not just a blind leap into unknown tasting territory, it helps to have a touch of the familiar. If you know you like the taste of Chardonnay, for example, try something close to it, only different. Here are some suggestions to start you on the road to vino nirvana.

IF YOU ENJOY . . .	TRY . . .
Chardonnay	French Chablis
	Pinot Blanc
	Pouilly-Fuissé
	Viognier
	Mâcon-Villages
Pinot Grigio	Sauvignon Blanc
	Pinot Gris
	Dry Riesling
	Soave
	Sancerre
	Pouilly-Fumé
White Zinfandel	German Riesling
	Chenin Blanc
	Gewürztraminer
	Vouvray
Merlot	Zinfandel
	Pinot Noir
	Beaujolais

IF YOU ENJOY . . .	TRY . . .
	Chianti
	Côtes du Rhone
Cabernet	Syrah/Shiraz
Sauvignon	Amarone
	Malbec

In a perfect world all restaurants would offer an endless array of wines by the glass. Sadly, that's rarely the case. Much as we hate to say so, there's a legitimate reason. Wine begins to deteriorate as soon as the bottle is opened. It's a problem for restaurants to preserve the wine that remains in all those opened bottles. Unless a restaurant can invest in an expensive preservation system, a lot of leftover wine is wasted, and profits are poured down the drain.

Of course, we're alluding here to restaurants that care about wine. Others take a more lackadaisical approach. At the end of the evening, the cork is slapped back into place and the bottle stands on the bar until business the next day. You walk in for lunch on day two and get a glass of wine that may have already suffered the ravages of time. Avoid this predicament by asking your server when the bottle was opened. Some waiters and bartenders mark the date the bottle was opened. Don't accept a wine you think won't be fresh. For some picky people this could be a couple of hours. For us, it's twenty-four hours for a white that's been refrigerated.

When you're ordering wine just for yourself, you have the luxury of selecting one that will pair perfectly with the food in front of you. For simple foods it's easy. This little rhyme we learned in childhood should help:

> White wine is fine with fish or fowl,
> Red is just right with charbroiled cow.

But what on earth do you choose to go with, say, a wilted baby spinach salad with sautéed onions, tomato, pancetta and goat cheese with a warm balsamic vinaigrette? If we were in a red mood, we might order a Pinot Noir or a Chianti. If it were a white day, we'd probably have a dry Riesling or a Sauvignon Blanc. We're not following any rules. We've just tasted enough wines to know what we like. We don't know if you'll like the same wines we do, but here's what we recommend to go with some popular restaurant fare.

Hamburger	Shiraz, Zinfandel, Chardonnay and Champagne
Steak	Cabernet Sauvignon, Amarone and Champagne
Pepperoni Pizza	Chianti, Sauvignon Blanc and Champagne
Chinese	Riesling, Gewürztraminer, Pinot Noir and Champagne
Sushi	Sauvignon Blanc, Riesling, Saké and Champagne
Mexican	Gewürztraminer, Rosé, Beaujolais Nouveau and Champagne
Broiled Lobster	Chardonnay, Chablis and Champagne
Barbecued Ribs	Pinot Blanc, Red Meritage and Champagne
Grilled Salmon	Merlot, Pinot Noir, Pinot Gris and Champagne
Chicken Caesar Salad	Pinot Gris, Chardonnay and Champagne

And here's the most useful wine-by-the-glass tip we can give you: If you and your dining partners are likely to drink more than three glasses of the same wine, order a bottle. You'll get four or five glasses of wine from a bottle for about the same price as three individual glasses. Cheers!

ORDERING A BOTTLE OF WINE WITH CONFIDENCE: 5 FOOLPROOF STRATEGIES

Whether you're entertaining prospective clients or trying to charm a new beau, ordering wine in a restaurant is a high-pressure responsibility. Even under ideal conditions, you're not going to please everyone. They've all got different personalities and different tastes. On top of that, each person will be eating something different. If you were choosing the entire menu—or if you were entertaining at home—you'd have much more control and an easier task of choosing the wine.

In a restaurant your wine selection has many parameters, not the least of which is your budget. Just remember this when making your choice: It's possible to drink more or less any wine with more or less any food. And while you may not choose the perfect wine for everyone at the table, it's almost impossible to choose a wine that's completely wrong.

Ultimately your selection will be judged not so much on the wine's merits but on the confidence you exude in ordering it. When you demonstrate authority in the selection process, your guests will believe you've made an outstanding choice long before the wine is even poured. They'll expect to like the wine and probably will. If they don't like it, they'll be too awed by your self-possessed style and obvious experience to speak up. We're here to offer you five different wine-selection strategies that will give you the confidence you need to wow any crowd.

The Easy Way Out

We're going to make this as easy as falling off your three-inch Manolo Blahnick stilettos. Only two wines to remember: Pinot Noir and dry Riesling. Pinot Noir if the group is in the mood for red. Riesling if everyone's clamoring for white. Period.

You don't have to worry about what everyone's eating. There's no matching to be done—just a simple choice between red and white. And if you suffer from serious indecision, order both. The wine will be drunk, we guarantee.

These wines are the sluts of the food world. They're indiscriminate about pairings. They pretty much like all foods and don't care if one is slathered in fat or another is all spiced up. They have no shame about having multiple partners simultaneously. And you better believe they show everyone a good time.

Ordering is simple. When handed the wine list, hold it but ignore it. Turn to the waiter and ask what Pinot Noirs or dry Rieslings the restaurant offers. He might begin to recite the names, but more than likely he'll refer to the wine list in your hand.

Aha! This is exactly what you want him to do. While he points out each listing, you can check out the prices without being obvious.

For Rieslings make sure they're labeled "dry" if they're American or "*trocken*" if they're German. Otherwise you may end up with a wine that's a little too sweet for most of your guests' palates. For the Pinot Noirs, look for wines from Oregon and California, which will usually mean good taste and good value.

The Three Little P's

Prescreen.
Preorder.
Pronounce.

A sneak preview of a restaurant's wine list will guarantee that you come across as an expert to your friends. It's like someone giving you the exam questions in advance. Having confidence is easy when you already know the answers.

Lots of restaurants have Web sites. And the ones that care about wine will have at least part of their wine lists there. If not, there's always the fax. Most restaurants will be happy to send their list to you. The other option is to visit the restaurant a day or two ahead and peruse the list right there. It's worth mentioning here that in order to get a gracious reception from the restaurant's management, *do not* call or visit during the height of business.

Prescreening the list gives you plenty of time, unobserved by others, to read, evaluate and compute. Then when the list is presented to you in front of your group, you'll appear cool, calm and obviously familiar with all of the wines.

A thoughtful hostess may occasionally preorder the wine. Call the restaurant in advance with your selection, and the wait staff will be prepared to pour at your direction.

An advance copy of the wine list will give you an opportunity to practice pronouncing unfamiliar wine names. Say words like Gewürztraminer (guh-VURTS-trah-mee-ner) and Pouilly-Fuissé (poo-yee-fwee-SAY) out loud and often so that, at showtime, they'll just roll off your tongue like you've been using them for years.

Shooting from the "Hip"

You're frantic to choose a wine that will match the cutting-edge chic of the Helmut Langs and Donna Karans draping the chairs around your table. What would be sufficiently avant-garde to impress this postmodern in-crowd? Certainly not the traditional old Bordeaux and Burgundies. You want something that screams "Look at me! I'm hot, hip and haut monde."

Just like the best designers take classic forms and colors and transform them into today's trends, winemakers use well-known grapes and give them their own spin. Some of them, like Merlot, take off and become their own phenomenon. But Merlot is so yesterday.

Fashionable whites that will show off your savvy must include Sauvignon Blanc from New Zealand. Sure, you can find good Sauvignon Blancs from elsewhere, but New Zealand has put a fresh new face on them. An Oregon Pinot Gris is an in-the-know choice. It's the same grape as the ubiquitous Pinot Grigio from Italy but with more substance. Viognier—from anywhere, including its French homeland—is a classy wine with voluminous flavor.

If your sartorial sense demands red, try on a Malbec from Argentina for size. It'll have a big and boisterous impact. A more subtle choice is a Cabernet Franc from California. No longer just one of many grapes in a blend, Cabernet Franc has won popularity as a varietal all its own. It's like a Merlot with cachet. Just like bell-bottoms keep coming back into style, so do wines. Order a Châteauneuf-du-Pape. It's full-bodied and retro-chic.

Playing the Midfield

Whether you're currently playing the field or are taking a time-out, we're sure you've honed a well-developed strategy for snaring a winner. After all, smart girls don't enter the game unless they know all the plays. The same holds true for choosing a wine. Deploying an artful strategy will help you select a wine winner every time.

Go for the midsection—the middle of the price range, that is. These can be outstanding wines. They're not as widely hyped as some of the top items, so are often a good deal for the price. Wines in this midsection tend to have lower markups—often only two times wholesale instead of three—than wines sold at the lower range.

More and more restaurants are boasting wine lists of hundreds and even thousands of different wines. But even selecting a wine from a list of only a hundred can be challenging. That's why we recommend the middle-of-the-list tactic. Once you've decided on the type of wine (Chardonnay, Cabernet, etc.), go to that category and head to the middle of the list. Choose two or three and ask your server which one he recommends.

This strategy is especially handy when you're playing on a foreign field, like when the list is all Italian wines and you don't speak the language. You can usually ascertain whether you're in red or white territory and go from there. And don't be shy about ordering by number. It'll probably get you to your goal faster.

Sommelier Knows Best

Men will not ask for directions. They want to find the way all on their own, even if they end up in a different state with an empty gas tank. It's a macho thing. Thank God that's not something we have to worry about.

We're confident enough to ask for help when we need it. Whether in the driver's seat or on a restaurant banquette, we look for the easiest and most efficient way to get us where we want to go. If that means taking someone else's advice, so be it.

The sommelier (saw-muhl-YAY) is the person at the restaurant whose advice you want. He's the one, after all, who put the wine list together. Who better to guide you? Of course, not all restaurants (in fact, very few) have a sommelier. Can you trust your server to recommend an appropriate wine? Sometimes yes. Sometimes no.

Before you relinquish your wine-selection responsibility and risk disaster, ask your server a question or two. Try something open-ended like, "This is an interesting list. Why were these wines selected?" There's no right or wrong answer. But you'll be able to tell by the intelligence of the response if you want to entrust your dining experience to this person.

A good sommelier, or a well-informed server who has passed your rigorous questioning, can be your best friend and coconspirator when you're about to buy a bottle of wine for the price of a Bulgari baguette. You'll want to impart two pieces of information to the sommelier: (1) the food you plan to order and (2) your price range. The food part is easy. Price may be a more delicate issue, and the sommelier is well aware of that. To be discreet, point to one or two affordable wines on the list and move your finger to the price. Say, "I was thinking about something along this line." The sommelier will understand. Pointing is also a helpful gesture when you don't know how to pronounce a wine's name.

This is the perfect opportunity to describe, as best you can, the kind of wine you have in mind. "I'm in the mood for a red. I've always been fond of Cabernets but would like to try something a little different." This gives the sommelier a direction but allows him to recommend a wine specifically suited to your meal.

Some people are intimidated by a sommelier and consider him a symbol of wine snobbery. But you'll likely find that he's an enthusiastic teacher whose mission is to make sure you're happy with the wine selection.

THE WINE-TASTING RITUAL STEP-BY-STEP

Is it thumbs-up or thumbs-down? You ordered the wine. Now you have to pass judgment on its drinkability. The purpose of this wine-tasting ritual isn't to determine the suitability of your choice. It's to determine if the wine has for some reason gone bad. You have two alternatives here: the wine is drinkable and should be served or it's not and should be sent back.

The either/or decision is pretty simple, but the ceremony attached to it has made otherwise fearless men melt into their upholstered chairs. As women we have a distinct advantage over the guys in this domain. After all, we've been faking things for years. We can fake this too.

You don't have to know much to come across like a pro and impress everyone at your table, including the solemn waiter hovering at your side. Consider this an acting job. With our stage directions, a few lines of dialogue and a little improvisation, you'll convince all observers that you're a wine master. Go ahead. Milk it for all it's worth.

- Action: Waiter approaches table, presents wine for your visual approval. You look intently at the label for a moment, then nod knowingly to the waiter in the affirmative.

  By these subtle movements you've indicated to the waiter that yes, indeed, this is the wine you ordered. At this point it's in your best interest to check the vintage date on the label. A vintage other than the one you ordered can cost you. A substitution may be from an inferior year, and you can count on being charged the price of your original selection. Your nod gives the waiter the go-ahead to open and pour the wine.

- Action: Waiter cuts the capsule, wipes the lip of the bottle, removes the cork and places the cork on the table in front of you. You ignore the cork. Or, for added drama, pick up the cork and examine all its surfaces.

  The cork isn't really going to tell you anything important about the quality of the wine inside the bottle. On occasion you might find crystals on the end of the cork that had contact with the wine. These are harmless tartrates that can unpredictably form during aging and can be ignored. Once in a dozen blue moons you might encounter a cork that's dry and crumbly or thoroughly wet. Either condition could signal that air has crept into the bottle and spoiled the wine. In any case, suspend judgment until you've tasted the wine.

- Action: Waiter wipes inside the lip of the bottle, pours a thimble-size portion of wine into your glass and stands back. You pick up the glass by the stem and hold it up to a light source—lamp, candle—or against a white background. Look admiringly at the bowl for several seconds.

  How you hold your wineglass has significance. Our observation is that the more a person knows about wine, the lower on the stem she holds the glass.

  The rationale is that holding the glass by the bowl will warm the wine and alter its taste. Whether that's the real motive or simply affectation, your glass-holding style will advertise your wine savvy. Tradition says you should visually inspect the wine for color and clarity. While the color may provide intriguing clues to a wine's background, it's not going to tell you whether the wine is good or bad. As for clarity, high-tech operations in winemaking have pretty much eliminated the cloudiness issue. So look all you want. But the real test is to follow.

- Action: Put the glass back down on the table. Now rotate it so that the wine swirls around the inside of the glass.

  At this juncture some wine geeks will make comments about the wine's "legs" or "tears"—the little streams of wine that slowly slide back down the inside of the glass after swirling. The legs may give some indication of a wine's alcoholic strength. But the primary purpose of swirling is to release the wine's aromas.

• Action: Pick up your glass, position your nose above the bowl and gently inhale.

Because smell and taste are related, just smelling a wine can reveal a lot about its character. If a wine has gone bad for any reason, your nose will likely detect it first.

• Action: Bring the glass to your lips and take a sip of wine. Hold the wine in your mouth for a moment. Then swallow.

Experienced tasters swish the wine around in their mouths because different parts of the mouth and tongue register the attributes of sweetness, acidity, bitterness and texture. Do this or not as you wish.

• Action: Pause for a moment as if reflecting. Turn to the waiter and in an authoritative voice say "very nice" or "that will do nicely" or "you may pour for the table."

The overwhelming chances are that the wine you selected is perfectly drinkable. You don't need to comment on the wine because (1) everyone will assume it's good because it passed your meticulous analysis, and (2) each guest will taste it differently anyway.

• Action: Waiter pours for the others at the table and finally pours a decent amount of wine into your glass.

Congratulations! You fooled them all!

SENDING WINE BACK

Oh, no! You followed the wine-tasting ritual script, but when it got to the part where you put your nose into the wineglass and took a big whiff, something gross happened. Rather than being

> ## WINE BAR:
> ### *The truth is uncorked*
>
> Presentation of the cork to diners goes way back to a time before labels, when there was no proof a bottle of wine actually came from the winery it was attributed to. Unscrupulous restaurateurs would pass off common French wine as having come from the famous châteaus. To halt this practice, the châteaus began branding the corks with their names. And waiters began presenting the corks to verify the wine's origin.

met with the fresh and fruity scent of berries, you were nearly gagged by noxious fumes. It's time to send the wine back!

Nine times out of ten, your nose knows. If you'd prefer to rely on your palate, go ahead and taste. It won't hurt you. It'll probably confirm what you already know: Anything that smells that bad isn't something you're about to gag down.

Now is no time to be timid or ashamed. In a polite but firm manner say to the waiter, "I think this bottle is bad, and I'd like to send it back." Be prepared for a variety of responses, but the bottom line is a good waiter will replace the bad bottle with a new bottle of the same wine.

If the waiter knows something about wine, he'll probably smell the offending wine himself. It could help determine the culprit responsible for the flawed wine—a tainted cork or a long ride in a hot truck. If the waiter knows little about wine, he might call over a manager for another opinion.

But even if you're the only one who recognizes the flaw, the restaurant should replace the wine—and, most likely, will. It's no financial hardship for the restaurant because the restaurant will, in turn, send the bottle back to the distributor for replacement. If you or the restaurant management is wary of another bottle of the same wine, just make another selection.

RESTAURANT FAUX PAS TO AVOID

You'd never be caught dead in Capri pants with knee-high boots—an obvious fashion faux pas that would have you shunned by anyone who recognizes style and good taste. You know better. But some social blunders are the result of just being unaware, like the woman returning from a trip to the ladies' room with her skirt tucked into her pantyhose. Wine faux pas in restaurants are committed either by people who genuinely have bad taste (not you, of course) or by those who are simply not yet acquainted with wine traditions.

- Asking the waiter for a bottle of Chateaubriand.

    Wine is often described as "chewy," but, for heaven's sake,

---

WINE BAR:
Cheap Wine Tricks

The Saucy Sisters are persistently in pursuit of bargains, and we love to share our finds with our girlfriends. Here are two little tricks to help you get more wine than you paid for.

"Share"—We order one glass of wine to share. When we get lucky, the bartender pours the wine into two glasses rather than one. We always end up with more than half a glass.

"Taste"—We ask for a taste of wine before ordering a full glass. We drink it up and either order a full glass or try another sample.

this is taking it too far. Chateaubriand, as we all know, is not sipped. It's cut into small pieces with a steak knife, accented with a small amount of bearnaise sauce, then masticated to a consistency such that it can be savored and swallowed. Chateaubriand is, after all, beef. When it comes to wine, you're looking for Château Something Else. Lots of wines—especially French wines from Bordeaux—use château in their names. While the literal translation is "castle," in winespeak *château* means "wine estate" or "vineyard" and refers to the actual land where the wine was produced. By the way, the châteaus whose names appear on the labels can range from shacks and modest farmhouses to sumptuous palaces. We often wonder if the châteaus pictured on the labels are real or the product of some artist's vivid imagination.

- Referring to the sommelier as "that piece of ass with the cute little silver cup hanging around his neck."

While the characterization may be accurate, why antagonize the person who holds the keys to the wine cellar? The sommelier is the wine steward in a fine restaurant whose job is to help you select an appropriate wine for your meal and budget and then to carry out the wine-serving ritual with a high degree of professionalism and a low level of pretension. And the cup hanging around his neck on a ribbon? It's called a *tastevin*—French for, you guessed it, "taste wine." The tradition goes back at least a couple hundred years to the cellar masters of Burgundy, who developed the silver cup to sample wines in the near-dark, candlelit cellars. The dimples in the silver were designed to catch and reflect light to make it possible to check the color and clarity of the wine. Alas, for today's sommeliers who might enjoy a small cup of wine at each table, the *tastevin* is more ceremonial than practical.

- Taking your favorite box wine to Le Cirque.

  Don't get us wrong. We'll tote our own wines to restaurants at every opportunity—especially if it's a restaurant not licensed to sell wine. If that's the case, go for it. Take anything you want. However, if the restaurant does serve wine, don't take a wine that's on its list. (Yes, we know Le Cirque has no wines in the box on its list, but that's a whole other discussion.) Let's face it, a restaurant makes most of its profits from alcohol. It's not really fair for you to deprive them of that profit. Here's what we suggest as an alternative: When you call for your reservation, express your intention to bring a "special" wine. Make sure it's not on their list and offer your reason for wanting to bring it. Maybe the occasion is important to you (like an anniversary or birthday), or perhaps the wine itself has a particular significance. Nine times out of ten, the restaurant will bend over backward to make you happy. Just remember that when you supply your own wine, you'll be assessed a "corkage" fee. It varies tremendously from restaurant to restaurant and can range from $5 to $35 a bottle and more. And, depending on the cost of the wine, the corkage could obliterate any savings you were expecting. If you decide to take your own wine anyway, the most important rule to follow is to tip the waiter as if you had bought the wine at the restaurant. After all, someone else still provided glassware, opened the bottle and served the wine.

- Sending a bottle of wine back because the color clashes with your dress.

  The only legitimate reason for sending a bottle of wine back is that it's bad. And by bad we don't mean it simply doesn't meet your expectations. While most restaurants will indulge whiners and exchange the wine in question for another bottle, it's totally bad form to complain without real justification. So when is a wine officially bad? You'll know it when you smell it. The main culprit for turning a charming and tasteful wine into a malodorous swine is the cork. In about 5 percent of all wines, the natural cork has been tainted with a chemical compound called TCA, which causes the wine to smell musty and moldy and to taste equally as noxious. This is what wine buffs mean when they say a wine is "corked." If a whiff of the wine reminds you of rotting socks in your old boyfriend's gym locker, send the bottle back. A wine can also be ruined if it's been shipped or stored at high temperatures. It will actually taste like it's been cooked. Send it back. Less likely, but not impossible, is chemical or bacterial spoilage. If it smells like nail polish remover or rotten eggs, send it back.

• Asking for a doggie bag for your leftover wine.

Unless you look particularly beautiful in an orange jumpsuit, you'll want to avoid this habit because in most states you'll be breaking a law by driving with an open container. But there are two even more important reasons: (1) Once the cork is out of the bottle and the wine is exposed to oxygen, the wine begins to deteriorate. You won't be able to keep it for long. By the time you get around to finishing the rest of the bottle, it probably won't be worth the effort of bringing it home; (2) Asking for a doggie bag for wine is just plain tacky and makes you look cheap. While the best way to dispose of leftover wine is to drink it, we don't want to encourage overconsumption. If you have a worthy wine, a better option— and a classy gesture—is to send a glass back to the chef.

• Sipping wine with a cheekful of Bazooka.

Besides demonstrating a lack of good breeding, chewing

gum while downing wine distorts the taste of the wine. Everything you eat—whether it's sweet, salty, sour or bitter—will affect the taste sensation of the wine. A sweet flavor will make a wine seem more bitter. It will also cause dry wines to taste fairly nasty and will bring out their acidity. Pairing wine with real food is tricky enough. Adding a wad of chewed-up plastic to the equation is too much to have to compute.

ASK THE SAUCY SISTERS

How much should I tip on wine?

We don't know, or care, what etiquette experts might say, but here's the Saucy Sisters' tipping rule: Add 15–20 percent onto the total bill, including wine. Some cheapskates might want to leave less if it's an expensive wine, but we don't believe in skimping on good service. And, besides, who ordered that expensive bottle anyway?

Should I be given a fresh glass when I order a second bottle of wine?

If the second bottle is a different wine, your server will bring clean glasses. If you order a second bottle of the same wine, your server will likely pour the wine into your original glass. Although they're not obligated to do so, some restaurants will provide new glasses regardless. We appreciate this practice.

What does "NV" on a wine list mean?

"Non-vintage." You'll see that most of the wines listed will have a vintage year associated with them. The non-vintage wines are a blend of grapes from two or more years. NV wines are not inferior in any way.

I overheard someone asking the waiter for a "reserve" wine list? What's that all about?

Some fancy-schmancy restaurants have a second, supplemental wine list with rarer, and usually pricier, wines. You'll have to ask your server if one is available. Perusing it is no obligation to buy.

Sometimes I'm served reds that are too warm or whites that are too cold. What should I do?

For whites, ask your server to remove the bottle from the ice bucket and put it on the table to warm up a bit. You can always put it back later. For reds, ask the server to bring an ice bucket to the table. He'll probably think you're crazy, but if the wine's too warm, it'll benefit from five minutes on ice.

If I'm ordering the wine for a group, am I safer to go with a white or a red?

If you're a group of three or more, we recommend you order both. We have two strategies. The first is to just order one of each and let each guest tell the waiter which one to pour. The other strategy is to order a bottle of white for the appetizer course and then order a bottle of red for those who want it with their entrées.

How much should I order?

About a half bottle per person is a good rule of thumb for most groups—unless it's our group, which always consumes more.

I've noticed that most wines by the glass are also available by the bottle. Are those the safest bets to order when choosing wine for a group?

Like most of life's decisions, there's an up side and a down side. On the positive side, the wine may have been put on the by-the-glass list because of its popularity. By ordering this "Miss Congeniality," you have the assurance that lots of people have tried it and liked it just fine. On the other hand, the wine may have been put there because it was really a "Miss Cheap" and could be marked way up. But here's our tip: Because the restaurant will have an already-open bottle of the wine, you can ask the waiter for a small taste before you commit to a whole bottle. If it doesn't meet your expectations, it's not too late to change your mind.

Why is it that the same wine will cost so much more at one restaurant than at another?

Like real estate, it's location, location, location. A New York City restaurant is probably going to charge more for that bottle than a restaurant in Franklin, Kentucky. It also has to do with the size of the restaurant and the price of the entrées.

Please tell me I was hallucinating. I thought I saw a waiter rinsing the wineglasses with the wine that he ultimately served.

We wish we could tell you it was only a dream. The way it works is the waiter pours a small amount of your wine into a wineglass and swirls it to coat the inside. Then he pours the wine from the first glass into another, swirls again and repeats the process until everyone's glass has been "seasoned." The usual reason given for doing this is to remove odors or soapy residue from the glass. Hello! How about a good water rinsing in the kitchen? More than pretentious . . . it wastes our wine.

Is there a way to find the best value on a wine list?

Look for lesser-known wines. They move more slowly than the popular Chardonnays, Merlots and Cabs, so they're likely to be priced attractively to get sold. Although there are many *others to choose from, try a Rioja from Spain, a Grüner Velt-liner from Austria, a Carmenère from Chile or a Pinot Blanc from California.*

I'm taking a prospective client to dinner, and I want to impress him in a big way. He's knowledgeable about wines. So what do I order? By the way, money is no object.

You could always just flatter him by letting him choose the wine. But if you'd rather impress him, go for a prestige red Bordeaux. They're blends of primarily Cabernet Sauvignon and Merlot grapes and reach their peaks after several years of aging. The highly celebrated—and expensive—châteaus to look for include Lafite-Rothschild, Latour, Margaux, Haut-Brion, Mouton-Rothschild and Pétrus. And, if he knows about wine, the vintage will matter. From the most recent, these are the years you want: '98, '96, '95, '90, '89, '86, and '82.

What does it mean when a restaurant advertises that it has a Wine Spectator Award?

It tells you that the restaurant cares enough about wine to submit its list for evaluation by Wine Spectator *magazine and that it was considered good enough for an award. Almost three thousand restaurants around the world have one. Although there are a number of criteria considered, such as regions represented and thematic match with the menu, "Award of Excellence" winners will have at least 75 wine selections, "Best of Award of Excellence" winners will have 350 or more, and "Grand Award" winners will have a list of 1,000 or more.*

Chapter 5

Champagne Sister ...

EVERYTHING BUBBLY

AH, CHAMPAGNE, nectar of the gods. With you we have rung in abundant New Years, blown out too many birthday candles, proposed to our beloved, toasted our best friends, cursed our enemies, grieved over our loved ones, consummated business deals, sung songs to whomever would listen, made the most passionate love of our lives, swung on swings and danced until dawn.

So, is Champagne the *special occasion* accompaniment to life events? It's something special, all right.

Just think about the times in your life when Champagne has played a role. Probably more than you would have imagined—yet it's still thought of as a *special occasion* drink. We think Champagne is an *every occasion* partner, with us at every milestone of our lives.

Champagne, sparkling wine, bubbly—whatever you call it—is the life of every party. Why? One taste will tell you.

CHAMPAGNE VS. SPARKLING WINE

We dare you to tell the difference between a Champagne and a quality sparkling wine. In a blind test, we doubt most pros could do it. But there's an important distinction and one that smart girls need to know. It's very simply this: Champagne comes from the Champagne district of France. Everything else is sparkling wine.

In Spain they call it *cava*. In Germany it's *sekt*. The most famous one emanating from the Piedmont region of Italy is *Asti*. In the United States, we're just cheeky enough to call it . . . champagne—with a little "c." The French are scandalized that we would do such a thing. Even their cousins in the Loire Valley can't call their sparkling wines Champagne. But we can't help ourselves. "Sparkling wine" is so cumbersome, and "champagne" just rolls off your tongue.

Champagne producers developed a winemaking process called the *Méthode Champenoise*. It's a laborious process of fermenting and blending and fermenting again in the bottle, then turning and . . . you get the idea. But it produces the most sublime beverage the world has known. (Do we make our prejudices obvious?) The wines are held in such esteem that producers of other sparkling wines duplicate the process to try to achieve the same quality levels.

Of course, producing champagne in the French method is time-consuming and labor-intensive; that's why the wines can be so expensive. When you see a bottle of bubbly in the store for, say, $5.99, you can bet that the bubbles were created in a different way, by the *Méthode Charmat*. The grapes used in this method are usually less expensive than the Pinot Noir and Chardonnay used in Champagne. And the second fermentation takes place in large, closed, pressurized tanks rather than in the bottle. Tank-fermented bubblies tend to be fruitier than their Champagne counterparts. Asti is a good and refreshing example of this method.

Producers in Champagne face strict guidelines, including what grapes they can use. Only Chardonnay, Pinot Noir and Meunier are permitted. Champagne is an area of striking geographical contrasts. It has a lousy, cold climate, chalky soil, and limited agriculture. Yet its valleys produce the best grapes in the world. Go figure! They say you must go to Champagne to truly understand and experience its nuances. Just ninety miles northeast of Paris, it's worth the trip. Besides—the greatest drink in the world is served round the clock in Champagne.

PRESTIGE CHAMPAGNE HOUSES

A Champagne "house" is a producer—or company—that produces and sells its individual style or styles of Champagnes. Many of the houses are under the same ownership, like perfumiers and couturiers. Like a scent, a Champagne is chosen by style. There are close to two hundred houses in the Champagne region. Approximately one-fourth of these houses sell their products in the United States. Some of the most well known and well respected ones are:

Billecart-Salmon	Louis Roederer
Bollinger	Moët & Chandon
Charles Heidsieck	Perrier-Jouët
Deutz	Piper-Heidsieck
G. H. Mumm	Pol Roger
Krug	Taittinger
Lanson	

Beginning with Moët & Chandon in 1974, several French Champagne houses have started up operations in California. Like their French counterparts, the California wineries are located in cooler climates and produce their sparklers with the same grape varieties—namely, Pinot Noir, Chardonnay and Meunier. These American branches of French Champagne houses include:

> Domaine Carneros (owned by Taittinger)
> Domaine Chandon (owned by Moët & Chandon)
> Mumm Cuvée Napa (owned by G. H. Mumm)
> Piper-Sonoma (owned by Piper-Heidsieck)
> Roederer Estate (owned by Louis Roederer)

MAKING THE BUBBLES

Here's a toast to all the bubble makers! The process of making champagne is long and tedious. But we suppose nothing that tastes so wonderful would come easy. These are the six basic steps.

1. The juice from the grapes ferments for about three weeks, producing a still wine—a wine without the carbon dioxide that causes effervescence.
2. The wines are blended according to the producer's style.
3. The wine is bottled and laid down to allow for a second fermentation and development of carbon dioxide inside the bottles. This takes up to nine weeks.
4. The wine is aged according to the producer's specifications.
5. The bottles are rotated from a horizontal position to a vertical, upside-down one. This process, known as riddling, allows the sediment to collect at the cork for easy removal.
6. The wine is disgorged, which means the neck of the bottle is frozen and the sediment is removed. At this point, sugar is added (called dosage). The amount of sugar depends on the degree of dryness or sweetness the producer wants to obtain. And the bottles are recorked.

Sounds easy enough on paper. But, as always, champagne makers have lots of variables to consider—what grapes to blend, whether to use grapes from one vintage or several, how long to age the wine, how much sugar to add. Each decision will have an effect on the eventual aroma, color and flavor—and, of course, price.

LOOKS *ARE* IMPORTANT: BUBBLES, BOTTLE AND CORK

Before you even take that first sip, there are three immediately obvious characteristics that distinguish champagne from other wines: bubbles, bottle and cork.

Bubbles are the essence of champagne—about 49 million of them in every bottle. They're formed during the second fermentation of the wine when the carbon dioxide is trapped inside the bottle.

Pour a glass and look for yourself. In fine Champagne the bubbles will be tiny and float upward in a continuous stream from the

WINE BAR:
May I have my bubbles in red, white and blue?

Americans' taste for champagne differs from that of the French, at least according to Gary Heck, president and chairman of Korbel Champagne Cellars. When his father first bought the company in 1954, he decided to produce champagne in a style that was lighter and more delicate and with more fruit flavor than the heavy, yeasty Champagnes of France. It caught on. Korbel went from producing 3,000 cases of champagne in 1954 to 1,150,000 cases in 2002.

bottom of your glass. If they're large and random, you might have a lesser-quality champagne. It's a subtle difference but easy to recognize. It's like spotting the difference between a real Rolex and a fake. (Real: The second hand sweeps in one continuous motion around the dial. Fake: It jerks around, stopping momentarily at every second.)

Now take a peek at the bottle. If we were to compare a wine bottle to a champagne bottle, it'd be like comparing a quarterback to a linebacker. The wine bottle is sleek and lean with gentle curves, while the champagne bottle is heavy, thick and formidable. Not necessarily pretty, but it serves its purpose—to protect the champagne. The design of a champagne bottle is one of necessity and function. The bottles need to withstand the high pressure, about ninety pounds per square inch, exerted by the carbonation after bottling. It also has a large punt, or indentation, in the bottom of the bottle to help reduce the pressure along the bottom of the bottle. Without it, the bottles would blow out and break much more frequently.

And the cork? Talk about big butts! How in the world do those big-bottomed corks fit into a champagne bottle? Well, just like some of us, at a younger age their shape was less expansive. The corks used for champagne are the same substance and cylindrical shape as those used for wine bottles, just a bit longer and thicker.

Cork is a springy material, so when it's squeezed into the bottle, the top part bulges out and the bottom part expands against the sides of the bottle. Since the cork remains in place for several years (sometimes decades), it becomes accustomed to its shape and stays that way even when removed from the bottle.

WINE BAR:
Sunken Treasure!

In 1998, about five hundred bottles of 1907 Heidsieck Champagne were rescued from the bottom of the Baltic Sea, where they had lain since 1916. The Champagne was part of a collection of thousands of bottles on board the Swedish ship *Joenkoeping* when it was struck by the Germans during World War I. The bottles had been destined for the court of Czar Nicholas II.

Salvage organizers who tasted the almost-century-old bubbly said it was well preserved by the cold temperature (35 degrees) and the darkness. The bottles were auctioned in London at an average price of $2,488. One bottle sold for $4,068, a world auction record for a bottle of Champagne.

STYLES: VINTAGE, NON-VINTAGE AND SWEETNESS LEVELS

Every Champagne house, large or small, works tirelessly to create its own style. Much of their success is owed to the tradition of using the best grapes and grape combinations and employing some of the top winemakers in the world.

Vintage and Non-Vintage

Champagne is designated as vintage or non-vintage. A vintage Champagne uses 100 percent of its grapes from the year indicated on the bottle—always a particularly good harvest year. Vintage Champagne isn't made every year—only the best years. Its flavor is usually fuller and fruitier than non-vintage. Vintage Champagne must be at least thirty months old before it's sold and can be kept for up to fifteen years.

Non-vintage Champagne comprises about 80 percent of the Champagne sold by the larger Champagne houses. It's a blend of wines from several vintages, sometimes using up to forty different wines. Although the majority of the grapes in one bottle might come from a single year, the producer may use as much as 40 percent from previous years. Champagne houses use this technique to create their own distinctive styles that can be re-created year after year. The producers are required by law to set aside at least 20 percent of their Champagne each year to be used for blends for future years. Non-vintage Champagne is sold ready to drink, but may maintain its integrity for up to three years.

Rosé

Rosé Champagne is sometimes called *pink* Champagne because the skins of the grapes are left in contact with the juice for a brief period, giving it a pinkish color. Alternatively, the color can be achieved by adding some red Pinot Noir wine to the base wine blend. Rosé Champagne can be vintage or non-vintage, and despite its color is usually dry in flavor.

Blanc de Blanc

Some Champagnes are made from just one of the three permitted grapes. A blanc de blanc (meaning white wine from white grapes) is made from 100 percent Chardonnay grapes and is lighter than Champagnes that also include Pinot Noir. It can be vintage or non-vintage.

Blanc de Noir

Another one-grape Champagne is blanc de noir (white wine from black grapes). It's usually made from the Pinot Noir grape.

Prestige Cuvée

These are referred to as luxury Champagnes because they are made exclusively from grapes grown in the best vineyards. They are not released until they are at least five years old and may keep for twenty-five years or more. This is the finest Champagne of the house. It may be vintage, such as Moët & Chandon's Dom Perignon and Louis Roederer's Cristal, or non-vintage, such as Krug's Grand Cuvée.

Levels of Dryness and Sweetness

Many factors influence the flavor of Champagne—such as the grape, vineyard, vintage and blend—some of which can be subtle and difficult to detect when tasting. One thing most of us discern, though, is the dryness or sweetness of a Champagne. The amount of sugar in a Champagne also determines its style. The designations of sweetness are indicated right on the bottle's label. Here's what they mean:

- Extra Brut—The driest of all and not a common style.
- Brut—The most common and popular style. It's considered very dry and to most experts has the perfect balance of sweetness to dryness.
- Extra Dry—A slightly less dry style than Brut, considered dry to medium dry.

- Sec—Medium dry to medium sweet. Rarely seen today.
- Demi-Sec—Sweet and great with desserts—or as dessert itself.
- Doux—Extremely sweet.

Sparkling Wines That Sparkle

Even the richest girls wear costume jewelry on occasion. They also buy bottles of bubbly from outside Champagne.

In the Loire Valley of France, sparkling wines are often made from the Chenin Blanc grape, the grape that goes into Vouvray. The result is refreshing and creamy. Sparkling wines are produced in the eastern regions of France, including Alsace, where they blend Pinot Noir, Pinot Blanc and Pinot Gris. The wines turn out to be quite crisp.

Spain produces *cava*, named after the word for cellar. Spanish winemakers traditionally used native grapes but are increasingly switching to Chardonnay. You'll probably recognize the names of the major producers: Freixenet, Codorniu and Paul Cheneau. Cavas are usually light and crisp and inexpensive.

Italy's sparklers come in a variety of styles and go by several names. One option is a Lambrusco. It's a bubbly that most Americans know as pink and sweet. But there are white and dry versions that are more popular in Italy. Another is Prosecco, which is available both fully sparkling (*spumante*) and lightly sparkling (*frizzante*). They're usually crisp and dry. Moscato d'Asti is another alternative and a good accompaniment to fruit-based desserts. It's lightly sweet and slightly fizzy. Then, of course, there's always the more well known Asti, the semi-sweet to sweet, fully sparkling wine that's available everywhere.

In Germany sparkling wine is called *sekt*. It can be made from

Pinot Blanc, but more than likely, will be made from Riesling grapes. Using Riesling gives *sekt* a bracing acidity.

Who'd think of Australia for sparkling wine? But winemakers there are creating some winners. One producer may blend Pinot Noir, Muscadelle, Chenin Blanc and Semillon, while another may produce a blanc de blanc from all Chardonnay.

In the United States, good sparkling wines abound, and not only from the French offshoots. In California, names like Korbel, Gloria Ferrer, Iron Horse and S. Anderson should ring familiar notes. You'll find good values from other areas—like Washington and New York states—too.

STORING AND SERVING THE BUBBLY

Storing Savvy

Champagne is sensitive to temperature and light. Like all wines, it maintains its character best when stored in a cool, dark location. Don't bother with expensive cooling units. A closet or basement with a temperature of about 50 degrees is fine. With the right environment your bubbly should keep for at least three to four years. If you don't have such a location for storage, champagne can be kept in the refrigerator for several weeks without harm. The worst thing for the champagne's quality is for a bottle to be exposed to extreme hot or cold temperatures or light.

Quick Chill & Warm Greeting

Ever notice how you're never prepared for that impromptu visit? He'll be here in an hour, and the bubbly is resting comfortably

WINE BAR:
Hold on to your cap!

You know that metal cap on top of the Champagne cork that's usually stamped with the producer's name? Well, don't throw it away. It may be worth a bunch. That little metal cap is causing one of the fastest-growing wine collectible frenzies in Europe—even bigger than Beanie Babies were in the United States. Well, almost.

The metal cap is called a *plaque de muselet*, and in France they're all the rage. In restaurants and bars, patrons quickly put them in their pockets or purses as soon as the Champagne is opened. If left on the table or bar, neighboring party girls have been known to abscond with them.

What's all the fanfare that would turn your regular law-abiding girl into a thief? Well, the plaques can be works of art. With the advances in printing and stamping, Champagne producers are becoming increasingly creative in their plaque designs. Portraits, coats of arms, slogans and varied colors are added to make each plaque unusual—and pricey. Some plaques are selling for hundreds of dollars. Plaque Web sites, where buying and selling goes on twenty-four hours a day, are hot.

In the United States not all producers of our sparkling wines have added their mark to the plaques yet. But it's probably just a matter of time before the craze catches on here.

in the hall closet. Here's a way to chill your champagne to its ideal temperature before you're even out of the shower.

Fill your sink with water and ice and immerse the bottle so that it's covered. Twirl the bottle for a couple of minutes and leave it there while you shower. When you've towel-dried yourself, towel-dry the champagne bottle and put it in the fridge. You'll both be ready when you open the door to greet your special guest.

Non-Lethal Approach to Opening the Bottle

Five, four, three, two, one—no, it's not Apollo 13, it's the champagne cork! It might be dramatic to open the bottle with a big pop and see the cork flying high, but it's unsafe. Ask anyone who's been attacked by a cork in orbit. Here's the safest and smartest way to open that bottle.

Remember, your mission is to control the cork. First, get a clean towel. Once you've removed the foil covering, point the bottle in a safe direction. Standing the bottle on the counter is usually safe. Keep one hand over the top of the cork with the towel between your hand and the cork as you untwist the wire cage. Corks can loosen and explode as soon as the wire is unwound. Remove the wire. Keep the towel on top of the cork with one hand and put your other hand on the bottle at a point where you have a good grasp. Turn the bottle—not the cork. You should feel the cork loosen a bit. (If not, keep trying. Some corks are stubborn. If it still doesn't budge after several attempts, you might want to get out the pliers!) Keep a downward pressure on the cork as it completely loosens and finally releases. The sound you hear should be barely audible, which means you've saved the bubbles. Hold the cork over the opened bottle for a few seconds to ensure the champagne doesn't escape. Now it's safe to pour.

The Champagne Serve

Wine pros pour champagne with such finesse and flamboyance. You can learn their one-handed technique, but it's a bit tricky. It takes strength (a full 750-ml bottle of champagne weighs three pounds) and coordination. We suggest practicing first with plastic cups and a champagne bottle filled with water until you've mastered the performance. Hold the base firmly in one hand with the thumb in the punt (the indentation on the bottom of the bottle) and the fingers spread out along the barrel of the bottle and pour. (This is actually a great workout for those biceps.) If you can't get and maintain a good grip this way, then don't try it with a full bottle. Better to use a two-handed pour than suffer the consequences of a dropped bottle.

Now the glasses. There's a reason for those long-stemmed flutes. The elongated shape and small opening at the rim enhance the flow of bubbles and minimize their escape, keeping the concentration of aromas inside the glass. Crystal, you'll be interested to know, produces more bubbles than ordinary glass due to its rough surface. Don't chill the glasses. They'll fog up and cloud your view of the bubbles. Pour champagne slowly so it doesn't overflow. Sounds simple, but because of the bubbles, the liquid rises quickly and you can overfill the glass before you realize it.

The temperature of champagne should be cold, from 43 to 48 degrees. After opening the bottle, keep it in a champagne bucket filled with ice and water to maintain its temperature. Warm champagne is (ugh) not at its best.

Leftover Bubbly?

The only reason we can imagine for not polishing off an entire bottle of bubbly in one sitting is . . . well, if something more urgent comes up in the bedroom. If you're that lucky, there are ways to store the bubbly so you can enjoy it again the next day. It will usually keep, sealed, for about twenty-four hours. A champagne bottle stopper is the best way to maintain the bubbles. It's made of metal with a spring and special lip to grab the rim of the bottle. Champagne stoppers are available in most wine or kitchen stores.

Even without a special stopper, you can still preserve your sparkling wine overnight. Wrap the opened end of the bottle with two layers of plastic wrap. Hold it in place and secure with a rubber band. Keep the bottle chilled in the refrigerator. And if you happen to have a raisin, drop it into the bottle before you close it. The bubbles should stay lively for a day or two.

Leftover champagne makes for a romantic breakfast the next morning. It goes with any food you're likely to be having. Serve it just like you did the night before or mix it with a special juice— peach-apricot, pineapple-tangerine or just plain orange. Even when champagne has lost its bubbles, we have a hard time just pouring it down the drain. If you want to make a last-ditch, desperate attempt to revive the bubbles, find a metal paper clip. Put one in each glass and watch as the bubbles enthusiastically—

albeit briefly—reappear. When your sparkling wine loses its sparkle, don't hesitate to use it in place of still wine for cooking.

Everyday Bubbles

It's almost impossible to think of any special occasion without champagne. Weddings, anniversaries, birthdays, promotions—and the two biggest champagne-selling days every year, Valentine's Day and New Year's Eve. While festive occasions call for a glass of bubbles, champagne is its own reason to celebrate. Just opening a bottle with a friend becomes a special event.

WINE BAR:
Christening Ships with Champagne

The practice of christening ships dates back thousands of years and across many nations. In the United States, ship launchings were always festive occasions, with some type of christening fluid (sometimes wine, water or even whiskey) used to bless the ship. But it wasn't until 1890 that champagne was used in the ceremony. On this occasion, the navy's first steel battleship, *Maine,* was the recipient. The exact reason for the switch to champagne is unclear, but it's believed to be because of its celebratory nature.

Prohibition played its role in U.S. ship launchings when it was dictated that only nonalcoholic liquids be used. The *Pensacola* and *Houston* were christened with water and the submarine V-6 with cider. And in 1931, Mrs. Herbert Hoover used no christening fluid at all. She opened a hatch that released a flock of pigeons.

Champagne is all part of a day's work for fashion models toiling up and down noisy runways. Backstage at their frantic, high-pressure fashion shows, they sip single-serving sparklers through straws. (Heaven forbid any lipstick become smudged!) They started the trend of the "mini"—what the rest of us always called a split—a 187-ml bottle of champagne. Jumping into and out of designer clothes and strutting your stuff in front of hundreds of pairs of eyes is no cakewalk. High fashion is high stress, and a girl needs a refresher that will keep a smile on her face. It's a good thing the minis come in multi-packs.

Champagne is travel-friendly for girls on the go. After a hard day on the road selling computers or scrutinizing balance sheets, a chilled bottle of sparkling wine offers an ideal invitation to unwind in a strange city. There are no roadblocks—like missing corkscrews—to get in the way of its enjoyment. And while a crystal flute might be preferable, a plastic cup will get you where you want to go.

BUYING FOR A SPECIAL OCCASION

Champagne can be intimidating when you're buying it for a really special occasion, like an engagement party or a wedding. You want everything to be perfect, but the bubbly comes in so many different varieties and prices that it's tough to pick just the right one.

Start your champagne planning by asking yourself these questions:

1. Do I want to serve champagne just for a toast or throughout the party as well?
2. When do I want the champagne toast to take place—for example, at the beginning of the party or with the cutting of the cake?
3. How much per bottle do I want to spend?

For a toast, you'll get eight glasses from a bottle of champagne. Served alongside other wines at the bar, you will only get four to five glasses from the same bottle. If you're planning the toast at the start of the party, a brut-style sparkler is in order. A champagne toast that coincides with serving wedding cake or other dessert may warrant a sweeter style, perhaps a demi-sec. When you're serving a large group, price is always paramount. Once you've established an upper threshold, it's time to put your expert shopping skills to work.

Here's one wedding scenario. You'll have 100 people at your reception (including you and your irresistible groom) and will serve champagne for the toast only. You'll need 13 bottles (100 people ÷ 8 glasses per bottle = 12.5 bottles). You've decided to spend $10 per bottle. Assuming you can buy your own champagne in the retail market (as opposed to having to buy directly from the restaurant or club), you'll be eligible for that 10 percent case discount. Your champagne expenditure, before state sales tax, is $117 (13 bottles × $10 = $130 − 10% = $117). That's for a standard-size bottle. Many producers make larger bottles, which are particularly suited to parties and can offer additional savings.

CHAMPAGNE BOTTLE SIZES & DESIGNATIONS			
MEASURE	SIZE EQUIVALENCE	SERVINGS	POPULAR NAME
187 milliliters	quarter bottle	1	split
375 milliliters	half bottle	2	half
750 milliliters	standard	4	fifth
1.5 liters	2 bottles	8	magnum
3 liters	4 bottles	17	jeroboam
6 liters	8 bottles	34	methuselah

MEASURE	SIZE EQUIVALENCE	SERVINGS	POPULAR NAME
9 liters	12 bottles (1 case)	50	salmanazar
16 liters	20 bottles	112	nebuchadnezzar

Make your champagne planning fun by staging your own champagne tasting with friends. Check out your favorite retail store and look for sparkling wines in your price range. Look for specials or lesser-known labels that might offer a bargain. Pick up several different kinds and serve them with the same kind of food you'll be having at the reception at the time of the toast—hors d'oeuvres, perhaps, or cake.

For you fashionistas who want to color-coordinate all aspects of your wedding, here's a knock-'em-dead tip: Personalize the label on the champagne bottle to match your flowers and bridesmaid dresses. Companies that offer that service or software to do it yourself are all over the Internet. *Mazel tov!*

WINE BAR:
Champagne's Role as Peacemaker

In 1783 the first recorded manned hot air balloon flight took off from Paris and landed miles away in the French vineyards. The local farmers were frightened and suspicious of this flying object that roared and spit fire. To appease them—and keep the farmers from shooting at them—the pilots offered them champagne. It's a tradition that's still carried on today.

COCKTAILS WITH A SPARKLE

How about some champagne cocktails that will tickle more than your nose? Not those overly sweet potions that make you wish you'd stuck with water. No, we're talking sophisticated, glammed-out, pull-no-punches cocktails.

CHAMPAGNE MARGARITA

1 oz. tequila
splash orange liqueur
splash lime juice
4 oz. champagne

Mix tequila, orange liqueur and lime juice and pour into a glass. Add champagne and serve.

CHAMPAGNE MARTINI

2 oz. vodka or gin
2 oz. champagne
splash lemon juice
orange twist

Pour vodka and champagne into a martini glass. Top with lemon juice, twist and serve.

CHAMPAGNE HAVEN

1 oz. Port
4 oz. champagne
splash orange juice

Pour Port and champagne into a glass. Top with orange juice and serve.

ASK THE SAUCY SISTERS

I hear so much about Dom Perignon. What is it?

Dom Perignon is the prestige cuvée of the Moët & Chandon Champagne house. It's named after the famous monk of the 1600s who, contrary to the popular legend, did not invent Champagne but played an influential role. Dom Perignon was a highly regarded winemaker and is credited with being the first person to successfully contain Champagne in glass bottles with Spanish corks. The Champagne house Moët & Chandon began production of Dom Perignon in the 1920s. Bottles of this fine bubbly usually start at about $100.

I've seen certain letters on the labels of Champagnes like "RM" and "NM." What do they mean?

The letters you see are the trade registration for the Champagne house. They indicate whether the producer grew his own grapes or purchased them from other sources. "RM" stands for Recoltant-Manipulant (grower-distributor); this is a grower who makes and markets his own wine. "NM," Negociant-Manipulant (merchant-distributor), is a producer who purchases grapes or wine from other growers and uses them for his wines.

My boyfriend and I really like sparkling wines that are on the sweet side. Neither of us knows much about buying these wines. What should we look for when shopping for these wines?

Look on the label. The words "demi-sec" or "medium dry," or even "doux," indicate that these are bubblies that contain more sugar—and hence are sweeter. In California, the word "cremant" also denotes sweet or dessert-style sparkling wines. If you're into sweet, stay away from bruts, which are very dry and probably not to your taste.

I'm having a dinner party and would like to serve different champagnes rather than wines. Would this be appropriate?

Definitely. Champagne and sparkling wines complement practically every food type. There are varying styles of champagnes with distinctive flavors that you could pair with every course. Start with a dry champagne and end with a sweet one.

Sometimes when I pour champagne into my glasses, there's lots of foam that's slow to subside. Is this normal?

What you're experiencing might be from residue on your glasses. If there's any soap or detergent on your glasses—even the slightest bit—it will cause the champagne to foam when the carbon dioxide mixes with the detergent. Cleaning your glasses by hand and rinsing them with lots of hot water is recommended. Dry them thoroughly before you start pouring.

Will you settle a debate I'm having with my husband? He says the United States is the biggest consumer of Champagne and I say it's France. Who's right?

We assume you're referring to Champagne with a capital "C"—the sparkler from the Champagne region of France. In which case . . . you're right! The French drink almost twice as much Champagne as the rest of the world put together. The UK and Germany are the first and second largest importers of Champagne, with the United States third. However, U.S. consumers purchase the most prestige cuvées.

I swear that champagne goes to my head faster than wine does. My husband says I'm crazy. Who's right?

You, our Saucy Sister, are right on! It's the bubbles. A recent study confirms your personal experience. A team of researchers in the human psychopharmacology unit at the University of Surrey found that blood alcohol levels in bubbly drinkers rose much faster than their counterparts who drank flat champagne. The same champagne, only flat, was used instead of a different wine in order to isolate the effects of the bubbles alone. After just five minutes, the volunteers who drank the fully fizzy drinks had an average of 0.54 milligrams of alcohol per milliliter of blood compared to 0.39 for the others. And in standard computer psychomotor tests, the fizzy drinkers took 200 milliseconds longer than when they were sober to notice peripheral objects, compared to 50 milliseconds longer for the others. But exactly *why* champagne gets you drunker faster is still a mystery.

Chapter 6

~~~~~~~~

Have Wine, Will Travel...

A TOUR OF THE WINE WORLD

LOUNGING ON THE DECK of your private yacht, you look back at Portofino enveloped in a crimson sunset and take a sip of the fragrant Dolcetto you picked up onshore. . . .

Okay, maybe your vacation is a day trip to the Jersey Shore. But a luscious glass of wine—Dolcetto or otherwise—can take you anywhere. Where do you yearn to be?

- On the banks of the Rhine surveying the ruins of a thirteenth-century castle? Take a sip of a delicate German Riesling and just close your eyes.
- On a safari capturing rare and stunningly beautiful wildlife on film? Try a Pinotage, the uniquely South African red.
- Exploring the crystalline waters and coral formations of the Great Barrier Reef? Savor a long-lived Shiraz from Down Under.

Winemaking—and drinking, of course—has been going on since the Bronze Age (that's five thousand years to you and us) and has spread around the world to areas where reasonably temperate climates can sustain grape growing. Everyone associates wine with France and Italy and Germany. But winemaking also thrives in places you'd least expect it—like Romania, Israel, Brazil, Lebanon and China. Some of these countries' wines will be difficult—if not impossible—to find at your neighborhood wine store. (Oh, darn! We're gonna have to get on a plane again.)

One of the great joys of traveling is getting to know an area through its wine and food. When a trip just isn't in the cards, there are still plenty of tasting options available from U.S. and imported wines. We call this *bar stool traveling*. Whether you go to the beverage or the beverage comes to you, wine is your ticket to travel.

OLD WORLD OR NEW WORLD?

If the term "New World" conjures up thoughts of Christopher Columbus and the *Nina*, *Pinta* and *Santa Maria*, drink . . . er, think again. Picture a winemaker wringing her hands over bubbling tanks of fermenting grapes. You got it . . . *Old World* and *New World* have their own meanings in the realm of wine. They

---

WINE BAR:
This should help with the labor pains!

Ancient Persia was truly wine country. Salaries were paid in wine—ten to twenty quarts a month for the men and ten quarts for the women. We don't think the women made an issue of equal pay back then. Besides, they were rewarded with extra rations after the delivery of each child. Ouch! The Persian ladies might have appreciated the wine *before* the delivery.

refer to different styles of winemaking. It all boils down to the difference between growing grapes where they want to grow and growing grapes where we want them to grow.

In the Old World—by which we mean Europe—grape vines were planted two thousand years ago by the Romans. Over time vines that didn't suit the specific soil or climate died off, leaving behind vines that were ideal for those particular sites. The Old World philosophy is to nurture these grapes and let the wine make itself. So for two thousand years, without too much tinkering by the winemakers, a wine's taste identity was attributed to the soil and climate of the individual vineyard. This is what the French call *terroir*. Old World wines are considered subtle and balanced with a taste of their basic ingredients, including the earth.

In the New World—meaning the Americas, Australia, New Zealand, South Africa and Asia—the great European grapes were transplanted to replicate the classic European wines. But different land, different climates . . . different results. Not to be foiled, the crafty New Worlders had technology on their side. New machines and modern chemistry allowed winemakers to build flavors into the wine. New World wines are considered big and aggressive—in your face with tastes of oak barrel treatment and other winemaker involvement.

New Worlders see the winemaker as the star. To Old Worlders, it's the dirt. One style isn't necessarily better than the other. They're just different. Any wine drinker can enjoy both styles. And as happens in real life, there's been crossover. Some Old Worlders have adopted New World technologies, and some New Worlders have gone back to Old World farming and winemaking techniques.

The Old World–New World divide is obvious when you look at the labels on the bottles. Old World countries always named their wines after the places where the grapes were grown. Aha! Dirt comes into play again. Wines had names like Beaujolais, Chianti and Rioja. Most of the time the labels won't even tell you what kind of grapes are in the bottle. First of all, Old World winemakers have always made their wines by mixing several different kinds of grapes. And, anyhow, after two thousand years, "everyone" in the Old World knew what kind of wine was produced where.

In the New World winemakers began making wines from single grape varieties and naming them after the grape. New World bottles carried names like Chardonnay, Cabernet Sauvignon, Chenin Blanc, Zinfandel, Pinot Noir, Viognier, Sauvignon Blanc. And those are just a few of the approximately ten thousand grape varieties winemakers could choose from.

Just as the Old World and New World have adopted some of each other's winemaking styles, there's also been crossover in labeling methods. Some New World winemakers have started labeling their wines with the name of the specific vineyard. Others have blended grape varieties and have given their new wines proprietary names, like The Novelist or Big Bitch Red. Old World winemakers have started to add the grape variety to the labels of wines for export, just to help out people like us who are accustomed to choosing our wines by the grape. So many wines . . . so little time!

WINE BAR:
Hop on board for a wine flight!
Just don't plan on getting very far

A "wine flight" is a grouping of several wines poured in 2- to 3-ounce servings and sold by a restaurant as a "set." The wines are usually grouped together because of a common element—country, region, vintage, varietal, winery or even label design. The advantage is you get to taste a number of wines without having to buy a full glass of each. If one wine in particular strikes your fancy, you can always move up to a glass . . . or a bottle.

SAUCY TOUR OF THE OLD WORLD

France

Oolala! Those French. You have to hand it to them, they're real trendsetters. A Chanel model strides down the runway and before you can say *"le vin rouge, s'il vous plaît,"* women around the world are sporting the same style. Fashion isn't the only thing that's imitated. French wines are emulated and used as the standard for judging quality. Most countries that produce wine have copied the wine styles and grape varieties that have been so successful in France. Even when the grapes are transplanted halfway around the planet, they retain their French names—Cabernet Sauvignon, Merlot, Sauvignon Blanc, Pinot Noir.

Wine is firmly embedded in the French culture, which is evidenced by how much of it the French people drink. They consume more wine per person than any other country, and nine times the amount Americans drink. Maybe that's why their system of defining and regulating wine regions—or appellations—is so unintelligible to the rest of us. Remember the underlying principle: French wines are named after places—not grapes; the place can be a region, a district, a subdistrict, a village or a vineyard, and the smaller and closer to the exact spot where the wine was produced, the better the wine is supposed to be. The only trouble is you have to be an expert in French geography to know the names and distinguish when the wine is named after a village or a district. And can you believe that this bewildering system of appellations is copied by other countries? All we want is a tasty bottle of wine, not a geography lesson.

Each wine region in France is recognized (at least by those in the know) for the distinct kind of wine it produces. In a nutshell, here are the premier regions and their wines ... and some geographical names to help identify them when you're strolling down the French aisle of your favorite wine store.

Region	Types of Wines Produced	Geographical Names
Bordeaux	Red wines made by blending Cabernet Sauvignon, Merlot and Cabernet Franc Dry white wines made by blending Sauvignon Blanc and Semillon Sweet dessert wines	Médoc Pauillac Saint-Julien Graves Saint-Émilion Sauternes
Burgundy	Red wines made from Pinot Noir Light and fruity reds made from Gamay White wines made from Chardonnay	Chablis Beaujolais Mâcon Pouilly-Fuissé Côte de Beaune Côte de Nuits Côte d'Or Pommard Meursault
Rhone	Full-bodied reds made from Syrah Robust Grenache-based reds Dry, rich whites made from Viognier Dry, full-bodied rosé wines	Hermitage Condrieu Côte-Rôtie Châteauneuf-du-Pape Côtes du Rhone Tavel
Loire	Dry, off dry and sweet whites made from Sauvignon Blanc and Chenin Blanc	Sancerre Pouilly-Fumé Vouvray Touraine
Alsace	Dry whites made from Riesling, Gewürztraminer, Silvaner, Pinot Gris, Pinot Blanc and Muscat	Alsace, perhaps influenced by its German neighbor, uses varietal names.

Region	Types of Wines Produced	Geographical Names
Champagne	Champagne, the world-famous sparkler	Champagne. It's all you need to know.

The French are *très* conscious about the quality of their wines. So they created a system for ranking (and regulating) quality, and the rank is printed, plain as day, on the label. There are four possible ranks. From the lowest to the highest, they are:

1. *Vin de table.* It means "table wine" and is also referred to as *vin ordinaire.* The only place name you'll see is "France."
2. *Vin de pays.* It means "country wine." The phrase is always followed by a place name.
3. *Vin Délimité de Qualité Supérieure* (VDQS). "Delimited Wine of Superior Quality." You'll find the words below the name of the wine.
4. *Appellation Contrôlée* (AOC or AC). The phrase appears in conjunction with the place name; for example, Appellation Bordeaux Contrôlée.

Bordeaux wines . . . Boy, have they got a lot of classé!

Just look at their labels. These wines come from châteaus! Some châteaus, though, have higher status than others. Back in 1855 Napoleon III called on Bordeaux wine brokers to come up with a formal classification of their wines. No problem, they said. They just rated the wines according to their prices—the theory being that the most expensive ones would be the best. (Sounds very nouveau riche to us, but we suppose the brokers had some kind of vested interest.) When all was said and done, sixty-one wine estates received the status of *grand cru classé* (which, literally translated, means "great classified growth"). The brokers divided the *crus classés* into five categories, which are still used today. The first—and highest ranked—group is called *premier cru* ("first growth"), and includes such recognizable and prestigious names as Château Lafite-Rothschild, Château Margaux and Château Latour. And so it went on down the line to number five, *cinquième cru*. The sixty-one ranked châteaus (out of eight thousand or so châteaus in all of Bordeaux) are a select group that can—and do—command top dollar for their wines.

Real Burgundies don't come in jugs

And you thought the wine you poured from those big bottles at college parties was the real thing just because the label said "Burgundy." Those mass-produced generic reds are frauds! (Which is not to say they don't make really good sangria.) True Burgundy comes from the French region of Burgundy, where the reds are made from Pinot Noir and the whites from Chardonnay. The demand for Burgundy wines far surpasses what the region can produce, so, for the most part, prices are high. As in Bordeaux, Burgundy vineyards can be officially rated, only in Burgundy the highest rating is *grand cru* followed by *premier cru*. (No one ever claimed that understanding the French mind would be easy.) The ownership of vineyards in Burgundy is crazy. One vineyard can be divided up between lots of small owners, each with a small parcel. The 125-acre *grand cru* vineyard Clos de Vougeot has around eighty different owners. The scuttlebutt is that the vineyard's soil is so prized that workers are required to scrape it from their shoes before they leave for home each night.

Bordeaux and Burgundy are certainly the superstars of French wines. They're famous. They demand big money. People fawn over them. But as coveted as Bordeaux and Burgundies are (especially the ones from prestige wine estates), there's still plenty of talent in France's other eight regions. Savvy girls with an eye toward value will head to the beautiful Loire Valley for their charming and light whites, or south to the Midi (Languedoc-Roussillon) for robust reds or even to Provence for some rosé to drink along with seafood from the nearby Mediterranean.

Is the subject of French wine now clear as ... mud? We thought so. Just remember that in France, it's all about location, location, location. You may not know whether Sancerre or Condrieu refers to a grape or a place, but when a word appears on a French label, you can be sure it's a place. So how does the label help us know what's inside the bottle? *It doesn't!* Not unless you already know something about French wine and geography. No wonder French wines are so exasperating and intimidating.

In the New World we at least know by its name whether a wine is red or white. Chardonnay ... it's white. Merlot ... it's red. But Bordeaux? Well, it's red (after all, Bordeaux is famous for its reds) ... unless it's a white Bordeaux. Ditto Burgundy and Rhone. In the United States, you'd hardly go into a store and ask for a Napa. You might ask for a Cabernet from Napa or a Chardonnay from Napa. While Bordeaux is known for its specific blends of grapes, Napa is known for a lot more than just its Cabs and Chardonnays.

Sometimes it's not as critical to understand a subject as it is to *appear* to understand it ... or to sound as if you understand it. So here is our pronunciation guide for the next time you're conversing with a waiter or store clerk about French wine.

LANGUAGE LAB

Beaujolais	boh-zhuh-LAY
Bordeaux	bohr-DOE
Borgogne	bor-GON-yuh
Brouilly	broo-YEE

Cabernet Franc	ka-behr-NAY FRAHNGK
Cabernet Sauvignon	ka-behr-NAY SAW-vee-nyohn
Chablis	shah-BLEE
Chardonnay	shar-doh-NAY
Château	sha-TOH
Châteauneuf-du-Pape	sha-toh-nuhf-doo-PAHP
Chenin Blanc	shen-in-BLAHNGK
Condrieu	kawn-DREE-yuh
Corton-Charlemagne	kor-TAWN shahr-luh-MAHN-yuh
Côte d'Or	koht-DOR
Cuvée	koo-VAY
Graves	GRAHV
Haut-Brion	oh-bree-OHN
Hermitage	Er-mee-TAHZH
Mâcon-Villages	mah-KAWN vee-LAHZH
Pinot Blanc	PEE-noh BLAHNGK
Pinot Gris	PEE-noh GREE
Pinot Noir	PEE-noh NWAHR
Premier cru	preh-MYAY KROO
Sancerre	sahn-SEHR
Sauvignon Blanc	SAW-vee-nyohn BLAHNGK
Semillon	seh-mee-YAWN
Syrah	see-RAH
Terroir	teh-RWAHR
Vin	VAN
Viognier	vee-oh-NYAY

Italy

Mangia! Mangia! Who can imagine savoring a forkful of pasta alla puttanesca without a lip-smacking, full-bodied Chianti to wash it down? Certainly not the Italians. For them, wine is made to be drunk with food. And no meal could possibly be complete without a bottle of wine on the table. We like the way they eat!

The Italians' love affair with wine goes way back. After all, it was the Roman legions who spread the art of grape growing and winemaking throughout what is now Western Europe. How odd, then, that just a few years ago the reputation of Italian wines hit bottom. Cheap jug wine was what people associated with Italy. But in adversity there is opportunity. And it sparked a revolution in Italian wine quality.

Modeled after the French system, Italy developed its own procedure for improving and controlling the quality of its wines as well as for classifying them by quality. Starting from the bottom and working our way up, here are the categories you'll see on the labels:

1. *Vino de tavola.* Italy's "table wine."
2. *Vino tipico.* Wines that are approved as being representative of their area.
3. *Denominazione di Origine Controllata* (DOC). Wines that meet certain standards and that come from specific geographic areas of production like Chianti. These wines are made from traditional Italian grape varieties using traditional winemaking techniques.
4. *Denominazione di Origine Controllata e Garantita* (DOCG). "Super" DOC wines. Eventually, DOC rules were considered to be not strict enough; hence, a new, higher level.

Italy produces more wines than any other country and has bragging rights for incredible diversity as well—more than two thousand kinds of wine made within its borders. Everywhere you travel in Italy you'll see grapevines growing, from the Alpine foothills of Piedmont to the Mediterranean coastline of

Sicily. The grapes are overwhelmingly and uniquely Italian—Sangiovese, Nebbiolo, Barbera, Dolcetto. But don't count on always seeing the name of the grape on the label. Like the French, the Italians name their wines after the places where they're produced. For Chianti Classico, which is named for the Chianti Classico winemaking district, you won't find the name of the Sangiovese grape or any of the other grapes that go into the blend. Yet you'll see that Barbera d'Alba (made near the town of Alba) and Barbera d'Asti (produced around Asti) use the Barbera grape name. Then again, not all Barbera wines use the grape name. If this name game is as frustrating for you as it is for us, follow us to a sampling of the wines themselves. Primitive as it may be, we divide our favorite Italian wines into four categories.

Big Manly Reds . . . are rich, full-bodied and complex with lots of tannin.

- Barolo (Sometimes called the "Elvis" of Italian wines. No, make that the "King" of Italian wines.)
- Amarone (A.k.a. Amarone della Valpolicella)
- Valpolicella Ripasso ("Ripasso" is a process that adds color, tannins and complex flavors to a regular Valpolicella.)
- Brunello di Montalcino

Easy-Swigging Reds . . . aren't necessarily light. Just easy to drink. Even though Italians favor drinking them with food, we're not so picky.
- Barbaresco
- Barbera
- Chianti
- Valpolicella

- Bardolino
- Dolcetto

Lean and Clean Whites . . . are fresh, fragrant and light. If you're looking for something with more body, get out of Italy and head to Burgundy or California.
- Gavi
- Soave
- Pinot Grigio
- Orvieto

Fizzies . . . are bubbly and sparkling.
- Asti Spumante (Now known as just plain "Asti." It's semi-sweet to sweet.)
- Prosecco (Can be lightly or fully sparkling.)
- Moscato d'Asti (Lightly sparkling.)
- Lambrusco (Red and semisweet.)

It's a bird. It's a plane. It's Super-Tuscan!

In the 1970s a bunch of rowdy but passionate winemakers in Tuscany ran afoul of the recently created DOC laws by experimenting with "new" French grape varieties (like—ohmygod!—adding Cabernet Sauvignon or Merlot to the traditional Sangiovese) and new methods not prescribed in the official regulations. Well, these lawbreakers got theirs. Their wines were labeled "Vino da Tavola"—lowest of the low! Only thing was, the wines turned out to be some of the best produced in Italy and quickly acquired a loyal and free-spending following. The wines are called Super-Tuscans. (As you probably guessed, the term "Super-Tuscan" doesn't appear on any label.) Perhaps as a result of the incongruity of a premium wine listed in a decidedly non-premium category, a new official quality category emerged, IGT (*Indi-*

cazione Geografica Tipica), whose rules are less strict than those of the DOC. The wines are made in the general style of the specific Italian regions and promise a combination of quality and value.

LANGUAGE LAB

Asti Spumante	AH-stee spoo-MAHN-teh
Brunello	broo-NELL-oh
di Montalcino	dee mawn-tahl-CHEE-noh
Chianti	kee-AHN-tee
Dolcetto	dohl-CHEHT-oh
Nebbiolo	neh-BYOH-loh
Pinot Grigio	PEE-noh GREE-zhoh
Sangiovese	san-joh-VAY-zeh
Soave	SWAH-veh
Valpolicella	vahl-paw-lee-CHEHL-lah
Vino	VEE-noh

Germany

One look at a German wine label is enough to drive you to drink . . . almost anything but a German wine. If the Germans wanted us to drink their wines, why would they make it so difficult? Of course, the Germans have always marched to their own drummer.

Achtung! While the rest of the Old World rates its wines by where the grapes are grown, Germany's highest-quality wines (labeled QmP, meaning "quality wine with distinction") are categorized by the ripeness of the grapes when picked. The riper the grape, the higher the sugar content and in Germany's opinion the higher the quality of wine. From the least ripe (lowest) to the ripest (highest) are:

Kabinett

Spätlese

Auslese

Beerenauslese

Trockenbeerenauslese

Eiswein

At the lower ripeness levels (*Kabinett* and *Spätlese*) the sugar in the grapes can be fermented completely to dryness. So for those wines, there's really no direct correlation between the ripeness level and the sweetness of the wine. At the three highest levels, however, the amount of sugar is so high that the wines can't help but be sweet. To achieve high ripeness levels, the grapes are picked late into the fall. Even though Germany has short summers, German autumns are often long and warm—and conducive to late harvesting of grapes. (Does it come as any surprise that the wines made from these grapes are called "late harvest" wines?) The grapes for a *trockenbeerenauslese* are picked one by one, and it can take a skilled picker all day to gather enough grapes for a single bottle.

When grapes hang on the vines longer than usual, they can be infected with a mold (*Botrytis cinerea*) that dehydrates them. You'd think this would be disastrous. Far from it! This mold is so beneficial to the resulting wine that it's called *noble rot*. Besides shriveling the grapes, noble rot concentrates and intensifies the sugar and flavor. The end product is amazingly rich, complex, sweet, of course—and super expensive. Try $100 plus per bottle!

Some wine drinkers complain that German wines are just too sweet. (This makes us laugh considering the millions of wine drinkers hooked on White Zinfandel!) But German wines are made in dry styles as well as off dry and sweet.

Finding the dry ones—if that's what you're after—has always been the challenge. The Germans are trying to make it easier. Dry wines, particularly for export, were (and still are) labeled "*trocken*"

WINE BAR:
Sightseeing Tip

Heidelberg tun, possibly the world's largest wine barrel, is on display in the cellar of Heidelberg Castle . . . in Heidelberg, naturally. It was built in 1751 from 130 oak tree trunks and holds 58,124 gallons of wine. If our calculations are accurate, that's more wine than we can drink at one sitting. Then again it doesn't really matter because the tun is empty. It's been filled only three times in two and a half centuries and has developed an irreparable leak.

for dry and *"halbtrocken"* for half-dry. Starting with the 2000 vintage, dry German wines may have alternate label designations. Wines indicated as "classic" will be dry, uncomplicated varietals with reliable taste and quality at affordable prices. "Classic" will appear next to the name of the grape variety. (Yes, those independent Germans buck the Old World traditions again. While other European countries eschew grape names on labels, Germany uses them in addition to place names.) "Selection" wines must meet additional quality criteria. The grapes have to come from an individual vineyard named on the label and have to be handpicked. These are premium dry varietals that are available in limited quantities and priced accordingly. "Selection" will appear on the label after the vineyard site. *Trocken, classic, selection*—they all signify a dry style of wine.

Because of Germany's climate, 85 percent of the country's wines are white. They're also relatively low in alcohol, which, to us, means we can have two lunchtime glasses of a German wine rather than one glass of a big Chardonnay from France or California. Riesling, held in high esteem around the world, is the signature grape of Germany. Rieslings can be dry or sweet, depending on the

WINE BAR:
Ice wine? You mean wine on the rocks?

Eiswein ("ice wine") is made from grapes that have frozen on the vines. It was first produced in Germany in the winter of 1794 when an unexpected frost forced the winemakers to produce wine from semi-frozen grapes. It's another way Mother Nature adds sweetness to wines. The grapes are pressed before they thaw, and the water separates out from the juice as ice. The juice left to be fermented has concentrated sugar and flavor. And so does the wine.

intent of the winemaker. They're light in body yet strongly flavored and can age beautifully. Other German whites you may come across are Ruländer (Pinot Gris), Weissburgunder (Pinot Blanc), Gewürztraminer and Scheurebe (Riesling-Silvaner cross). The real snob appeal of German wines is directed less at the dry wines than at the big-bucks sweet dessert wines. Germany produces reds as well, but tasting them may require a passport. Not many are exported. But if you get a chance, try their Spätburgunder. It's made from the Pinot Noir grape, with a lighter taste than you'd get from a Pinot Noir from Burgundy. Germany has thirteen wine-growing regions, which, for the most part, stretch along the banks of rivers, the most famous ones being the Rhine and Mosel.

LANGUAGE LAB

Auslese	OWS-lay-zuh
Eiswein	ICE-vine
Gewürztraminer	guh-VURTS-trah-mee-ner
Halbtrocken	HAHLP-troe-ken

Kabinett	kah-bih-NEHT
Riesling	REEZ-ling
Spätlese	SHPAYT-lay-zuh

Spain

The rain in Spain stays mainly in the . . . vineyards? *Not!* Drought is a persistent problem, especially in central Spain. Growers adapted to the lack of rainfall by widely spacing their vines, reducing both the density of the vines and the grape yield. That explains why Spain has, by far, more land devoted to vineyards than any other country yet comes in third or fourth in actual wine production.

At one time Spain had a reputation for making inexpensive, unremarkable reds. But several events changed that. Wine laws, similar to those in France, were adopted to improve the quality of the wines. Irrigation was legalized. Modern production methods were instituted. And winemakers expanded into new regions—all of which enhanced the prospects for Spanish wine.

Spain has a four-tier rating system for wines. From the lowest quality to the highest the tiers are:

1. *Vino de Mesa.* The equivalent of "table wine."
2. *Vino de la Tierra.* Regional wine similar to France's vin de pays.
3. *Denominación de Origen.* DO.
4. *Denominación de Origen Calificada.* DOCa.

Only one region has met DOCa standards, and that's Rioja, Spain's oldest and most famous winemaking area. Three-quarters of the wines from Rioja are reds from the Tempranillo grape in combination with others. The wines range from delicate to big and alcoholic.

WINE BAR:
So you'd like your wine personally delivered?

In addition to its wines, Spain is known for a unique wine-delivery system: the bota. It's a goatskin bag that holds about a liter of wine. Squeeze the bag and a stream of wine is forced out through a nozzle and into your mouth—sometimes by a compatriot a considerable distance away.

The common denominator of Riojas is the characteristic vanilla aroma that comes from aging in American oak barrels. The French introduced Spanish winemakers to oak barrels in the nineteenth century, but Spain uses American oak, which is not only cheaper but imparts a stronger flavor to the wine. These oak-aged reds are denoted as *crianza* when they've aged for two years at the winery, as *riserva* when they've aged for three years, and as *gran riserva* when aged for five or more years. Riojas, with their oak dominating their fruit, weren't made to appeal to anyone outside the national borders. Recently, however, winemakers have started making more fruit-driven wines to attract a more international palate.

Probably the most exciting white wine from Spain is Albariño, which is one of the few whites that are produced as a varietal. The grapes are so thick skinned that only a small amount of juice can be extracted. The wines are rich and complex with high levels of alcohol and acidity. As you'd expect, they're also fairly expensive.

LANGUAGE LAB

Albariño	ahl-bah-REE-nyoh
Crianza	kree-AHN-zah

Rioja	ree-OH-hah
Riserva	ree-ZEHR-vah
Tempranillo	tem-prah-NEE-yoh
Tinto	TEEN-toh
Vino	BEE-noh

Portugal

R-E-S-P-E-C-T. Sure, Portugal gets its share—but more for the cork that goes into the bottles than for the wines inside. Portugal is the dominant producer of those ubiquitous bottle stoppers. The country's also responsible for Port and Madeira, two of the world's best fortified wines. But its reds and whites? Outside of Portugal's borders, few people are familiar with the country's table wines.

Portugal is no newcomer to winemaking. In fact, the Portuguese were the first to establish an appellation system, back in 1756—179 years before the French created their much-ballyhooed and respected system. But Portugal's appellation system has, in some ways, become less important. Because the old-time winemakers were so tied to tradition and failed to modernize, a new generation of winemakers armed with new ideas and new techniques began producing wines outside the appellation system, giving their wines proprietary brand names and forgoing regional names.

One Portuguese wine that's regularly exported and that you're likely to find on your wine store shelf is Vinho Verde—literally "green wine." No, you won't mistake it for margarita mix. The name refers to the ripeness (or, rather, lack of ripeness) of the grapes when they're picked. The wine is light and high in acidity and—outside of Portugal, where they drink the red version—white. The better Vinho Verde whites are made from the same grape as Spain's rich and creamy Albariño wine. (The districts where each is produced are just across the border from each other.)

Portugal is undergoing a winemaking revival, and most of the exciting new wines are red. In the Douro region where Port is made, winemakers are using the same grapes to make reds that are full-bodied, intense and concentrated. And just to the south in the Dao region, the wines are rich with lots of alcohol.

LANGUAGE LAB

Colheita	kuhl-YAY-tah
Quinta	KEEN-tah
Vinho Verde	VEE-nyoh VEHR-deh

WINE BAR:
Put a cork in it!

Portugal grows about 30 percent of the world's cork trees and processes more than half of the world's cork. Cork trees are a species of oak with thick bark that can be stripped from the trunk and large branches without hurting the tree. By Portuguese law, the trees can't be stripped more than once every nine years. Once stripped, the bark is processed, graded and branded. Cork has certain properties that have made it a good bottle stopper since the seventeenth century. It has compressibility, so that it can be inserted into the thin neck of a bottle, and elasticity, so it can swell back up to form a tight seal that keeps the wine in and the air out. A wine cork made from pressed cork scraps costs about ten cents. The extra-long corks used in wine from one of the famous wine estates cost about forty-five cents.

Austria

Maria von Trapp would have been scandalized! Some un-scrupulous wine producers from her homeland adulterated their wines with diethylene glycol (a substance related to antifreeze that makes the wine taste sweet) in an attempt to pass them off as ex-pensive late-harvest wines. But quicker than Captain von Trapp could blow his whistle, the Austrian government stepped in. That was 1985. Since then, perhaps the world's strictest regulations for wine production and labeling were implemented. This near disas-ter inspired a renaissance in the Austrian wine business, and today more and more Austrian wines are available outside its borders.

With Austria's proximity to Germany and a shared language, you might expect their wines to be more similar than they actu-ally are. Austria has warmer seasons, longer summers and differ-ent winemaking traditions. The result: full-bodied and mostly dry wines more like you'd find in Alsace.

Grüner Veltliner, Austria's secret for generations but now its most famous white wine, is finding its way to appreciative palates elsewhere. Often abbreviated "GV," Grüner Veltliner is typically dry and spicy and is lauded as a highly adaptable accompani-ment to food. Other white varieties you may run across are Welsch-riesling (not to be confused with *real* Riesling which, in Austria, is called Rhine Riesling), Gewürztraminer and Weissburgunder (Pinot Blanc).

Austrian reds, harder to find than the whites, are usually light. Be on the lookout for Blauburgunder (Pinot Noir), Blaufränkisch and Zweigelt. Like their German neighbors, Austrians pride them-selves on their dessert wines, primarily late-harvest Rieslings. The level of quality and sweetness is expressed by the terms (in ascend-ing order) *Spätlese, Auslese, Ausbruch* and *Trockenbeerenauslese.*

LANGUAGE LAB

Blauburgunder	BLOW-ber-guhn-der
Grüner Veltliner	GROO-ner FELT-lee-ner
Weissburgunder	VISE-ber-guhn-der

WINE BAR:
May I see some identification, please?

The legal age to drink wine varies from country to country (and sometimes within a country). Here's a sampling.

Australia	18
Austria	16
Canada	18 or 19
Chile	18
China	no minimum age
Denmark	18
France	16
Germany	16
Greece	16
Italy	16
Japan	20
Mexico	18
New Zealand	18
Philippines	18
Portugal	no minimum age
Saudi Arabia	alcohol forbidden
South Africa	18
Switzerland	16
Ukraine	21
UK	16 with meals, otherwise 18
USA	21

SAUCY TOUR OF THE NEW WORLD

Australia

For a country that produced few table wines before the 1970s, Australia has more than caught up with the rest of the wine world. *Goodonyermate, Oz!* (Translation: Well done, Australia!) Australia's wines have had a meteoric rise, thanks in part to a warm, dry climate that's conducive to growing grapes. But most of the credit goes to the Australian winemakers who latched on to technology and, using traditional European grape varieties, pioneered new techniques to produce wines that are uniquely theirs.

Australia's wines are a lot like the Australian people: friendly, confident and open. The wines are usually meant to be drunk young. Australians have been used to drinking their wines at the point of sale—at a restaurant or just a short drive home from the store. (And who isn't used to doing that, you may rightly ask.) So the wines had to be good as soon as they were released. Australian wines are easy to drink and full of the flavor of the grapes.

Every wine region has a signature grape. For Australia, it's Syrah, the red-wine grape that earned its reputation in France's Rhone region—only the Aussies call it Shiraz. It's thought that the Syrah grape originated in Persia, whose medieval capital was Shiraz. Hey, maybe that's where they got the name! Shiraz is generally full-bodied and less tannic than a Cabernet—perhaps closer to a Zinfandel. It's become so popular and recognized worldwide that other countries have begun labeling their Syrah "Shiraz." (Do we hear Doris Day in the background? "Que Syrah, Shiraz . . . ")

Australia's white counterpart to Shiraz is Semillon, a dry wine that's emerging from the shadow of Chardonnay. Outside of Australia, Semillon is used primarily for blending because it produces an unexciting wine on its own. However, the winemakers in Australia have been able to produce a memorable wine that's been highly praised. Just so you know when you're ordering it: Outside

WINE BAR:

Take two glasses of Shiraz and call me in the morning

"Wine doctors" play an interesting part in Australia's history. Since 1818, over 160 physicians have established vineyards. This list includes some of Australia's largest and best-known wine companies, such as Lindemans, Penfolds and Hardys. Of course, the most unusual vineyards were the ones planted at lunatic asylums. The more enlightened doctors of the nineteenth century tried to alleviate the boredom of their patients in such austere surroundings by engaging them in meaningful outdoor activities like gardening. But the grapes and wine also provided some variety in their monotonous diets as well as supplemented their vitamin C intake.

Australia, Semillon is pronounced seh-mee-YAWN. Down Under they say SEH-meh-lon.

Australia's fiercely independent winemakers aren't afraid to try new things. While tradition dictates winemaking in other parts of the world, not so Down Under. The winemakers invented two entirely original blends—Shiraz with Cabernet Sauvignon and Semillon with Chardonnay. Australia's wines are labeled with the grape variety, and these blends are named after both grapes with the dominant variety first, as in Shiraz/Cabernet Sauvignon or Cabernet Sauvignon/Shiraz. The label has to say *exactly* how much of each variety is in the bottle.

LANGUAGE LAB

Semillon	SEH-meh-lon
Shiraz	shee-RAHZ

WINE BAR:
*Please fasten your seat belts. Beverages will be
served when we're safely off the ground.*

"Flying winemakers" are wine consultants who travel
the globe providing winemaking expertise wherever
needed. The term was spawned by a group of Australian winemakers in the '80s who went to France in
their "off-season" to advise French wine cooperatives.
Conveniently for all parties, the Northern and Southern
hemispheres have opposite seasons, and winemakers
can work two harvests a year.

New Zealand

Pack your bag and don't forget your waterproof boots. It's a
gold rush in New Zealand! Okay, nobody's actually panning for it.
But farmers, who just ten years ago guffawed at those crazy people
wanting to buy worthless grazing land to grow grapes, are now
counting their gold as they sell their land for more than they ever
dreamed possible.

New Zealand, where sheep outnumber humans thirteen to one,
once had an economy dependent on the export of dairy and sheep
products. Those traditional exports have dwindled, but wine exports have skyrocketed.

New Zealanders have made wine since the early 1800s, but it's
only been since the 1980s that they've received any critical acclaim. The year was 1986, to be exact, when the country won "best
wine" three days in a row in international competition. The winning wine was a Sauvignon Blanc from the Marlborough region,
New Zealand's largest and most important wine-producing area.
And thus began the country's reputation for producing a mother

lode of outstanding Sauvignon Blanc. The wine is considered so distinctive that it's being hailed as the world's best example of the style.

How did New Zealand wine come so far so fast? Many young winemakers travel to Europe during the Northern Hemisphere's harvest season to gain experience in the classic wine regions, then return and adapt what they've learned to the conditions back home. They've applied their expertise to more than Sauvignon Blanc. Chardonnay is the second most produced variety, and it comes in a number of styles, many of them unoaked. Another well-done white is Riesling.

The Kiwis produce red too. Merlot and Cabernet dominate. But Pinot Noir is making inroads. It's the country's most planted red grape but has been used primarily for bubbly. Now it's being made into a varietal. Wine production in New Zealand is small by world standards, but it's positioned to play a key role in the country's economic future.

WINE BAR:
If you want first-class wine, don't fly economy

Passengers on Air New Zealand flights drink 800,000 bottles of wine a year. And the powers that be want to put their best foot . . . uh, bottle forward. They blind taste hundreds of New Zealand wines and assess them in light of altitude, cabin pressures, passenger stress and humidity. Complex wines are out. Ditto tannins. First-class passengers get wines selected for their excellence. Business class gets solid flavors, variety and trendiness. Economy gets durability.

South Africa

There's more than one way to safari in South Africa. Forget the wild animals. Put away your telephoto lens. Just pick up a wine-glass and go. Most of South Africa's vineyards are clustered on the southwestern coast near the Cape of Good Hope in an area known as Cape Winelands—and all within ninety miles of Cape Town. How convenient for visiting wine tasters.

Unfortunately for South Africa's early Dutch settlers, there was no wine to greet them. So, in 1655, the Dutch governor planted vines of his own, and four years later he was drinking the fer-mented fruit of his labors. The Dutch, though, had no real wine-making tradition. Enter the French Huguenots in 1680. Fleeing religious persecution back home (and armed with winemaking skills), they started arriving. Voilà! Winemaking flourished. "Flour-ished," it turns out, is something of an understatement. By the eighteenth century, the Cape was producing an incredibly lus-cious and concentrated dessert wine called Constantia. It became all the rage in the royal courts of Europe and commanded princely sums. Even Napoleon ordered it from his exile on St. Helena.

The next two centuries were not so good for Cape wines ... another understatement. In spite of an illustrious winemaking past, South Africa was back at square one in the eyes of the world. The mission was twofold: Improve the quality of the wines and overcome years of trade sanctions that were lifted only when apartheid was abolished in 1991. It appears that the country and its winemakers were up to the task. Among other things, they im-ported improved vine cuttings and began oak aging.

These days the Cape produces wines from lots of different grape varieties. The most common is Chenin Blanc—called *Steen* locally—which is made in different styles and as sparkling, late-harvest and rosé wines. Meanwhile, Sauvignon Blanc and

Chardonnay have become very popular. As for reds, Cabernet Sauvignon, Merlot, Pinot Noir and Shiraz are important varietals.

But not to be completely overshadowed are two varieties that are associated primarily with South Africa. The white—variously called Cape Riesling, South African Riesling and Paarl Riesling (but not Riesling at all because it's made from the Crouchen grape)—can be dry or off dry. The red is Pinotage, which came into existence in 1925 when Pinot Noir was crossed with Cinsaut (which the South Africans call Hermitage). The first international assessment of Pinotage was scathing, collecting descriptions such as "rusty nails" and "acetone." But over time it has earned respect, developed a following and become South Africa's ambassador to the rest of the wine world. Pinotage is medium-bodied and subtly flavored—an easy-drinking wine.

South Africa has an appellation system, its Wine of Origin—although participation is voluntary and only about 35 percent of Cape-bottled wines are certified. The most recognized appellations that you'll see on labels are Paarl, Stellenbosch and Constantia (yes, home of that once-great dessert wine). "Estate" on a label is similar to the French *Château* or *Domaine*, only the rules governing its usage are more loosey-goosey than the French. An estate is defined broadly so that blends can come from different vineyards and can be bottled at locations apart from the estates.

LANGUAGE LAB

Crouchen	kroo-SHEN
Pinotage	pee-noh-TAHJ

Now here's a tip to wine lovers who like to be on the cutting edge. . . . Ever wish you had visited Napa back in the days when it wasn't so big and commercial and crowded . . . back when you could walk into a winery and end up sipping something special with the winemaker himself? That's the South African Winelands today. It has unaffected charm and hospitality, and world-class wines, yet remains relatively undiscovered by North American travelers.

Chile

It can take a heapa money and a lotta sloggin' to make a star look cheap. Just ask Dolly Parton . . . or the winemakers of Chile. Their wines sure are cheap. Try $5 to $7 a bottle for some! But making flashy wines at Wal-Mart prices took hefty investment and years of effort. It all paid off, though. Like Dolly, Chile's wines have attracted a worldwide audience of fervent fans.

The Spanish conquistadors planted vines in Chile back in the sixteenth century. From that point on, Chile has had a thriving wine industry, producing wines for the country folk from the common Pais grape. But it was France that, ultimately, had the most influence on Chilean winemaking with the introduction of Bordeaux and Burgundy grape varieties.

By the 1960s winemaking had fallen on hard times out of ne-glect. Wineries had not modernized. Some were still making wine in concrete vats. Grapes were trucked in mighty high tempera-tures without regard to oxidation. Then an infusion of capital and a renewed commitment to quality changed all that. Winemakers developed a global strategy and began exporting their inexpensive varietals to foreign markets. Chilean wine climbed the charts from North America to the UK to Australia.

Most of Chile's wines, and its best wines, are produced in the Central Valley, which looks east to the Andes and west to the Pa-cific Ocean. This region is home to the bigwig wine exporting companies, such as Concha y Toro, Santa Rita and Santa Carolina. Cabernet Sauvignon and Chardonnay are the dominant varietals coming from Chile. Some naysayers complain that Chile has no identity of its own, depending as it does on French grape varieties. Ever resourceful, some winemakers are producing wine from Carmenère, reviving a long-forgotten grape and claiming it as Chile's unique gift to the world of wine.

Nothing breeds success like success. Chile attracted the attention—and investment—of winemaking icons from around the world, like Robert Mondavi from California and Baron Philippe de Rothschild from France. New ventures and new partnerships have formed to produce not only the highly marketable varietals but wines that will achieve the excellence of a *grand cru*. Look out! Prices on the rise!

LANGUAGE LAB

Carmenère	kahr-meh-NEHR

Argentina

Once forced into servitude, a French tart finds true love and a new home in Argentina. It's a story of hope, of happiness. It's the story of Malbec. This French red-wine grape was not appreciated for her full potential back in Bordeaux. No, she played a subservient role to Cabernet Franc, Cabernet Sauvignon and Merlot. She was the blending grape. Sure, there are those who never make it onstage. But Malbec . . . she knew she could be a star!

Argentina gave Malbec her big break. She didn't disappoint. Her performance produced a wine that was deeply colored, robust and fruity, with enough flexibility to be drinkable at release, yet capable of aging. In return, Argentina gave her fame and adoration. Malbec shares the stage with a troupe of talented, and mostly red, players—Cabernet Sauvignon, Merlot, Bonarda,

WINE BAR:
Even wine gets jet-lagged!

Imagine this. You've met your *dream man* on the Internet. (Yes, you've seen his picture, verified his portfolio, and he checks out.) Now it's time to fly across the country to get up close and personal. He wants to pick you up at LAX. What do you say? *Don't do it!!!*

Sure you think you're prepared. You get up before dawn to allow hours for hair and makeup. You've had a manicure and pedicure and selected the perfect outfit. Your accessories make a statement without being pretentious. You leave for the airport.

Here's what happens en route. Sidewalk check-in is a mile long. You stand in 90-degree heat while dark, wet circles form under your arms. Once past security (and just why did they make you remove half your clothes?), you think a Bloody Mary sounds good. Oops! Just a small stain on your blouse. He'll never notice. An hour at the gate and two hours flying time, and you arrive at DFW to change planes. Another hour on the ground. No Bloody Mary this time. Safely on board, aisle seat, mother and (of all the luck!) child to your right. Toy falls, mother retrieves, run in your stocking. Two-plus hours later—exhausted, mascara smeared, hair wilted, nails chipped—you arrive. So . . . you want to greet Mr. Right at the concourse or freshen up at the hotel first?

The same thing happens to wine after a long journey—say, from the winery to your wholesaler. They get off the truck and, frankly, they're outta whack. Or, as a wine professional might say, "out of balance." No fruit. Harsh tannins. Just not ready for proper presentation. They need some time—maybe a few days, a

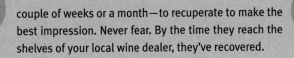

couple of weeks or a month—to recuperate to make the best impression. Never fear. By the time they reach the shelves of your local wine dealer, they've recovered.

Sangiovese, Torrontes, and even the Criolla grape, dating back to the early days of the Spanish missionaries. But everyone knows who the real star is.

Argentina ranks fourth or fifth in worldwide wine production. (Rankings vary from year to year.) And even though most of the country's wine is drunk at home, Argentina has become a major exporter. With the prices for wines from other New World countries on the rise (even the wines from neighboring Chile), Argentina may be the place for value-conscious consumers to look.

Wine drinkers aren't the only bargain hunters looking toward Argentina. Vineyard land is certainly a deal compared to other wine-producing areas. Some of the larger Chilean wine companies are crossing the Andes and investing in Argentinean real estate. They must know something. . . .

LANGUAGE LAB

Malbec   mahl-BEHK

United States

Americans have always been boozers. Our colonial forefathers were really into rum, whiskey and beer. Some things haven't changed much. "Bartender, give us a piña colada, a whiskey fizz and a Coors Light." It's not that the early settlers didn't want to drink wine. In fact, winemaking was an official aim of the colonies.

But the wines they produced from indigenous American grapes turned out be—how shall we say it?—not agreeable to their European palates. The settlers were used to wine made from vinifera grapes, the species responsible for all the classic wines. So the colonists imported vine cuttings from Europe. Two problems cropped up: either the vines couldn't survive the extremes of climate here or, if they could handle the weather, the vines were destroyed by native pests. What was an enophile to do?

A chance discovery in the early 1800s of a hybrid that could thrive in American conditions led to the first successful commercial production of wine in the United States—in, of all unlikely places, Indiana. Other hybrids were discovered or created and winemaking centers emerged in Missouri, on the shores of Lake Erie and in the Finger Lakes region of upstate New York.

Meanwhile, in what would later become California, Franciscan monks successfully planted vineyards with vinifera vines as they moved up the coast establishing their missions. In the mid-1800s winemaking in America really started to take off. Through the years the winemaking business had its ups and downs—caused by economics or disease—but in 1920 it crashed and burned. Prohibition marked the death knell for winemaking in America. Even though homemade wines and "sacramental" wines were permitted, commercial wines were banned. Prohibition caused most American wineries to shut down their presses forever and caused the country to lose two generations of wine drinkers.

It wasn't really until the 1960s that the industry began to revive. Ah, yes, the '60s . . . Julia Child showing her TV audience not only how to cook like the French but how to enjoy a glass of wine like the French. Never mind that most wine-drinking Americans were downing Boone's Farm Strawberry Hill or Gallo Hearty Burgundy, or exotic imports like Mateus and Lancers. But "times they were a-changin'." Instead of generic wines labeled "Burgundy" or "Chablis" or "Chianti," wine drinkers were increasingly

---

WINE BAR:
Danger: Fermentation Ahead!

During Prohibition a shrewd product called the Grape Brick was introduced. It was a block of dried and pressed wine-grape concentrate with an attached packet of yeast whose warning label read "Do not add yeast or fermentation will result."

---

offered new "varietals," wines named after the variety of grape they were actually made from. "I'll have a glass of white wine" was replaced with "a glass of Chardonnay, please."

Varietals grew in popularity—consumption as well as production—as the wine-drinking habits of Americans evolved toward greater complexity. It wasn't until 1976, though, that American wines earned real respect from the Old World. At the Paris Tasting that year, a California Cabernet and a California Chardonnay beat out the best red Bordeaux and white Burgundy in a blind tasting by a panel of *all French judges.* The world took notice.

Today, all fifty states produce wine. But wouldn't you know, the same state that's responsible for introducing us to beach volleyball, oxygen bars and organic cooking is also the one best known for its wines. And for good reason. California produces well over 90 percent of all the wine made in the United States. Unlike in other winemaking regions of the world, the climate in California is so consistent that it's rarely a problem to get enough sun to ripen the grapes every year. Because of the fully ripened grapes, California has established a style of wine that many would consider "fruit forward."

Napa Valley and Sonoma County north of San Francisco are certainly the state's most famous winemaking regions. Tourists by the millions flock there to take advantage of the shopping and restaurants as well as sample the creations of their winemakers. But top-quality wineries have popped up all over California, from Mendocino to Monterey to Santa Barbara and even farther south toward the Mexican border. California's hot Central Valley is a huge grape-growing area and is responsible for three-quarters of the state's total wine production. Those grapes used to be destined primarily for jug wines, but new facilities and technology have improved the wine's quality.

In addition to its reputation for Chardonnay, Cabernet Sauvignon, Merlot, Pinot Noir and Sauvignon Blanc, California can lay claim to "introducing" Zinfandel. Even though Zinfandel isn't a native American variety, having recently been traced through DNA testing to a wild vine that grows on the Adriatic Coast in Croatia in the former Yugoslavia, California was responsible for popularizing the wine—in all its forms.

Perhaps the newest—and hottest—movement to come out of California is the production of so-called Cal-Italia wines; that is, varietals and blends from classical Italian grapes like Sangiovese, Barbera, Nebbiolo, Moscato and Pinot Grigio. Super-Tuscan-style wines have attracted a following and are considered to have big potential because of the fruity nature of California grapes.

The second-largest wine-producing state behind California is New York. Most of New York's wines come from the Finger Lakes area, including some of the country's best Rieslings. But Long Island is the state's most recent success story. Some people are calling the area New York's Bordeaux because the land and climate of the two wine-producing regions are so similar. Long Island has become best known for its reds, particularly its Merlots and Meritage blends.

The Pacific Northwest is a hotbed of premium wine production. In Washington both warm-weather and cool-weather grapes can flourish. You'll find Merlot, Riesling, Cabernet Sauvignon,

WINE BAR:
Which way to the vineyard, Kee-mo-sah-bee?

In the 1980s several maverick California winemakers got together, calling themselves the Rhone Rangers. Based on their fondness for the French wines of the Rhone and their shared desire to make something other than Cabernet and Chardonnay, they decided to pool their experiences in producing wines made from Rhone varieties. Among the Rhone-style varietals you can happily taste today are Syrah and Viognier.

Meanwhile, another group of Francophile winemakers who felt that using just one grape variety didn't necessarily produce the highest quality wine formed the Meritage Association. They began making wines that were blended from the traditional "noble" grapes of Bordeaux. A meritage wine has to blend at least two of those grape varieties, and no single variety can make up more than 90 percent of the blend. It also has to be the most expensive wine the winery makes.

Chenin Blanc, Sauvignon Blanc and Semillon all coming from the state. You may also run across a little-known red called Lemberger. Don't give even a passing thought to the stinky cheese with the similar-sounding name. The wine is fruity and dry and smells just fine.

Oregon ... well, talk about Pinot envy! Oregon's got two Pinots: Pinot Noir and Pinot Gris. They're very much admired and sought after. But Riesling and Chardonnay hold their own there as well.

With every state in the Union on the winemaking bandwagon, you might think they're all newcomers just following the lead of the biggies. *Au contraire.* Take Florida. A century before the Pilgrims landed at Plymouth Rock (and three hundred years before California became a state), Spanish settlers were making wine out of the native American Muscadine grapes. The most popular variety, Scuppernong, is still used to this day to make a sweet white wine drunk mostly by Southerners.

With the big fuss everyone makes over France's Château This or Domaine That, you might wonder if the United States has an appellation system. Well, it does. But its rules are much more lax. An AVA (American Viticultural Area) is a geographic designation only—compared to the French AOC, which regulates what grapes you can grow, how much you can grow and how much alcohol the wine can have. The only requirement for using an AVA on the label is that 85 percent of the grapes have to be grown in that area. The term "AVA" doesn't appear on any label. But if you see "Napa Valley," for example, on the label, that's the AVA. There are AVAs within AVAs—kind of like those cute Russian dolls that contain progressively smaller and smaller dolls inside. Winemakers will sometimes choose a larger AVA because it gives them more options in buying grapes and in blending grapes from other AVAs. So instead of Mt. Veeder (an AVA within Napa) or Napa Valley, a winemaker might select "North Coast" as the AVA because it encompasses Napa, Sonoma County, Mendocino County and Lake County.

LANGUAGE LAB

Meritage	MEHR-ih-tihj (Rhymes with Heritage)
Muscadine	MUHS-kuh-dihn

> ### WINE BAR:
> *Space-Aged wines are so de rigueur, darling!*
>
> Just when you thought barrel aging and bottle aging were the secrets to quality wine, enter the Space Age. Using images taken from satellites and planes, NASA is mapping vineyards to help growers grow better grapes. Winemakers have always known that grapes from different parts of their vineyards produce distinct flavors and tastes. Now they're learning from the photographs which specific sections of the vineyards are doing better than others in terms of ripening, disease and soil drainage.

THE REST OF THE WINEMAKING WORLD: A QUIZ

Kampai! Na zdorovie! Serefinize! Cheers, old girl! Here's a toast to countries that are giving it (winemaking, that is) a go. Wine may not be queen, but it's at least a lady-in-waiting.

1. The citizens of what country typically mix white wine with Coca Cola or red wine with Sprite to make the drink more palatable?

   a. Romania   c. China

   b. Peru   d. Tunisia

2. In what country was it fashionable to play a party game where revelers would toss the remaining few mouthfuls of wine in each other's glasses into the air in an attempt to hit a delicately balanced dish on a pole?

   a. Japan   c. Hungary

   b. Greece   d. Turkey

3. Where is the per capita wine consumption two glasses per year?

    a. Mexico   c. Russia

    b. Bulgaria   d. Romania

4. In this country the consumer is looking for the effects of the alcohol rather than the taste of the beverage. Hence, the biggest seller isn't wine—it's brandy.

    a. Japan   c. Mexico

    b. China   d. All of the above

5. What nation produces Bull's Blood, a robust style of red wine?

    a. Bolivia   c. Hungary

    b. Greece   d. Mexico

6. What country is home to the Temple of Bacchus, built by the Romans as a tribute to the god of wine?

    a. Israel   c. Greece

    b. England   d. Lebanon

7. In what country did a television show called *Paradise Lost* popularize the drinking of red wine by showing the main characters committing suicide by mixing poison with Château Margaux?

    a. England   c. Russia

    b. Canada   d. Japan

8. About what country is it predicted that global warming will benefit its winemaking?

    a. Switzerland   c. Canada

    b. England   d. Venezuela

9. What country during the Roman era consumed an average of 350 liters of wine per year per family, compared with a current consumption of 6 liters per person per year?
    a. Luxembourg
    c. Israel
    b. Slovenia
    d. Greece

10. What country is the largest producer of ice wines?
    a. Russia
    c. Luxembourg
    b. Canada
    d. Switzerland

11. What country has such a heavy Moslem population that it exports 80 percent of its wines?
    a. Bulgaria
    c. Turkey
    b. Morocco
    d. Algeria

12. Where is the oldest winery in the entire Western Hemisphere?
    a. Brazil
    c. Mexico
    b. Uruguay
    d. Canada

Answers: 1. c, 2. b, 3. a, 4. d, 5. c, 6. d, 7. d, 8. b, 9. c, 10. b, 11. a, 12. c.

FORTIFIED WINES

Hey, sailor, how 'bout we spend a whole rapturous night of fortification? Those fortified wines are a guarantee of pleasure every time. How could they fail with all that extra alcohol added as a performance enhancer?

If we were making regular table wine, we'd crush the grapes and just let fermentation take over until the process was complete. The result would be a dry wine with about 12 percent alcohol. For a fortified wine, we add straight alcohol of some kind during fermentation, before all the natural fruit sugar is consumed. This stops fermentation and we end up with a sweet wine with an alcohol content boosted to around 20 percent.

Port

Let's pull into port and discuss one of the all-time great fortified wines . . . Port. It's made by adding brandy to red wine. Now have we got your attention? Port came into being thanks to one of the many wars between England and France. The British just loved their Bordeaux wines, fondly calling them "claret." But then war was declared and the French ports were blockaded: voilà, no more French wine. The British turned to their friend Portugal and set up trading companies on Oporto to ship Portuguese wines back to England. This British connection is one reason so many of the Port makers have English names.

The wine shippers in Oporto originally added a couple of buckets of brandy to the wine to stabilize it for the long trip to England. Then, as the story goes, they started adding the brandy earlier and earlier to expedite the shipping process, until it began to be added during fermentation. The wine, quite appropriately, was named Oporto, after the city from whence it was shipped.

True Port—or Oporto, as it says on the label—may have up to thirty grape varieties combined (although eighty varieties, mostly red, are officially authorized), but only five traditional grape varieties are considered Port's mainstay. Real Port has to come from the Douro region of Portugal. It's a lot like Champagne in that regard, which has to be produced in the Champagne region of France to be labeled "Champagne." Also like Champagne, Port is copied by wines from around the world produced in the same style. As good as the copies might be, they're not true Port.

Port can range from a crisp, bright white Port to a dark, sweet Vintage Port. Port enthusiasts make a big deal over Vintage Ports.

WINE BAR:

What does an all-American girl drink from a claret jug?
Beer, of course.

In 1871 the British Open golf tournament needed a new trophy. Considering the popularity of claret, it was decided that the winner of the tournament would receive a claret jug, hand-engraved with a golfing scene.

When 1996 British Open champion Tom Lehman hosted a gala charity dinner in Minneapolis, the claret jug was used as the centerpiece for the head table. Tom got busy signing autographs after dinner and forgot about his trophy. A friend remembered it and gave it to Tom's wife, who, in turn, gave it to her friend Alissa to hold.

About 2 A.M. Tom gets a call from the police. A young woman, it seems, was swilling beer from the venerable jug at a local bar, and someone suspected she had stolen it. Tom had just one question for the officer on the phone: "Does the suspect have blond hair, big dimples, and is her name Alissa?"

Only a couple of minor problems: They're unbelievably expensive, and you have to wait years before you can drink them. Vintage Port is made from the best grapes from the best growing seasons and is bottled after only two years in wood barrels. That means the wine in those bottles is harsh and tannic, qualities that make it difficult to enjoy young but perfectly suited to aging over a long period of time. We mean *long!* The rule of thumb is at least fifteen to twenty years. And three and four decades is not uncommon.

If you're going to invest in a Vintage Port, make sure you're getting the real thing. The label will say "Vintage Port" (or "Vintage Oporto") in big letters on one line without anything printed between those two words. This distinguishes it from two other types of Port that are also vintage dated.

If you're the kind of person who can buy a new outfit and put it in the closet for weeks or months waiting for the perfect occasion to wear it, then Vintage Port is right for you. The rest of us without any discernible patience have alternatives. Other Ports (and there are quite a few) share two qualities: They're aged in wood longer than Vintage Ports to mellow them out, and they're ready to drink as soon as you remove them from the liquor store shelf. These are some to try:

Late Bottled Vintage (LBV)	Probably the next best thing to a Vintage Port. It's vintage dated, but the grapes aren't from the best years. Or the grapes could come from younger vines. Unlike Vintage Ports, which develop a sediment after years of aging, LBVs are normally filtered before bottling and don't produce a sediment.
Tawny	So called because of the amber-brown color it develops as it ages in the barrel. There's usually an indication of its age on the label— ten, twenty, thirty years old. These are approximations, however, because Tawny Ports are blended from grapes from several years.
Ruby	One of the least expensive Ports. It's bottled young while it still has its deep ruby color. "Reserve" or "Special Reserve" indicates it has aged longer.
Colheita	Like a Tawny Port from a single year. It's the only one, besides Vintage Port and LBV, that's vintage dated.

Vintage Character	A premium Ruby made from higher-quality grapes. "Vintage Character" probably won't appear on the label. Instead, you'll find Proprietary names like Bin 27, Six Grapes and Boardroom.
White	Made from white grapes in a dry style.

Madeira

Now let's set our sails for Madeira, a Portuguese island off the coast of North Africa. Its location in the Atlantic made it an ideal port of call for ships traveling to South America and around Africa to Asia.

The ships picked up wine on Madeira for their voyages to the faraway lands. The only catch was by the time they reached their destinations the wine had become undrinkable. So, just like Port, alcohol was added to stabilize the wine. This time it wasn't brandy but alcohol distilled from cane sugar.

Before long an odd discovery was made. The wine actually tasted better after it had made the long journey—rocking and rolling its way through tropical heat—than it did before. In fact, round-trip Madeira tasted better than one-way Madeira. Merchants began putting casks of their wines in the hold of ships as ballast and sending them on sea voyages for the sole purpose of developing their flavors. Alas, the trips got too expensive. So new techniques for heating the wine were conceived to treat and age the wine at home. Today, all but the highest-quality Madeiras are still subjected to heat in the winemaking process.

Another odd—but very practical—discovery was made about Madeira. It will last almost indefinitely and is nearly indestructible. Maybe because it's already been subjected to the humilities (for a wine) of heat and oxygen and hanging around in a cask for twenty years, there's nothing you can do to ruin it. Go ahead . . . open it, store it in a hot closet, let it sit there for years. Just try doing that to any other wine!

Madeira usually starts out as a white wine and, through the heating process and maturation, becomes an amber color. The wines were traditionally named after the noble grapes grown on the island that they were made from—Sercial, Verdelho, Bual (or Boal) and Malvasia (or Malmsey). The names also denote increasingly sweet styles. When those names don't appear on the label, the style will be indicated by the words "dry," "medium dry," "medium sweet" and "sweet." Quality designations in ascending order are:

1. Granel. Bulk wine that's been colored and sweetened
2. Finest. Blended 3-year-old wine
3. Reserve. Blended 5-year-old wine
4. Special Reserve. Youngest component in the blend is ten years old
5. Vintage. Aged twenty-plus years in a cask and comes from a single year

Sherry

Now let's set our sails and sights for the home of Sherry. England, you say? Nope. While historically a lot of Sherry has been consumed there, not a drop is produced there. Sure, you hear the word "Sherry" and you think of upper-crust Englishmen standing around a paneled library discussing strategy for the upcoming fox hunt, or a tea room full of English matrons haughtily sipping this innocent beverage as if they weren't really imbibing.

No, we're headed for Spain. Jerez, Spain, to be exact. It's the town that gave Sherry its name and the only region that produces legitimate Sherry. You may wonder how "Jerez" became "Sherry." We did. The Moors who ruled the area for seven hundred years—and the ones who originated the Sherry trade with England—called the town "Seris." "Seris" evolved into "Jerez" for the Spanish and probably evolved, at the same time, into "Sherry" for the English. (At least Sherry is closer to Seris than it is to Jerez.) A bottle of authentic Sherry will be labeled "Jerez-Xeres-Sherry"—the Spanish, French and English names for the town.

Unlike Port and Madeira, Sherry is fortified with alcohol after fermentation is complete. So, until they're sweetened afterward (and several are), Sherries are dry. Some are lightly fortified (called *fino*), others more heavily fortified (called *oloroso*). But what you'll find on the labels are indications of their style.

- Manzanilla—An extra dry *fino*-style Sherry that's light and delicate with a salty tang and a pale straw color.
- Fino—A *fino*-style (duh!) Sherry that's dry, light and delicate with a pale straw color.
- Amontillado—An aged *fino* that's rich, almost amber in color with a nutty taste.
- Oloroso—*Oloroso*-style (ditto duh!) Sherry that's dry, deep gold to deep brown and has a rich raisin flavor.
- Palo Cortado—Sought after by Sherry connoisseurs. It's a cross between a *fino* and an *oloroso* with a *fino*'s tanginess and the nutty character of an *oloroso*.

Then there are the sweet Sherries with some kind of sweetening agent added—mainly dark, syrupy wines.

- Pale Cream—A *fino* that's been lightly sweetened.
- Cream Sherry—An *oloroso* that's been heavily sweetened.

• Brown Sherry—An extremely sweet and very dark *oloroso* Sherry.

Sherries are, for the most part, non-vintage and maintain their consistency from year to year through a unique blending procedure called the *solera* system. Picture rows of casks stacked on top of each other—up to fourteen levels—with the oldest wines on the bottom tier and the youngest on top. Sherry producers will take one-quarter to one-third of the wine from the bottom (oldest) barrels and bottle it. Then they'll replace what they've removed with Sherry from the next tier up—the next oldest. They'll continue this all the way to the top. It's like a cascade of Sherry. (If only this could replace the ubiquitous punch fountains at wedding receptions!) By the way, you've heard of Spain's "running of the bulls." This blending method is referred to as "running the scales."

Sherry is so versatile. Drink it before dinner or after—or both. Dry ones should be served chilled, sweet ones at room temperature.

VISITING WINERIES

Hey, Fern! Come take a slug of this here Penis Nar. Looks okay but tastes like old Duke lifted his leg over a vat of Mama's red pepper jelly.

Repeat after us: I promise . . . no matter how many wine samples I've downed . . . no matter how bad I think the wine is . . . I will never . . . behave in such a manner . . . that will embarrass me . . . when I sober up.

Visiting a winery can be like standing in line at Disneyland, or it can feel like you're an invited guest in someone's home. It all depends on where the winery is located and how big or small it is. A winery is a reflection of both a region's culture and the personality of the owners.

The idea of a winery visit is simultaneously appealing and daunting. Will I know what to say about the wines? Will I have to buy something? Let's clear that up right now. You don't have to know or buy nothin'. Genuine interest and enough sincerity to fill a wine bottle will get you everywhere.

Where to Go

Follow your passion. If you like wines from a particular region, go there first. You're familiar with the wines of Napa and gravitate to them at the wine store? For goodness sake, go to Napa. You can't tell the difference between a Riesling from the American Northwest and one from Germany, but you happen to have a business trip scheduled for Stuttgart? You'd be an idiot not to take advantage of the proximity of German wine country. "Gesundheit" is the only word of German you know? Don't let that stop you. More often than not, you'll find someone who speaks English. But, really, the language of wine is universal. Somehow, enthusiasm and sign language can overcome most barriers. We say "most" because some French wineries can be ... well, French.

What to Expect

Different size wineries are geared up differently to receive visitors. Larger wineries will undoubtedly have tasting rooms, shops and visitors' centers. Your visits may be somewhat regimented. But the advantage is you just show up during regular business hours, and you'll be accommodated. You'll have a list of the wines available for tasting and should feel no compunction about trying them all.

Small wineries offer more adventure—like you're discovering a place no one else knows about. Chances are, you'll be the only visitor and end up talking with the proprietor and winemaker herself. You may have only a couple of wines to taste. For small wineries, especially in Europe, you may have to call ahead for an appointment.

Some wineries charge a small fee for tastings. We suppose it suppresses the wino traffic. It also eases our conscience when we don't plan to buy anything. Then again, we've never met a wine we couldn't drink, and we've never left a winery without buying a bottle of *something*.

BAR STOOL WINE TRAVEL GUIDE

Whether you're on a worldwide wine safari or just want to select the right bottle of wine for one moment in time, here's an abbreviated travel guide to help you make a choice that will be in your favor. These are some of the top wine-producing countries' most popular wines, and a few well-priced suggestions from us.

COUNTRY	RED	WHITE	WINE SUGGESTIONS
Argentina	Malbec	Torrontes	Catena Cabernet Sauvignon
	Cabernet Sauvignon	Chardonnay	Balbi Malbec
	Merlot	Chenin Blanc	

COUNTRY	RED	WHITE	WINE SUGGESTIONS

Australia	Shiraz
	Cabernet Sauvignon
	Grenache
		Semillon
		Chardonnay
		Riesling
			Penfolds Bin 2
			  South Eastern Australia
			  Shiraz-Mourvèdre
			Craneford Edna Valley Riesling

Austria	Blauburgunder	Grüner Veltliner Gewürztraminer Riesling	Domane Wachau Grüner Veltliner Federspiel Terrassen Bründlmayer Riesling
Chile	Cabernet Sauvignon Merlot	Chardonnay Carmenère	Alpaltagua Estate Carmenère Caliterra Merlot
France	Graves Médoc Pomerol St. Émilion Beaujolais Hermitage Côte-Rôtie Châteauneuf-du-Pape Côtes du Rhone Chinon	Chablis Champagne Condrieu Graves Hermitage Muscadet Sancerre Pouilly-Fumé Vouvray Sauternes	Barton & Guestier Vouvray Domaine Manoir du Carra Beaujolais-Villages

Germany	Spätburgunder	Riesling
		Ruländer
		Weissburgunder
			Georg Breuer Terra Montosa
			  Riesling
			Kreusch Twist River
			  Gewürztraminer

COUNTRY	RED	WHITE	WINE SUGGESTIONS

Italy	Barolo
	Barbaresco
	Bardolino
	Valpolicella
	Brunello di Montalcino
	Chianti
	Montepulciano
	  d'Abruzzo
	Vino Nobile
	  di Montepulciano
	Dolcetto
		Gavi
		Orvieto
		Pinot Grigio
		Soave
		Asti Spumante
		Verdicchio
		Frascati
			Banfi Principessa Gavi
			Masi Valpolicella Classico
			  Superiore

New Zealand	Merlot Cabernet Sauvignon Pinot Noir	Chardonnay Sauvignon Blanc Riesling	Spy Valley Sauvignon Blanc Crossings Pinot Noir

Portugal	Port (fortified wine)	Vinho Verde
		Verdelho
		Madeira
		  (fortified wine)
			Caves Alianca Vinho Verde NV
			Ferreira Dona Antonia Personal
			  Reserve Port

South Africa	Pinotage Cabernet Sauvignon Merlot Pinot Noir Shiraz	Steen Sauvignon Blanc Chardonnay	Cloof Pinotage Baobab Sauvignon Blanc

COUNTRY	RED	WHITE	WINE SUGGESTIONS
Spain	Rioja Sherry (fortified wine)	Rioja Albariño Cava	Martín Códax Albariño Allende Rioja Crianza
USA	Cabernet Sauvignon Merlot Zinfandel Pinot Noir Meritage	Chardonnay Sauvignon Blanc Riesling Chenin Blanc Pinot Gris Sparkling Wine Meritage	Arcadian Bien Nacido Chardonnay Cosentino The Zin

ASK THE SAUCY SISTERS

What are "white table wine" and "red table wine"? Some of them are pretty expensive. I thought table wines were just ordinary wines.

In some European countries like France, Italy and Spain, "table wine" does, indeed, indicate the lowest quality. But in the United States "table wine" is practically every wine you drink. We look at it this way: You open the bottle, you put it on the table; thus, "table wine." The designation has no bearing on quality. It has to do with the amount of alcohol in the wine. Essentially all the wine we drink—if it's not a sparkling wine or a dessert wine—is a table wine. For American wines it means that the level of alcohol is between 7 and 14 percent.

I'm curious about Johannisberg Riesling. I thought it might be from South Africa, but the label says it's from California. Is it different than just plain Riesling?

First of all, the Johannisberg referred to on the label is a village in Germany's Rheingau region. The other Johannesburg (different spelling) is in South Africa. Riesling and Johannisberg Riesling are exactly the same thing. We think it's just a marketing ploy to make you think it's from Germany where Riesling reigns supreme.

I'm really into Zinfandels and have been experimenting with different ones. I keep seeing "old vines" on some labels like it's a big deal. Are these wines any better than Zins from young vines?

Remember, "better" is always in the eye (or palate) of the beholder. But here's the explanation. As grapevines get older, they produce less fruit. The same theory that says low-yielding vineyards achieved through pruning produce more flavorful and intense grapes (and, ultimately, higher-quality wine) applies to these old vines as well. Labels, however, may not tell the whole story. The term "old vines" isn't regulated. Anyone can use it. While legitimately "old" vines can be a hundred years old, a producer could use the term for much younger vines.

What's the difference between a château and a domaine?

They both refer to a wine estate in France. Château (literally, "castle") is used most often in the Bordeaux region. Domaine is used in Burgundy.

I've enjoyed the couple of winery tours I've taken. Next time I want to buy a few bottles while I'm there and ship them home. Will all wineries do that?

Most wineries are prepared to ship wine to you, but there's a big if—and that's if you live in a state where that's legal. Many states won't allow personal shipments of wines across their borders. And states with "dry" counties pose a problem for even intrastate shipments. In our opinion, the situation is a mess. It's best if you can carry the wines with you. And if not, stretch out a blanket and enjoy them where you are.

I'm not what you'd call an experienced traveler. Are there any wine tours I can take so someone else can handle the planning and logistics?

Even seasoned travelers appreciate what a good tour operator can offer—namely, access to wine estates (and their proprietors) that may not generally be open to the public. Of course, not all tour operators are created equal. We suggest looking for ones that specialize in particular wine regions. Two respected (and women-operated) firms are classic-wine-tours.com for Bordeaux and capewinetours.com for South Africa.

Is saké a wine or a beer?

Good question! The answer is "neither" and "both." It's made from grain (rice) and tastes better the fresher it is—both qualities of beer. Yet, like wine, its alcohol ranges from 12 to 16 percent, and it's consumed by connoisseurs from wineglasses. (If you're looking for a more definitive answer, the U.S. Bureau of Alcohol, Tobacco and Firearms categorizes saké as a wine.) Premium sakés are chilled. The cheaper sakés are served warm in small porcelain cups. We happen to enjoy warm saké and the charming Japanese custom of always filling one another's cup, never your own.

What's the significance of "bin" numbers on Australian wines? Are high numbers better than low ones, or vice versa?

Don't waste your time trying to interpret the numbers. It's just the traditional way the Australian wineries store their bottled wines before they're sold. A Shiraz goes into one bin, a Chardonnay goes into another. The real importance to you is to remember the ones you liked. Let's say you particularly enjoyed a Wyndham's Bin 55 Shiraz. You'll know to be on the lookout for each year's release of that wine.

Chapter 7

~

It's My Party and I'll Wine If I Want To...

ENTERTAINING LIKE A WINE DIVA

W E   S A Y if there's no wine, there's no party. We've endured volleyball beach parties with beer as the sole libation and Cinco de Mayo celebrations with only margaritas. But how many beers and margaritas can a girl drink? Never mind . . . forget we asked that. The point is we love our wine and know you do too. So, at our parties, wine reigns.

The first question everybody asks is: How much wine should I buy? It depends on lots of factors: what kind of party it will be, what types of foods you plan to serve, what other beverages you'll have available and how many wine drinkers there will be.

STAND-UP PARTIES

A stand-up party by any other name is a cocktail party, open house, reception, meet 'n' greet, mixer, meat market. It's the kind of party where guests mingle (or are supposed to) and have the freedom and mobility to abandon one conversation in search of another when the first one becomes unbearably boring.

Your first wine-related decision as hostess is whether to serve other beverages—mixed drinks, beer, sodas and waters. If you decide it'll be a wine-only party, you can be sure everyone will drink wine. If you'll be offering alternatives, the calculations get a little less precise. Estimating the number of wine drinkers is about as clear-cut as divining how many Episcopalians will be there. Who knows? But we figure one-third to one-half of your guests will be drinking wine.

Let's assume for a moment that you'll have twenty wine drinkers. Whether that's twenty wine drinkers out of twenty guests at an all-wine party or twenty wine drinkers out of forty guests at a cocktail party, it doesn't really matter. We're doing our calculations on twenty.

Assume your wine-drinking friends will consume about one 5-ounce glass each half hour of the party. (We always estimate on the high side.) That's 10 ounces per person per hour. So with twenty guests, figure on 200 ounces per hour times three hours—or 600 ounces of wine. A regular size (750 ml) bottle contains 25.4 ounces. (*Now* we come to appreciate our early math training.) So 600 ounces divided by 25.4 equals 23.6 bottles. The equation is:

Number of wine drinkers	$\times$ 10 oz. $\times$	Number of hours the party will last	=	Total amount of wine consumed	$\div$ 25.4	ounces in a bottle	=	How many bottles to buy

For large parties (or for very intimate ones) you may decide to buy wine in containers other than the standard 750 ml bottle. Here's a chart to help you determine the amount and number of glasses contained in each bottle (or box) of wine you buy.

SIZE	OUNCES	5-OZ. SERVINGS	4-OZ. SERVINGS
5 liter	169.0	34	42
3 liter	101.4	20	25
1.5 liter	50.7	10	12
1 liter	33.8	6	8
750 ml	25.4	5	6
375 ml	12.7	2	3
187 ml	6.3	1	1

At a typical stand-up party, guests will come and go. You probably won't have all the wine drinkers there for the entire duration of the party. As a result, you'll have leftover wine. And that's one *very* important reason to select wines that you personally enjoy . . . because you'll end up drinking them.

DINNER PARTIES

What better way to show off your culinary skills and wine-matching prowess than a dinner party? Unlike entertaining at a restaurant, here you're in absolute control. You're the star chef, the renowned sommelier and the famed hostess all wrapped into one. Being in charge also means you have the final say over the budget. No surprises at the end of the dinner when the check is presented. You can choose ingredients that are in season and priced accordingly. You have time to shop for out-of-the-ordinary wines in your price category. If you're lucky, you might unearth a real treasure in the bargain corner of your wine store. This is not skimping. It's being inventive and practical.

Tell the truth. Haven't you always wanted to have one of those

WINE BAR:
And be sure to count the silver too!

If you're serving four types of hors d'oeuvres, count on each guest eating three of each. Plan on buying fifteen pounds of ice for every ten people. Between food and beverages, guests will go through three napkins apiece.

glamorous gourmet dinners where you serve a different wine with each course? This is your chance. We'll walk you through it.

We like to start by offering our guests a glass of Champagne when they arrive. We're always prepared with backups in case they demur. But the only people to date who've turned us down are nondrinkers. Even our beer-drinking, martini-sipping and scotch-imbibing friends who say they "never drink Champagne" always ask for a second glass. Light hors d'oeuvres are in order at this stage.

The wines you serve at dinner should, of course, be coordinated with the foods you prepare. And there's another factor to consider: the sequence. In general, serve white wines before reds, light wines before heavy ones and dry wines before sweet ones. But don't let these rules drive you crazy. If you want to serve a light red before a rich, full-bodied white, go ahead. If you want to serve all whites—hey, it's your party. There's a corollary rule that says you should serve lesser wines before increasingly better and better wines, the theory being that the entire dinner production is a crescendo with the big payoff at the end. Our experience is that after about the third wine, our friends like anything we put in front of them. Perhaps that says something about our friends, but we don't think so.

How many bottles of each wine you should buy for your dinner party depends on how many different wines you plan to serve, the pacing of the courses and your guests' enthusiasm for wine. Do you want to pour one glass per person of each wine—or more? Do you want extra in case one of the wines becomes the darling of the evening? Let's make this as easy as possible.

We recommend you buy the total bottle equivalent of one bottle per person. That's total. Now let us break down how many bottles of each wine to purchase according to the number of wines and the number of guests.

Number of Wines	Number of Guests				
	4	6	8	10	12
2	2	3	4	5	6
3	1	2	2	3	4
4	1	1	2	2	3
5	1	1	2	2	3

Bottles of Each Wine

HOLIDAY PARTIES

The holidays present their own special challenges—and we mean more than Aunt Ethel's constant complaining and cousin Wally's irritating habit of showing up unannounced with his latest bimbo. Take Thanksgiving, for example. Turkey is a given. But every family has its own traditions and recipes passed down through the generations. For our family, it's *kartoffelklosse*, a potato dumpling so big and heavy and dark that, way back, it was nicknamed "shot-put." For other families the traditional dishes could be orange praline sweet potatoes, sausage apple stuffing, cranberry-pear relish or pumpkin cheese roll. How do you pair a wine with all those competing flavors?

One approach is to just throw up your hands and not bother trying to find the perfect match. Not a bad solution, really, particularly if you have an exceptional bottle of wine worthy of a family celebration. On the other hand, there are a number of wine options that taste good with turkey and with the mostly sweet accompaniments. This is our Thanksgiving-Christmas wine list:

> Sparkling wine (of course)
>
> Chenin Blanc
>
> Riesling
>
> Gewürztraminer
>
> Rosé
>
> Beaujolais
>
> Pinot Noir
>
> Chianti
>
> Zinfandel

The Passover Seder has as one of its traditions the consumption of four glasses of wine (kosher, of course), with one special cup left untouched on the table for the enjoyment of the Prophet Elijah. We know what you're thinking: Kosher wine—that thick, sweet, grapey stuff—doesn't go with anything and certainly not with gefilte fish and brisket.

Kosher wine has come a long way. When Jewish immigrants first settled in the northeast over a century ago, they had easy access to Concord and Niagara grapes. The wine they made from these grapes tasted like grape jelly once they sweetened it up a bit. This is just a style of wine—not a religious requirement. Today, kosher wines made from traditional grape varieties are produced in Israel, France, Italy, South Africa, Morocco, Australia and the

United States. So for your next Seder (or anytime, for that matter, because they're just good wines), look for red and white blends and table wines from Israel, Merlot from France, Chenin Blanc and Chardonnay and Cabernet from California—even Moscato d'Asti from Italy. *L'Chaim!*

The Fourth of July is two-thirds of a wine holiday: red, white and . . . well, you get the idea. What wines pair with hamburgers, hot dogs, fried chicken, corn on the cob and potato salad? In short, picnic wines. Wines that are at their best chilled to beat the heat. Wines that are easily transportable to picnic sites—the beach, the purple mountains, the valleys, the fruited plains, from sea to shining sea. Are we sounding all-American here? You bet! And this is the occasion for all-American wine in all its forms. Yes, you catch our drift—even jug wines and box wines. Some are better than others. And some are downright good. The benefits, as we see them, to mass-produced, big-container wines:

- You don't have to worry about running out.
- There are fewer containers to dispose of.
- Lifting them while full is more of a workout than those small sissy bottles.
- It's easier to catch underage drinkers trying to covertly pour a glass for themselves.
- The airtight plastic inside the boxes keeps the wine fresher longer.
- No corkscrew required (usually).
- If they're cold enough, it doesn't matter what they taste like.

DESSERT WINES

When we think of desserts, we think in terms of pounds and inches—the ones around our hips. Oh, the sweet, guilty pleasure!

WINE BAR:
Come kosher. You make me feel unleavened!

"Kosher" means "right" or "proper" in Hebrew. A wine—or any food—that's made according to Jewish dietary laws and produced under the supervision of a rabbi can be labeled as kosher. For wine to be certified as kosher, the winemaking equipment must be used solely for kosher products, and only workers who are Sabbath-observant Jews may handle the wine throughout the production. In addition, wines described as "kosher for Passover" have not come into contact with bread, dough or unleavened dough.

Who can turn down just a forkful of New York cheesecake or a spoonful of Cherry Garcia? We used to fool ourselves into thinking it would be only one bite—but, of course, it never was.

We've turned over a new leaf. We've given up desserts completely—in favor of dessert wines. Some people try to create good pairings by matching sweet wines with sweet foods, but we think dessert wines are best as desserts in themselves. Not only are dessert wines sweet and satisfying, a three-ounce serving has less fat and fewer calories than a serving of any other dessert (an average of 130 calories and *no* fat compared to 300 calories and 18 grams of fat for a slice of cheesecake). We know it's just a rationalization, but it works for us.

You don't have to memorize a lot of rules about dessert wines because there aren't any. Serve whatever strikes your fancy, whether it be sparkling, still or fortified wine. They all work. When sparkling is your choice, consider one of the less dry versions to end the meal. Look to Italy for an Asti or a delicate semi-sparkling Moscato d'Asti. Or to France for a Doux ("sweet") Champagne.

Do any of these names sound familiar? Beerenauslese, Tokay, Barsac, Sauternes. They're all sweet still wines perfect for dessert. So are wines you'll see labeled "late harvest," referring to wines— particularly Riesling and Gewürztraminer—made from grapes picked late in the harvest when they're ripe and sweet. You don't remember seeing them on your frequent sojourns through the wine store? Perhaps you overlooked them because they come in such small bottles and carry such high price tags. The bottles are half the size of a regular bottle. No, you don't have to buy twice as many. The normal serving size for dessert wines is only about two or three ounces. Debate endures over whether to chill these wines. Serving them cold tends to reduce the sweetness. However, good dessert wines have enough acidity to balance the sweetness. So decide for yourself.

Fortified wines—like Port, Madeira, Sherry, Marsala and Malaga—have brandy or a neutral spirit added to them, which, needless to say, boosts the kick. The serving size is smaller than for table wine and so is the glass. (A large glass and a small pour only makes us look cheap.) Like red wines, fortified wines are at their best at cellar temperature.

Port is at the center of much tradition, including the "Laying Down of Port" for a child, when a father or godfather buys a few cases of Port at the child's birth that will be drinkable years later. Starting at the age of twenty-one, the now-matured child can enjoy the now-matured Port, and can continue doing so throughout her life.

We're obviously talking here about Vintage Port that benefits from age. When it comes time to open and pour the first glass of wine, the recipient will have to decant the Port because it will have thrown a sediment. Not all Ports have to be decanted, however. Many Ports are stabilized and filtered before they're bottled and are ready to drink as soon as you buy them, so sediment isn't an issue. A quick way to tell if your Port requires decanting is to

WINE BAR:
Are you going to just leave me hanging there?

As we've seen, sweet wines can achieve their sweetness in a number of ways.

- The grapes can be left on the vine longer than usual to ripen and increase their sugar concentration. These are called *late harvest* wines.
- The grapes can be left on the vine even longer until they shrivel up and their flavors become concentrated. This applies especially to German wines that are labeled "auslese," "beerenauslese" and "trockenbeerenauslese."
- The grapes are allowed to develop a mold (*Botrytis cinerea*), called *the Noble Rot*, which concentrates the grapes' flavors and adds some of its own. This procedure is associated with Sauternes, Barsac, Tokay and the sweetest German wines.
- The grapes can be left on the vine until they freeze. These are called *ice wines* and come from northern vineyards in Germany, Canada and the United States. As an alternative, the grapes can be artificially frozen to produce less expensive ice wines.
- Sugar can be added to the finished wine. Almost all Champagnes and sparkling wines undergo this process of "dosage." Sparkling wines with no dosage are labeled "Natural."

check the cork. Ports that require a corkscrew to open are meant for long aging and will need decanting. Ports with a stopper cork that looks like it's wearing a plastic hat are ready to open and pour immediately.

The generous hostess always considers her guests' appetites and desires as well as her own. A liquid dessert may be your definition of heaven, but your guests might be longing for something sinfully solid. And so we offer these dessert wine pairings. The philosophy behind the matches is that the dessert wine should be sweeter than the dessert it accompanies.

WINE	DESSERT
Sauternes	strawberries
	pear tart
	angel food cake
	raspberry cheesecake
	crème brûlée
	butter cookies
Muscat	apple pie
	poached pears
	spice cake
	New York cheesecake
	raspberry gelato
	toasted almond biscotti
Late-harvest Riesling and Gewürztraminer	peaches
	bread pudding
	lemon custard fruit tart
	trifle
	pound cake with strawberry sauce

WINE	DESSERT
Port	almond tart
	chocolate cake
	brownies
	chocolate cheesecake
	coffee ice cream
	tiramisu
	caramel soufflé
Madeira	chocolate soufflé
	coffee cake
	peanut butter cookies
	pecan tart
	cannoli
Banyuls	dark chocolate desserts

WINE-TASTING PARTIES

So you think a wine tasting is a bunch of old farts sipping and spitting and talking in reverent tones about carbonic maceration and chapitalization? Well, not after the third glass of wine it isn't . . . and definitely not if it's *your* wine tasting.

A wine-tasting party can be anything you want it to be. Let it reflect your personality and the rowdiness quotient of your guests. We differentiate between structured and unstructured wine tastings—the latter is really more wine "drinking" than tasting. (Nothing wrong with that!) Working our way from the more formal to the less formal, permit us to give you some examples of our parties.

WINE BAR:
And you thought you were too mature for drinking games

Port is more than a drink. It's a social activity with a set of established rules. Long ago, British naval officers would pass the Port from "port to port"—that is, clockwise around the table. Women didn't participate in the tradition back then. (Women were expected to drink the "lighter" Sherry.) But we've come a long way, baby. Here's how the game is played.

1. The hostess begins by pouring a glass for the guest on her right.

2. The hostess then passes the Port to the guest on her left, who, in turn, pours for the person to *her* right (the hostess). The port is passed again to the left until the entire table has been served in this manner.

3. A guest never asks directly for more Port. Bad manners, you know. She asks the person nearest the decanter if he or she knows the Bishop of Norwich, a cleric who was notoriously stingy with his Port.

4. The above question is a signal that doesn't require an answer. The proper response is to pass the decanter to the left around the table until it reaches the person wanting the Port.

5. Should a guest fail to understand the signal and reply, "No, I don't," the appropriate response is, "The Bishop is a terribly good chap, but he never passes the Port!"

Oh, what fun we have. . . .

Structured

We usually reserve the more structured parties for people who are looking for more than just catching a buzz. (We have very high standards.) They don't have to know anything about wine (and, in fact, often don't)—they just have to have an interest in learning something about it. We seat guests at tables with empty wineglasses in front of them. The more glasses we set up, the wider the smiles on our guests' faces. More glasses means more wines. We have to admit to being more, uh, frugal with our glasses on occasion. Instead of setting out dozens (or hundreds) of glasses, we limit the number to two glasses per person—one for red, one for white—and add a pitcher of water to rinse the glasses between wines. And, of course, a dump bucket. (No one's going to drink rinse water when there's wine to be had.) A tasting portion of wine is much smaller than the normal 4 to 5 ounces. In fact, you'll get up to fourteen tasting portions out of one 750 ml bottle.

Who wants to work at her own party? So we find a person knowledgeable about the wines we're serving to lead the tasting—to talk about the wines, facilitate conversation (like that's ever a problem with wine being consumed) and answer questions. We know lots of informed wine people. But you can locate one of your own with a simple phone call to your wine store or local restaurant. We know this should go without saying, but it really helps if this person has a sense of humor. Generally, you serve the wines from white to red and from dry to sweet.

We've mentioned the terms "vertical tasting" and "horizontal tasting"—and remember, it has nothing to do with whether the guests are standing or reclining at the end of the party. When you want to see if you can tell the difference among vintages, have a vertical tasting. Serve several bottles of the same wine from the same winery, but from different vintage years. You'll probably be amazed by what you taste. For a horizontal tasting, serve the same kind of wine from the same year from the same general area—say, a 2000 Chardonnay from California—but from different wineries. This kind of tasting will show you how different regions (in this case, different parts of California) and different winemakers influence the end product.

"Blind" tastings add another dimension. None of the guests knows the identity of the wines being poured. That way, their opinions will be objective. At professional tastings, participants try to distinguish variations in regional traits and differences among specific wineries and châteaus. That's asking *way* too much of our guests. We like to include a jug wine or two at blind tastings just to see how they score against the competition.

Less Structured

We ask guests to bring a bottle of wine and be prepared to tell the group a little something about it. ("The wine is named after the winemaker's dog." Or, "It cures PMS.") Guests get one wineglass. We place wines on tables and counters along with pitchers of water and buckets. Periodically throughout the evening, we call on guests to describe the wine they brought and explain why they brought it. ("It's red. Someone left it at my house last year. It beat having to go out and buy another bottle for tonight.") Two hours after the start of the party (all guests' wines having been consumed) we bring out our house wine. It's usually the consensus that this is the best wine of the evening. (Tells you something about our guests.)

It's important that guests know at the outset how serious or laid back your tasting will be. Your invitation can set the tone.

Here's an invitation we sent out for what we hoped would be a fun and relaxed event.

The Saucy Sisters invite you
to taste an array of
specially selected wines from their cellar

Meeska Mooska Muscadet	Slightly juvenile wine with a highly animated character.
Disturbed Graves	Partially-bodied, full bouquet.
Gay Beaujolais	Fruity and sibilant, matured in San Francisco cellars.
Côtes du Kmart	Familiar U.S. vintages, inexpensive yet durable.

THEME PARTIES

Sometimes you want to drink a bunch of different wines with friends without the formality of a "tasting"—a party where guests can pour for themselves from bottles that range from respectable to novel. We've discovered that wine parties based on a theme create the ideal atmosphere.

Bridesmaid Revisited

It was the best of times. It was the worst of times. Your best friend's wedding. You were deliriously happy for her. (Of course, not as happy as if it had been you with the three-carat diamond and Mr. Right waiting at the end of the aisle.) She looked gorgeous in her exquisite Vera Wang. You were . . . well, a vision of contrasts. She was Sharon Stone to your Bridget Jones.

Whom to Invite:	Your girlfriends
Dress Code:	Nightmare bridesmaid dresses
Elements:	Wedding cake, ugliest dress contest, wedding albums
The Wines:	Guests bring a bottle of wine related to their weddings or weddings in general. Suggestions:
	Iron Horse Wedding
	Diamond Creek Cabernet
	Hope Estate Verdelho
	Jerman Dreams
	Cupid Chardonnay
	Pucker Grape
	Any Rosé (to match a pink bridesmaid dress)
	Any wine with a vintage matching your wedding date
	Murphy-Goode Liar's Dice (to depict your gambling, cheating ex-husband)
	Fat Bastard (to describe the father-in-law)

And the Winner Is . . .

We know. One day you'll be strutting down that red carpet with your Serengeti shades, Armani gown and million-dollar Harry Winston broach. In the meantime, you'll have to make do watching Joan Rivers schmoozing up the stars along the runway— and making your own judgments about whose hooters need lifting. Oh, this is too much fun to have alone. . . .

Whom to Invite:	Your gay male friends and your straight girlfriends
Dress Code:	Black Tie (or come as your favorite celebrity)
Elements:	Red carpet, lots of TVs, ballots for voting, fancy-schmancy hors d'oeuvres
The Wines:	Guests bring a bottle of wine related to movies, Hollywood or celebrities.

Suggestions:

Nova Wines Marilyn Merlot (with Marilyn Monroe on the label)

Nova Wines Norma Jean (a young Merlot)

Spring Mountain wines (where *Falcon Crest* was shot)

Celebrity Cellars wines

Two Paddocks wines (owned by actor Sam Neill)

Niebaum-Coppola wines (owned by producer Francis Ford Coppola)

Château de Tigne wines (owned by actor Gerard Depardieu)

Creston Vineyards wines (owned by TV's Alex Trebek)

Okay, it's not exactly showbiz, but . . . Greg Norman Estates wines (owned by the golfing great)

Bottle of Red, Bottle of White

If only you had Billy Joel's number to send him an invite. Music's the name of the game tonight. Crank up that karaoke machine and let the singing begin. Not just any songs . . . wine songs! "Kisses Sweeter than Wine" . . . "Strawberry Wine" . . . "Wine Colored Roses" . . . "Red Red Wine" . . . "It Was a Very Good Year." Better invite the neighbors.

Whom to Invite:	All but the terminally tone-deaf
Dress Code:	Whatever (Any Elvis impersonators in your crowd?)
Elements:	"Talent" contest
The Wines:	Guests bring bottles of wine with a musical name or musical-themed label.

Suggestions:

Grateful Red

Red Zeppelin

Jessie's Grove Zinphony

Opus One (in your dreams!)

Eight Songs Shiraz

Beachhaven Jazz

Fortissimo

Ironstone Obsession California Symphony

POST-PARTY CLEANUP TIPS

The party's over. What a mess to clean up! The only way to deal with it is . . . *yes,* leftover wine. (This could almost be fun. Oh, get a grip.)

Leftovers

The best thing to do with wine that's left in an open bottle is drink it. Oxygen and heat have already begun to ravage the wine's natural beauty, and nothing can stop the process of deterioration. (Are we going to have this same feeling when we look in the mirror in the morning?) Then again, even though you can't stop the decline completely, you can at least slow it down and buy some time.

Close the wine back up and stick the bottle in the fridge. That goes for both reds and whites. Refrigeration decelerates the chemical reaction that spoils wine, so that's the minimum you should do. No sitting the bottle on the counter overnight. It's the oxygen in the air that degrades the wine. Anything you do to reduce the contact between the wine and the air will help prolong the life of the wine. Bottle stoppers create a better seal than just reinserting the cork.

Bottles that are half full of wine are also half full of air. The trick is to remove the air. Specialty stores and mail-order catalogs offer all sorts of devices to reduce a wine's contact with oxygen once the bottle is open. They work to a degree, and in different ways. The most common systems involve either a reverse pump that removes air from the bottle to create a partial vacuum or a spray can of inert gas that you squirt into the bottle.

There are a couple of home remedies that will do the job too. One option is to get yourself a half bottle, drink the contents and clean the bottle well. Pour your leftover wine gently into the smaller bottle, leaving little or no air space at the top. Seal it and refrigerate it. The other option is to buy some marbles and clean them. Drop the marbles into an opened bottle until the level of the wine rises to the top. Seal and refrigerate.

Bottom line—what kind of time frame are we looking at here? How long will the wine last? Weeks? Months? Sorry to be the ones to deliver the news: We're talking *days*. The wine won't get rotten and moldy like the other foods you leave sitting in the refrigerator, but after a few days it'll taste dull and flat. Eventually it will oxidize, turn brown and taste foul.

Not all wines have staying power. Some will last for several days—others won't. For a wine to remain drinkable once it's been exposed to the air, it needs to be capable of aging in the first place. Reds that are high in tannins are the most durable because they were designed to age. Whites won't last as long. And then there are some wines—White Zinfandel and other light and fruity wines—

that are made for immediate drinking that won't survive at all. Age is also a factor. The younger the wine, the better equipped it is to survive. Older wines are just too frail to last.

The news is better on the fortified front. Except for older Vintage Ports that will deteriorate in a day, other fortified wines can last for weeks or even months. Light, dry Sherries are good for about a week. Ports and the richer, sweeter Sherries will last for several weeks. And Madeira will still be good after months on the pantry shelf.

Out, Damned Spot!

If only Lady Macbeth had known our spot-removal secret! A red-wine stain is a real-life melodrama. But thanks to the folks at UC Davis Department of Viticulture and Enology (and who might have spilled more wine than they have?), an effective remedy is at hand. Mix equal parts of 3% hydrogen peroxide and Dawn liquid dishwashing soap. Pour it on the stain, let it sit as you would any other pre-soak and then launder. It's good for colors and whites, and for cotton, polyester and nylon. Warning: Do not wear silk while drinking red wine. Even this foolproof trick can't rescue silk. In an emergency—when you don't have those ingredients at hand—try white wine as a cleaning agent. You may be surprised.

Getting into Hot Water

All those dirty glasses! And unless they're cleaned well, they can impart traces of detergent and dirty towel smell to the wine the next time you use them. We know you don't want to hear this but hand-washing is best for your fine crystal. (You don't put your mom's best silver tray in the dishwasher, do you?) Use the hottest water possible and only a hint of detergent. Rinse well. If you're going to use the dishwasher no matter what we say, wash the glasses by themselves—no dirty plates or pots—without detergent. Not only can detergent leave an odor, it can etch the surface of your crystal. When an odor is noticeable, rinse your glasses first in a mixture of water and baking soda, then rinse again in plain hot water.

Now . . . put up your feet, relax and relive your party's success. You deserve a nightcap. Well done!

ASK THE SAUCY SISTERS

What should I do when someone brings wine to my dinner party?

Unless you've asked your guest to bring the wine, you're not obligated to serve it. A gracious "thank you" will suffice.

I've been to wine tastings where water and plain crackers were served to "cleanse the palate" between wines. What's up with that?

We're not sure whether you're asking why cleansing the palate is necessary or why something more appetizing wasn't served instead, so we'll answer both. The purpose is to eliminate any lingering taste from one wine before you move on to the next sample so that you can fairly judge each wine. Eating something really yummy like shrimp dip or a bite of cheese tart will affect your impression of the wine to come. That's the reason something so simple and benign is served.

Assuming I had money to burn and wanted to impress someone, what's the most expensive wine I could buy?

According to the Guinness Records folks, the most expensive commercially available wine is Château d'Yquem Sauternes 1787. The tab will be between $56,000 and $64,000, depending on the retailer. At a less pricey level, a jeroboam (a 4.5-liter bottle) of Château Pétrus was recently auctioned at $28,750.

Do you have any suggestions for sophisticated hot-weather wines besides the typical picnic whites?

If you want to avoid whites altogether, there are some reds that taste great with a little chill on them, like a Beaujolais or a light Pinot Noir or a Spanish Rioja. But our highest recommendation goes to the essentially dry rosé, which has the depth and earthiness of a red and the refreshing acidity of a white. Plus, we like the color. You'll find quality rosés from the Provence region of France as well as from the Rhone Valley.

For pairing wine and food for a dinner party at home, do I start with the food or the wine?

It's really your choice. If you happen to be an incredible cook—or even have a special recipe you want to showcase—start with the food and choose the wines to match. On the other hand, if you have some exceptional bottles of wine you want to share with friends, select your menu to complement the wine.

~~~

Chapter 8

Wine Buff ...

MAINTAINING HEALTH AND BEAUTY
THROUGH WINE

Wine is the most healthful and hygienic of beverages.
—Louis Pasteur

AH, LOUIS . . . is it true? Wine and health. Hardly a day goes by without news of the latest study on the benefits—or ills—of wine consumption. What's a woman to believe? Should we or shouldn't we? And does it or doesn't it? And if we should and it does, how much is okay? Sounds like sex-education class.

For the past decade or so the medical community has been telling us how wine is good for our hearts. The American Heart Association links moderate drinking to a reduced risk of cardiovascular disease. Recent studies have also associated wine with a reduction in strokes among young women, a decrease in lung disease, increased bone mass in the elderly, and improved digestion.

The benefits of wine drinking may not be merely physiological. Health attitudes and lifestyles of wine drinkers are different from those who consume other kinds of alcoholic beverages or none at all. On the whole, women who are predominantly wine drinkers tend to eat a healthier diet, smoke less and exercise more than those who prefer beer, spirits or are alcohol abstainers.

But there can be too much of a good thing. Wine contains alcohol: 8 to 12 percent of a typical bottle. And for people at any age, too much alcohol can cause serious health problems, not to mention the dangers of drinking and driving. Excessive alcohol consumption also dehydrates our bodies and plays havoc with our skin.

So what's a girl to do with all this mixed information? Have no fear. We'll get to the bottom of it all. First, test yourself to see how savvy a sister you are.

HOW BUFF ARE YOU?

Okay, so you read everything that is available about drinking wine and its effects on your health. You devour your monthly women's health and fitness magazines as soon as they arrive in your mailbox . . . over a glass of Riesling, of course. You talk with your girlfriends about wine, dieting, health and all those other things . . . over a bottle of Riesling. You even admit to your doctor that you might, on occasion, overindulge on the wine just a bit, in hopes that she will impart some useful health information that you don't already know. Sounds like you could be a wine buff! But how buff are you really? Take our quiz and find out.

1. The use of wine for medicinal purposes dates back four thousand years.
True   False

2. White wine has the same positive effects as red wine in reduction of cardiovascular disease.
True   False

3. Moderate wine consumption for women is considered to be one to three glasses (4–12 ounces) of wine per day.
True   False

4. Wine has been linked to a lower incidence of Alzheimer's disease in women over fifty-five.
True   False

5. A red-wine headache is caused by the sulfites added to the wine.
True   False

6. Wine drinkers are less likely to catch the common cold.
True   False

7. Wine drinkers have higher IQs than beer drinkers.
True   False

8. A glass of blush wine has more calories than a glass of white or red.
True   False

9. The alcohol in wine reduces your bad (LDL) cholesterol level while raising your good (HDL) cholesterol level.
True   False

10. Alcohol-free wines are a safe alternative for women who should not consume any alcohol.
True   False

Answer Key:

1. *True.* Clay tablets unearthed by archeologists depict the use of wine as medicine in 2100 B.C.

2. *False.* While white wine consumption has been shown to have many health benefits, including reducing heart disease, red wine is made with the grapes' skins, which contain polyphenols, known potent antioxidants that help prevent clogged-up arteries.

3. *True.* Most medical and scientific professionals agree that moderate wine consumption for women is up to 12 ounces per day. One glass contains 4 to 5 ounces of wine.

4. *True.* Moderate alcohol consumption in individuals aged fifty-five and over has been associated with a decreased chance of developing dementia-related diseases, such as Alzheimer's and Parkinson's. Nondrinkers have shown the greatest incidence of dementia.

5. *False.* Sulfites, which have been added to wine for hundreds of years as a preservative, are more plentiful in your glass of white wine than red and are found in many canned fruits, vegetables and fish. The red-wine headache is more likely due to a reaction to histamines or phenolics, which are found in the grape skins used in red wines.

6. *True.* Drinking up to fourteen glasses of wine per week has been shown to be a strong preventative against the common cold. The flavonoids (anti-oxidants found in grape skins) have the ability to combat rhinoviruses (a major cause of colds).

7. *True.* So says a recent Danish study that found that the average IQ of wine drinkers was 108 points, compared to 97 for their beer-drinking counterparts and 101 for abstainers.

8. *True.* A 5-ounce glass of blush contains slightly more calories (110) than a glass of white (96) or red (102). The sugar content in blush wines is higher than fully dry whites or reds. Also, wines with a higher alcohol content, like Chardonnay or Zinfandel (13.5 percent), will usually have a few more calories than those with 8 to 12 percent alcohol. The same glass of dessert wine packs a whopping 226 calories. Guess that's why it's called *dessert*.

9. *True.* Wine lowers the low-density lipoprotein (LDL) so that there are less fatty deposits in the blood vessel wall, while it also raises high-

density lipoprotein (HDL) by clearing away the LDL and taking it back to the liver to be metabolized and reused.

10. *False.* Alcohol-free wines are actually *not* alcohol-free—they contain .5 percent alcohol. For women who must, because of health concerns, totally restrict their alcohol intake, these wines may not be safe.

So, how buff are you?

YOUR SCORE (AWARD YOURSELF ONE BUFF POINT FOR EACH CORRECT ANSWER.)

9–10:	Buffest of Them All
6–8:	Big-time Buff
4–5:	Passable Buff
2–3:	Buff in Need
0–1:	Totally Un-Buff

WHAT SCIENCE TELLS US ABOUT WINE AND HEALTH

Wine—of all colors and flavors—has been used for medicinal purposes for over four thousand years. Historians have recorded uses of wine as an antiseptic, sedative, diuretic and dysentery preventative through thousands of years. It was used widely for surgery and the treatment of wounds. Paracelsus, the father of modern pharmacology and originator of the word "alcohol," promoted wine as a tonic in the early sixteenth century. And in the nineteenth century, European wine drinkers were mostly spared from the cholera outbreak, scientists believe, because the wine wiped out the bacteria causing the disease.

It wasn't until the early 1900s that wine was studied and chronicled for its positive health effects. Raymond Pearl, a noted American biologist, studied the relationship between alcohol consumption and mortality in 1926. He wrote what is considered the first significant report on the benefits of moderate alcohol consumption to overall health. His timing couldn't have been worse. Facing a country heading toward Prohibition, the medical community didn't welcome his findings until decades later, when more headlines were appearing across the Atlantic about wine consumption and health.

In 1961, French scientist Jack Masquelier conducted research that demonstrated the benefits of red wine and reduction of bad (LDL) cholesterol. And in 1991, another famous Frenchman, Serge Renaud, coined the phrase "the French Paradox." Renaud stated that moderate and regular wine consumption was the explanation for low coronary heart disease rates among the French, despite high-risk factors such as a high-fat diet and high incidence of smoking.

The French Paradox spawned numerous research projects on wine and our hearts, our lungs, our brains, our bones and, basically, our overall heath. The findings have certainly helped to boost wine consumption and the popular belief that it really is good for us.

Heart Disease

There is very little dispute these days that moderate wine drinking is good for our hearts. Even the American Medical Association says that moderate alcohol consumption appears to lower the risk of certain complications of heart disease. Women who drink moderately and practice a good diet and exercise routine have a 30–40 percent reduced risk of coronary disease.

Alcohol works to alter blood lipid levels by lowering bad (LDL) cholesterol and raising high-density lipoprotein (HDL, or good cholesterol) levels. Wine's antioxidants help prevent the forma-

tion of plaque in our arteries. Additionally wine acts as an antico-
agulant, which keeps the blood from forming clots.

Wine contains resveratrol, the strongest antioxidant found in
nature—five times stronger than Vitamin E. It is present in all colors of wine—red, white and blush. Red wine has been further
linked to reducing heart disease because of the pigments in red
grape skins called polyphenols. While white and blush wines may
be somewhat lower in antioxidants because they don't contain
grape skins, they are just as effective in reducing the bad cholesterol and elevating the good.

Lung Disease

Many of the studies on wine suggest that one to three glasses of
wine per day is beneficial to the heart. A recent study conducted
at the University of Buffalo suggests that the same amount of
wine may help protect our lungs. The study showed that while
wine drinkers demonstrated greater lung function than non–wine
drinkers, those who consumed white wine had higher lung function than either red wine drinkers or nondrinkers. Again, it's the
antioxidant molecules in wine that help reduce inflammation in
the airways, thus protecting the lungs. Research is still going on to
determine why, but white wine drinkers were shown to have
higher levels of vitamin antioxidants in their blood and had the
best pulmonary function.

Strokes

Antioxidant flavonoids found in wine again seem to be the
hero in helping to reduce the risk of stroke in women under
forty-five. Separate studies conducted at the Centers for Disease

Control and Brigham & Women's Hospital show that moderate wine drinkers have a lower risk (up to 40 percent lower) than nondrinkers for hypertension and stroke. Beer drinkers and spirits drinkers showed no correlation to stroke reduction. Even the American Heart Association's Stroke Council has chimed in on the benefits of moderate levels of alcohol, saying that one glass a day may reduce the incidence of stroke. It's believed that the antioxidants prevent blood from clotting and increase the level of good cholesterol, helping to lower the overall cholesterol levels in the bloodstream.

Common Cold

All smart girls know to take extra vitamin C during cold season to help reduce our incidence of the common cold. But contrary to popular belief, there is no vitamin C in wine. So what is the reason for recent findings that wine drinkers have a lower rate of the common cold? Again, the anti-inflammatory compounds and antioxidants are believed to be responsible. Researchers at the University of Santiago de Compostela in Spain found that drinking up to fourteen glasses of wine per week acts as a strong preventative against the common cold. Beer and spirits drinkers, drinking equal amounts of alcohol, showed no reduction in colds.

Alzheimer's Disease

A recent study in Europe at the Erasmus Medical Center in the Netherlands found that two to five glasses of alcohol a day can help decrease the risk of brain deterioration in people over age fifty-nine. Brain deterioration leads to diseases such as Alzheimer's and Parkinson's. The findings revealed that those who drank moderately (and in Europe that is up to five glasses a day!) had a 50 percent lower risk of developing dementia than both the nondrinkers and those who drank fewer than two glasses per day. Researchers speculate that the alcohol may stimulate a brain chemical known to facilitate learning and memory.

Bone Mass

Common belief has been that alcohol lowers a woman's bone mass, which may lead to osteoporosis. However, a recent study in France indicates that drinking one to three glasses of wine a day may have a positive effect on bone density in women over seventy-five. The study was conducted to determine the relationship between alcohol and the bones of elderly women and how that relationship compares with estrogen-replacement therapy. Moderate drinkers' bones showed the greatest mass, with light drinkers next, followed by nondrinkers. Caution: Heavy drinkers had the lowest bone density.

WINE BAR:
Wine drinkers are smarter, richer
and psychologically healthier

The same Danish study that found that the average IQ of wine drinkers was higher than that of beer drinkers or teetotalers tells us that wine drinking is associated with higher parental education level and higher socioeconomic status. The study also found that wine drinkers were less neurotic, less anxious and less depressed. Wine drinkers also tend to have a lower risk of becoming heavy drinkers and a lower mortality rate than beer drinkers.

WINE BAR:
Nutrients and Calories in Wine

A 5-ounce glass of white wine contains about 96 calories. Are we getting any nutrients for those calories? Unlike most of the food and beverage industry, winemakers don't have to disclose on the label the ingredients or nutrients in their bottles. So, here's what you're getting—or not—in each glass of white wine.

Total Fat	0
Calories from Fat	0
Saturated Fat	0
Cholesterol	0
Sodium	7.09 mg
Carbohydrate	2.41 g
Daily Fiber	0 g
Sugars	0 g
Protein	.28 g
Vitamin A	0
Vitamin C	0
Calcium	0%
Iron	0%
Thiamin	.01%
Riboflavin	.04%
Niacin	.11%
Folate	0%

Weight and Body Mass

News we've been waiting for. Moderate and regular wine consumption is not associated with weight gain, according to a study by the American Cancer Society. And compared with nondrinkers, women who drink alcohol regularly and moderately tend to have a lower body-mass index (BMI), despite higher caloric intakes. The study found that consuming two glasses of wine a day does not influence body weight and it does not promote the development of obesity.

Moreover, for those who are already obese, the addition of moderate amounts of red wine to their diet may reduce their risk of heart disease. Significantly overweight people are at a greater risk of developing heart disease than leaner folks.

Digestion

Just dined at a local dive and are a little skittish about what you ate? Hopefully you downed the questionable cuisine with some wine. Researchers at West Virginia University found that wine

---

WINE BAR:
Can a wine be too fat or too thin?

Yes. Distinguishing between a fat wine and a thin one is as easy as . . . well, seeing the difference between Ally McBeal and Bridget Jones. In the wine world, Bridget wins out.

A fat wine is a big, silky and full-bodied wine that is usually high in alcohol content. It's known to fill the mouth with its richness. Examples of fat wines are the Pomerols from Bordeaux, rich and usually expensive wines.

A thin wine is one that lacks fullness, flavor, depth and complexity. You might think you're drinking flavored water. And for the price, go for the water.

consumption with food helps wipe out bacteria responsible for food-related ailments. And a recent study at Oregon State University found that wine, particularly white wine, can kill E. coli, salmonella and other potentially deadly bacteria. Great news for those of us who love those sidewalk food carts. And another reason to never leave home without a bottle of wine.

Colorectal Cancer

More women over the age of seventy-five die from colorectal cancer than from breast cancer, and men and women over fifty are at equal risk of developing this second-leading cause of cancer deaths. So it's great news that moderate wine consumption may

WINE BAR:
Keep your man seeing red!

A diet rich in tomatoes is associated with a reduction in prostate cancer risk in men. (What's that got to do with us? *His* prostate plays an important role in *our* sexual lives.) And red wine has one up on the tomato. Recent studies have shown that compounds found in red wine not only inhibit the growth of prostate cancer, but may also help destroy the cancer cells. The compounds belong to a class of polyphenols known as flavonoids, which have been shown to contribute to lowered cancer risk.

So here's to your next rendezvous in honor of prostate health: with a bottle of your favorite red and your favorite tomato dish. And how about a little red outfit? While no scientific studies have proven red clothing improves prostate health, we think it couldn't hurt.

protect against colorectal cancer. Beer and spirits did not show the same benefit.

So now you know what wine can do for you. Drink wisely, for pleasure and for your health. Know the facts—understand the difference between chatter over the water cooler and the findings in the latest medical journal. Evaluate your relationship with wine. It should make you feel good in mind and body. When, and if, it ever ceases to play that role, you've either been a bad girl or something is amiss.

Dr. Michael Talbot, a physician specializing in women's health and weight management, says moderation is the key. Wine has been proven to have health benefits in women, but there's a fine line between just the right amount and too much. Each of us needs to know our limits and listen to our bodies . . . then enjoy!

THE SAUCY SISTERS' HEALTH SOLUTIONS

So, you've been a bad girl? Had one glass too many and are singing the hangover blues? Or you've been getting these miserable headaches lately when drinking wine of all kinds? Or your doctor just told you that you're pregnant and must abstain—yes, totally abstain—for a while? Or maybe you think you might be allergic to something in your favorite wine? Well, here's your chance for rehab, buff rehab, that is. Information on the good, the bad and the ugly of wine's side effects.

Oh, What a Party . . . Hangover Culprits

The juice was flowing, your guests were having a ball—dancing, singing, laughing—and after they left, the lovemaking with your man went beyond your wildest fantasies. Problem is, right now you can't think of anything except your pounding headache, desperate thirst and occasional waves of nausea. Why is the outcome of something so delicious so dreadful? Girl, sounds like you have a hangover!

While you're hating whoever offered you that last glass of wine (oh, now you remember, it was you . . . the one you poured yourself to take to the bedroom), you're saying never again. Famous last words. While our intentions are good, there's every likelihood we'll be feeling this way again.

Any girl who loves wine knows what a hangover is. And unlike your recent party, a hangover isn't necessarily brought on by how much wine you drank. But it's a sure bet you'll get one if the number of glasses you consume in one day exceeds your ring size.

A hangover is a complicated biological event that is affected by many physiological factors. Other than the total amount of alcohol consumed, possible contributors to a hangover are the types of alcohol consumed, what you did or did not eat, if you are premenstrual, take oral contraceptives or just had an argument with your lover.

Our body is amazing. In its attempts to process alcohol and rid our system of it, we are made to feel the pain. Alcohol is a drug. When the level of alcohol exceeds our body's ability to metabolize it, we experience the vile symptoms of a hangover.

Alcohol is a diuretic and causes dehydration. There's justification for those many trips to the girl's room . . . it's not just to refresh our lipstick. A physical need is present. When your body loses fluid and you don't replenish it (in this case more wine doesn't count), the loss of fluids from the body plays a major role in a next-day hangover.

Dehydration is not the only cause of hangovers, however. Another offender is something called *congeners*, which are toxic chemicals created during the alcohol fermentation process. They give flavor, smell and appearance to alcohol and exist in varying amounts in wines. Methanol is a congener commonly found in wines and is the most likely cause of the notorious hangover headache. Some people claim that higher-quality wine has fewer impurities and thus fewer congeners.

If you find yourself feeling wine's alcohol effects more dramatically right before your period, there's a reason. Women may actually get inebriated faster during this time because our menstrual cycle significantly increases the rate of alcohol absorption in our body. Additionally the balance of sex hormones and our changing moods contribute to the alcohol's intensity.

Oral contraceptives can also affect the rate of alcohol absorption into the body. Studies have shown that women who take birth control pills can absorb alcohol quicker than women who don't. Again it is believed that the hormonal balances play a role in this.

Lack of sleep can also contribute to a hangover. When you have high levels of alcohol in your system, your brain does not enter its dreaming stage of sleep, which you need in order to feel rested.

Drinking more than one type of wine will not normally cause you to become more intoxicated or contribute to your hangover. Alcohol is alcohol. However, some wines, like Chardonnay and Zinfandel, have a higher alcohol content than others, so a glass of Riesling may not have the same effect on you as a glass of Zin.

The Saucy Sisters' Hangover Helpers

Food, glorious food. We should have it when we're drinking and shouldn't when we're hungover. The food in your stomach does help absorb the alcohol when you're drinking. No wonder wine with our meals feels perfect. However, when the alcohol has left our stomachs, food does not help. Those cravings we have for fast food on hangover days are misguided. The fat actually irritates our stomach and only adds calories to an already alcohol- and calorie-laden body. Water and a piece of dry toast may be your only salvation.

Okay, we've all tried it at least once: "hair of the dog." Does it help? Probably not. Adding more alcohol to your system, which has already had enough, may make you feel better for a few minutes, but the relief is only temporary. You're just postponing the inevitable.

As you know, there's no miracle cure for a hangover. Time— and lots of water—are your only allies. But there are some precautions, other than not drinking, that you can take to minimize the day-after effects of your next party.

Before the party: Eat something high in fat. We know you want to wear that gorgeous Armani black dress that fits you like a glove, but if you want to minimize the alcohol's effects, a high fat concentration in your stomach will help to delay its absorption.

During the party: Drink a glass of water between every glass of wine. This will not only help keep you hydrated, it will minimize alcohol's intoxicating effects on your body.

After the party: Eat something salty. Your wine consumption has probably flushed out lots of salt from your body. Drink a glass of water and then another glass of water and get some sleep. Many sports-minded, wine-drinking women are consuming their favorite sports drink—like Gatorade—to help attack their after- party thirst. The idea is that the electrolytes contained in most sports drinks (basically a salt that carries an electrical charge) can help restore your body's salt balance and help replenish the fluid lost during your partying.

WINE BAR:
Your Blood Alcohol Level

All wine divas know that drinking and driving do not mix. According to Mothers Against Drunk Driving (MADD), Americans rank drunk driving as their primary highway safety concern.

Knowing each state's legal limit of blood alcohol level before driving in that state is smart. In most states the limit is .10% blood alcohol level, although several have reduced the limit to .08% and more are considering doing so.

What is more important is how those numbers apply to you, since the estimated percent of alcohol in the blood is affected by your gender, height, weight and number of glasses of wine consumed in a period of time. Blood Alcohol Level (BAL) is the amount of alcohol present in your blood as you drink. It's calculated by determining how many milligrams of alcohol are present in 100 milliliters of blood.

There are several do-it-yourself breath tests on the market that provide an immediate estimate of your blood alcohol level. But most importantly, if you are even considering whether you're legal to drive, it's best to not drive at all.

Brain Shrinkage

This is for you serious party girls. Are you consuming more than four glasses of wine a day? Maybe an entire bottle all by yourself, seven days a week? Sure, we love our wine, but at this rate, we may not remember how to pronounce Gewürztraminer by the time we're fifty. The problem is that heavy alcohol consumption (and, yes, a bottle a day is considered "heavy") is associated with brain shrinkage.

Our brains shrink as a natural part of aging. But heavy drinking speeds up the shrinkage because alcohol affects the frontal lobe of the brain—the part that controls our cognitive functions.

The good news is that moderate alcohol consumption (three glasses or less) does not appear to affect the brain's volume. While this is an area of ongoing research and debate, we do know one thing: The fifth glass of wine is never as memorable or satisfying as the first. So why drink the extra calories?

Headaches

What an outrage! Here you are sipping a lovely Pinotage and—*boom*—your head starts pounding. Or worse, it feels like it's going to explode. You pop your favorite pain pill hoping for quick relief. A headache is bad enough, but who wants to waste a perfectly good glass of wine?

According to Dr. Fred Freitag, a physician with the Diamond Headache Clinic in Chicago, headaches are one of the most common complaints of women seeking medical care. Fourteen percent of the female population gets migraines. But what about wine headaches? Dr. Freitag has been specializing in headache care for over twenty years and is a wine enthusiast and winemaker. He says there may be several potential causes, but one you can count *out* is sulfites.

Sulfites occur naturally in many fruits and vegetables—including grapes—and help preserve the plant. Winemakers have added sulfites to wine for hundreds of years to preserve it and allow it to age. It's a common misconception that sulfites cause headaches. Sulfite headaches actually occur in only 1 percent of the population, usually asthmatics. The sulfite warning on the labels of U.S. wines was put there for those sulfite-sensitive people among us.

Dr. Freitag says the jury is still out as to the exact causes of wine headaches. But here are some possibilities:

- Congeners are organic compounds found in wine that are part of the fermentation process and give the wine its characteristic flavor. There are hundreds of them present in wine in varying amounts depending on the type of wine. The medical community has suspected these compounds to be part of the headache source.

- Histamines are chemical substances found in wine, predominantly reds. They are a natural occurrence and are found in many foods, such as eggplant, which has more histamines than red wine. The problem they may create is that they dilate our blood vessels, which may cause some people to get headaches. Also, some people lack the enzyme needed to properly metabolize histamines, compounding the problem.

- Prostaglandins are substances found in our bodies that cause inflammation and pain. It is possible that these contribute to our wine headaches.

- Tyramines are substances found in grapes and can cause blood pressure to rise in some people. The amount of tyramine differs depending on the type of grape, which may be why some people get a headache from one type of wine and not another.

- Woods used for aging wine may cause a woman to experience a headache. For example, some women are more sensitive than others to oak.

- The soil where the grapes are grown is also a likely factor. Soil contains varying types of chemicals. You may be able to drink a Cabernet from California, but not one from Australia.

- Physiology of the drinker is another factor to consider when you're trying to figure out this complicated area of wine and headaches. Our moods may play a role, and also our ability—or inability—to metabolize alcohol.

What's a headache-prone girl to do? About the only thing you can do is experiment with different wines. If one gives you a headache (and you'll know within fifteen minutes of your first sip), try another. Keep a journal and do your own study of which ones are the culprits and which ones you can enjoy headache-free.

If you're getting headaches from drinking Riesling, you may be sensitive to tyramines. Rieslings have one of the higher concentrations of tyramines. Try a Chardonnay or Sauvignon Blanc, because they are low in tyramines. However, stay away from Chianti, because it's even higher than Riesling.

If it's histamines you're sensitive to, vitamin B6 might be the answer for you. Vitamin B6 helps us metabolize histamines. Taking it before consuming wine could help prevent a headache, and if it's already too late for that, it could help you get over it.

Without detailed data and analysis, it's difficult to determine which wines may affect you, because every woman's physiological makeup is different. Until additional medical and scientific research is conducted, your best bet is to keep track of the wines you and your body can tolerate.

Alcohol-Free Wine

Congratulations, you're pregnant! You can make it through nine months without your favorite Pinot Noir, no sweat. But what do you do when your doctor tells you to cut out the wine for some other reason? Will it be spring water at all your upcoming dinners? Alcohol-free wine sounds like a good alternative. How does it taste? And will it complement your grilled salmon as well as a glass of Viognier? Well, here's the good news and the bad. Yes, the flavor hasn't been compromised too much, and you'll most likely enjoy it with your favorite meal. However, the alcohol-free wines on the market are not totally alcohol-free.

When so-called alcohol-free wine is made, the alcohol essence is reintroduced to the dealcoholized wine and blended with un-fermented grape juice. The result is a drink that contains up to .5 percent alcohol. If you have been advised not to consume even the slightest drop of alcohol, skip anything with the word "alcohol."

Give Me a Glass of Unleaded, Please

Is it true that lead crystal glassware can be dangerous? Here's the scoop:

Lead crystal glasses and decanters may release lead into your wine. Wine, because of its acidity, will absorb more lead than wa-ter or milk. The longer the wine remains in the crystal, the more lead will be released, so a glass of wine over the course of a meal will absorb minimal lead compared to wine stored in a decanter over a period of weeks.

According to the experts, lead crystal should not pose a threat to wine drinkers. However, to reduce your exposure, here are some tips:

- Don't store wine in a decanter. Use the decanter for onetime serving, and then wash it with vinegar and mild detergent.
- Soak new crystal in vinegar for twenty-four hours. Rinse thoroughly before using.
- Don't use harsh detergents on the crystal. They may increase the release of lead.

Purple Teeth

This is a problem more common to professional wine tasters and judges, who may sample eighty wines in a day, but you may have experienced it yourself, in which case you know how embarrassing it is.

Tooth discoloration is caused by the staining of saliva, which covers all the surfaces of your mouth, including teeth, tongue and even lips. Usually the staining is temporary and disappears when you brush your teeth. But over time, consistent red wine consumption may cause purpling of your teeth that's not eliminated by simple brushing. That's when a trip to the dentist is in order for some professional teeth-whitening procedures.

However, there are some quick fixes and preventative measures you can take. Don't brush your teeth immediately after drinking wine—wait an hour or so. All wines have acidity, which helps preserve the wine and increase its flavor, but the high acidity leaves your teeth sensitive to abrasion. Brushing too soon could ruin your tooth enamel. If you're in a hurry to brush, eat some cheese, which will help restore your mouth to its natural balance.

Drink water between sips of wine. It will help reduce the acid and the ultimate staining of your teeth. Rinsing with a pinch of bicarbonate of soda prior to brushing is also recommended. And if you're planning some colossal tasting, use a fluoride rinse in your mouth at least two to three hours before.

BUFF BEAUTY

Women are so creative. We'll try almost anything in search of the perfect beauty treatment. We've spread oatmeal on our faces, whipped eggs into our hair, slathered vegetable oil all over our bodies and laid tea bags on our eyelids.

So what about wine? Something so good for our bodies when consumed must have value for our outer beauty. Well, the question was asked and answered ages ago.

Wine, and its by-products, have been used by women for beauty treatments since the ancient Romans. Cleopatra answered the question by using the oils from grape seeds for eye makeup. Red wine was used for hair color and white wine was used for blemish control. Dyes made from red grape skins were used for cosmetics. And champagne, well, we all know it's to bathe in.

Use of wine for beauty treatments has not changed much today. There continues to be a proliferation of products espousing "natural" ingredients that use grape seeds or skins in their ingredients.

Grape-seed oil is one that continues to demonstrate benefits to our face, body and hair. It's rich in vitamin E and has linoleic acid, which serves as a great moisturizer for the face and body and is especially good for treating dry hair.

And while we can attest to champagne baths and dry white wine as a facial astringent, we haven't put the red wine into our hair yet. But next time you might want a few red highlights, why not give it a try? Just don't use the whole bottle. If you don't like the color, at least you'll have something to drink.

ASK THE SAUCY SISTERS

What is the alcohol content of an average glass of wine and does the alcohol affect the wine's quality?

Most bottles contain 8 to 12 percent alcohol. However, the alcohol content can be higher—like a California Zinfandel, which may have up to 16 percent. And, yes, alcohol is a major component in a wine's quality. It gives you the impression of its body and weight. It contributes to how the wine feels in your mouth. A full-bodied wine is one that is heavy or weighty. Just remember, the higher the alcohol, the higher the calories.

Are there any health advantages to drinking organic wines?

Organic farming avoids the use of industrial pesticides, herbicides and fungicides. The health benefits of organic wine are the same as with other organic crops, so you may see this as an advantage. Organic wines are made using the same methods as other wines, so you should not be able to detect a taste difference.

Why are women's recommended alcohol consumption levels lower than men's?

Women, on average, have less body weight and absorb alcohol more quickly. We have different enzyme levels in our stomachs and lower body water content, which results in alcohol becoming more concentrated in our body tissues. The term "moderation" varies throughout the world, but the majority of medical professionals say it is up to 12 ounces of alcohol per day.

Chapter 9

~~~

Fashion-Forward Wine...

ON THE CUTTING EDGE
OF WINE DIVAHOOD

WINE AS A FASHION STATEMENT? Absolutely! Look at it this way: One particular wine, because of its style, creator and reputation, is equivalent to wearing a Chloe velvet bustier, Prada beaded skirt and Fendi logo mules. It screams trendy, in demand and expensive. On the other hand, the wine standing next to it on the shelf with the Kathie Lee skirt & tee ensemble and Naturalizer pumps says dependable and reasonably priced. There's no wrong choice. But the wine you buy and how you serve it speak volumes about your ability to spot (or start) hot trends and entertain with panache.

Now that you've mastered the basics, it's time to enter the ranks of wine maven. Discover the fine art of unearthing wine jewels for peanuts, selecting the ideal gift for wine-drinking sisters and brothers, and faking whatever wine knowledge you haven't yet acquired. Now grab your Kate Spade bag and come undercover with us to learn the secret handshakes of wine divahood.

WINE BAR:
A wine's color "palate" reveals its age

When wine ages its color changes. For whites, the older they get, the darker they become—almost amber in some cases. It's just the opposite for reds. They fade with age (don't we all . . .) and develop a tawny or brick-red color. Pour yourself a glass of red and tilt it away from you. The browner and paler the rim, the more mature the wine. When you notice a color change in a young wine, it may be premature aging (like finding that first wrinkle).

SHOPPING STRATEGIES FOR THE WINE DIVA

Girls sophisticated in the ways of the vine have more than a few tricks up their sleeves when it comes to getting good quality for less. We're here to share some of those off-the-rack bargain tactics with you.

Buy from lesser-known, less-popular and emerging regions. Bordeaux, Napa and Tuscany are prime winemaking real estate. And you'll pay the price for their wines. Look next door— or halfway around the world—for real value.

France	Languedoc-Roussillon
	Provence
	Loire
	Savoie
Italy	Calabria
	Campania

	Puglia
	Sicily
	Sardinia
Spain	Navarra
	Penedes
	Priorato
South America	Argentina
	Chile
United States	Paso Robles (CA)
	Sierra Foothills (CA)
	San Luis Obispo (CA)
	Oregon
	Washington State
Other Good Bets	Portugal
	Greece
	Eastern Europe
	South Africa
	Australia
	New Zealand

Buy second labels. Wines that aren't the quality to be bottled under a winery's primary label are bottled under a second label. Château Lafite is said to have started this practice in the eighteenth century, and many of Bordeaux's other châteaus followed suit. The rejected wine wasn't bad—it was actually very good—it just didn't pass the rigorous selection process. These second-label wines are considered excellent wines. In great vintage years the gap in quality between a château's primary wine and its second label can be very narrow. On top of that, they offer an incredible deal—especially in light of the astonishingly high prices in Bordeaux. You won't find a Bordeaux second label for under $10, but $25 should get you in the door. These are the names to look for.

CHÂTEAU	SECOND LABEL
Château Lafite-Rothschild	Carruades de Lafite
Château Margaux	Pavillon Rouge
Château Lynch-Bages	Haut-Bages-Averous
Château Talbot	Connetable Talbot
Château Pichon-Longueville-Lalande	Réserve de la Comtesse
Château Haut-Bailly	La Parde de Haut-Bailly
Château Haut-Brion	Château Bahans-Haut-Brion
Château Cos d'Estournel	Marbuzet
Château Gruaud-Larose	Sarget de Gruaud-Larose
Château Lagrange	Les Fiefs de Lagrange

In the United States many wineries jumped on the bandwagon. When they realized they had more wine than they could sell under their flagship brands, they created their own second labels, which often showcased the winery's characteristic style. Some American second labels:

WINERY	SECOND LABEL
Caymus Vineyards	Liberty School
Stag's Leap Wine Cellars	Hawk Crest
Duckhorn	Decoy
Rex Hill Vineyards	Kings Ridge
Chateau Montelena	Silverado Cellars
Iron Horse	Tin Pony
Chappellet	Pritchard Hill
Cuvaison	Calistoga Vineyards
Raymond	La Belle
Monticello	Jefferson Cellars
Markham	Glass Mountain
St. Supery	Bonverre
J. Lohr	Cypress

When the second labels first appeared here, most of the wine used was excess wine that would have been a hard sell at a higher price. But knock a few dollars off the price, and they became a good value.

Big wineries with big budgets have taken second labels a step further. Rather than relying on excess product, they produce wines specifically for the budget-minded. They blend grapes from various regions to produce a wine they can sell at a low price. Beringer's Napa Ridge, Mondavi's Woodbridge, Sebastiani's Talus and Fetzer's Bel Arbor are all examples of this marketing strategy. Their second-tier wines are sold on price and easy access. Their primary brands are still sold on quality and limited availability.

Buy "shadow" vintages—the year following a block-buster vintage. After all the hoopla surrounding a great vintage, the next year is underappreciated and less in demand.

Shop for bin end sales. Throughout the year wine merchants have to get rid of their excess stock, and they reduce the prices of "leftover" bottles. These are not always schlock. There are treasures to be found.

Copy what the 4-star restaurants do. Call your favorite restaurant with a good wine list and ask what their "house" wine is. It's usually selected for its quality, value and widespread appeal.

WINE GIFTS FOR EVERY OCCASION

Another bridal shower! Forget Victoria's Secret. Get her something she'll really be able to use (not that sexy lingerie doesn't have its practical side). Buy something she'll remember you for long after the honeymoon's over. A stemware washing brush, and, yes, some stemware to go with it.

A woman's gift-giving life is eternal. There's always another gift for yet another occasion. The perfect gift is elusive—if not impossible. So make it easy on yourself and think "wine." Here are our suggestions for celebrating the occasion with wine accessories.

Bon Voyage: She's headed to Club Med. Her goal is to catch a man. Gift: Wine backpack with settings for two, including tablecloth and matching blanket.

Wedding: You're confident the marriage will last at least as long as a case of wine. Gift: A case of wine with personalized labels with a picture of the loving couple.

House warming: You know it'll take her weeks to unpack all those boxes. She'll need quick access to a glass of wine. Gift: Wine and glass wall rack with room for six bottles.

Bridesmaid: Your attendants can't even keep track of their own wineglasses. But somehow you trust them to be organized for your wedding. Gift: Wine charms in distinctive styles to match their personalities—and to keep them from drinking your wine.

Get well: She's under the weather, can't leave the house and has been living on saltines and chicken soup. Gift: Six-pack of single-serving Champagnes to lift her spirits and wash down the aspirin.

Groundhog Day: It's the rare and generous friend who would consider this day a worthy occasion for gift giving. You want to select something that will really cast a shadow. Gift: A Tiffany-style stained-glass lamp with a vintage grape motif.

Easter: You know she'd love to have a cute little bunny to call her own, but she can't even keep a cactus alive. Gift: A Rabbit Corkscrew named for its bunnylike profile. It opens a bottle of wine in three seconds . . . and requires no fertilizing.

April Fool's Day: You present her with an exceptional bottle of her favorite wine. Gift: Wine Bottle Puzzle that locks the bottle of wine inside a wooden block. Can she figure out the secret of the ropes and pulleys to liberate the object of her passion?

Mother's Day: By now, Mom has received her share of flowers. Perhaps this year she deserves something longer lasting? Gift: Champagne Bouquet. These tulip-shaped flutes have long stems but no base. Like cut flowers, they rest in a vase just waiting to be plucked out.

For him . . . just because: He rarely dresses up, but he looks so tempting when he does. Maybe with a little incentive . . . Gift: Cluster and grape tie and suspenders.

CORK AND LABEL ART

Pop Art

Pull the cork from a bottle and what do you see? Sometimes corks are branded with the winery's name and the vintage date of the wine. Back in the days when glues and inks weren't what they are today, paper labels on wine bottles would disappear or become illegible in damp cellars. The cork was the only means of identification.

There's no consistency about what you'll see branded on corks

WINE BAR:
And you thought diamonds were the perfect gift!

Crystals that form in wine when it gets too cold are called "wine diamonds." Two natural elements in wine, tartaric acid and potassium, bind together under chilly conditions and form potassium bitartrate crystals. They look like sugar crystals, but they don't dissolve. Don't panic when you find wine diamonds in your Chardonnay. They won't hurt you or the wine. They tell you that the wine was made from ripe grapes and has an accompanying acidity that keeps the wine fresh and long-lived.

Wine diamonds form more often in white wines than in reds. That's because the crystals develop only when the wine gets very cold, and red wines are usually served at warmer temperatures. To prevent you from the shock of discovering diamonds in your wine, some winemakers perform cold stabilization—in essence forcing the crystals to form at the winery instead of in your home. Should you find these precious nuggets in your wine, just stand the bottle upright until the crystals fall to the bottom, and pour gently.

these days. It may be a country code or a winery's name. On French wines you'll see "Mis en Bouteille" followed by a phrase such as "au Domaine," meaning "bottled at the estate." Laurel Glen Reds has pictures of tyrants and despots. Probably the funniest message delivered on a cork comes from Frog's Leap Winery: ribbit.

Without saying a word, a cork can give clues about the bottle's contents. The narrower and more out of shape a cork is when it's removed from the bottle, the longer it's been there—a clue to the age of an unlabeled wine. The length of the cork will tell you about the winemaker's intentions. A short one says the winemaker had little faith in the aging ability of the wine. A long cork says just the opposite—or says that at least the winemaker was an optimist.

Take It Off . . . Take It All Off

Wine label art is no harbinger of what's in the bottle, but it's often enough to stop you mid-aisle for a look-see. Some of it is comical and some of it's just plain stunning, suitable for framing or collecting. But getting the label off for any purpose is a sticky problem. If you're removing the label to put into an album, the best product we've seen is a five-inch-by-six-inch clear adhesive strip that actually splits the wine label and removes only the printed surface, leaving you with a laminated label you can then adhere to a page of your album.

How you remove a label that you don't plan to mount depends on the adhesive the bottler used. As a simple test, use your fingernail or a razor to take up the corner of the back label. If the back of the label is sticky, fill the empty bottle with the hottest water you can and let it stand for several minutes. Test the back label again by carefully sliding a razor under the label to start it. Then, if you're lucky, it'll peel right off.

If the back of the label isn't sticky, you'll have to add at least one other step. After you've filled the bottle with hot water, submerge the bottle into a pail or other container of hot water. Wait for several minutes and try to remove the label, starting it with the razor.

When these steps aren't enough to do the job (and more often these days they're not), here are some other tricks to try.

• Instead of submerging the bottle in plain water, add ammonia to it.

WINE BAR:
It ain't exactly clip art

Starting in 1945 Baron Philippe de Rothschild commissioned great artists of the day to design the top two inches of the labels for his famous vintages. Picasso, Chagall, Vertès, Salvador Dali and Andy Warhol were among the legends to grace this space. The 1993 label with a pencil sketch of a naked girl was banned in the United States. Bottles with blank labels were sent here instead.

- After submersion, use a hairdryer to apply extra heat to soften the glue.
- Instead of filling the bottle with water, add only a small amount, then microwave the bottle on its side (label side down) for a minute or two.

When all else fails, call the winery and ask them for an unused label.

WINE TRENDS ALL DIVAS SHOULD KNOW

Any sister worth her Jimmy Choos recognizes trends when she sees them. Not that she has to follow any of them. Just being able to identify them and talk about them over lunch at The Ivy is enough to establish herself on the cutting edge. These are some trends she might bring up to impress her lunch pals.

Screw caps: The fashionistas are doing it. Kim Crawford . . . Bonny Doon . . . PlumpJack. They—and a host of other forward

thinkers like Fetzer, Sonoma-Cutrer, Argyle and Murphy-Goode—
have replaced corks with screw caps. And not just on their $10 Ries-
lings, but $100 Cabernets. Unlikely as it might have seemed only
a couple years ago, screw caps are gaining momentum. Wine
drinkers in Australia, New Zealand and the UK have already welcomed them into their hearts. And pocketbooks. With one out of
every twenty bottles of wine ruined by a tainted cork, some consumers were tired of getting screwed, and started unscrewing instead. We're not talking about mere twist-offs, you understand.
They're state-of-the-art screw caps (called Stelvin closures, in case
you do want to impress your lunch companion) from a fancy
French company. After all, this is wine, not Budweiser.

Speaking of Budweiser . . . We don't think this is as much of a
trend as a marketing experiment, but at least one Aussie winery is
putting its wine into cans.

Bottle design: Ask anyone who's received a box from Tiffany's.
The packaging can be almost as good as the gift. In some cases,
wine bottles are too good to throw away. Use them again for olive
oil or flowers. Other bottles are more than just decorative. The
Glaxa bottle, which holds wines from Villa Sandi in the Veneto region of Italy, keeps the contents chilled without having to go into
an ice bucket. It's like a bottle within a bottle, with two layers of
glass and air in between that acts as insulation. Once the wine is
gone, you can use it again for any liquid you want to keep chilled.

Cult wines: Cult wines are not weirdos in robes; they're wines—
mostly Cabernets from Napa—that are made in small quantities,
sold almost exclusively by mailing list, and have a resale value of
at least twice their initial price. They're down from their stagger-
ing price heights in the '90s but are still going strong. Rich girls
like them because it gives them something showy to spend their
money on at auctions. Status-conscious girls like them because

they're practically impossible to get. Some wineries have waiting lists just to get on the mailing list. Stock-market girls like them because, when they can get their hands on an initial offering, they can cash in on the open market. A bottle that sells on the mailing list for $100 has been known to go for as much as $1,000 or $1,500. Some of the wineries in that elite club are Harlan Estate, Screaming Eagle, Bryant Family Vineyard, Dalla Valle Vineyards, Araujo Estate Wines, Colgin Cellars and Grace Family Vineyard. The ultimate trophy wines.

REMEMBERING WHAT YOU'VE LEARNED

You don't necessarily have to *be* a wine expert to look like one. No, just a few facts rolling off your tongue at an opportune moment will do it. And you don't have to be standing at a party with a glass in hand to toss out your jewels. Ideal moments for wine talk can arise any time during your day. Say you're on an elevator, the doors open and a real hunk of a guy walks in. It's just the two of you. You want to say something brilliant. The weather? Geez, that's something your grandmother would bring up! Why not a little wine chat? With thirty stories to ride to your floor, ten seconds should take care of it. How about:

"Have you ever heard of the Viagra of grapes? It was a grape jelly called 'Vine-Gro' used by home winemakers during Prohibition to accelerate the wine process and when mixed with water made a really strong wine in only two months."

You get the idea. Find any wine trivia that interests you, memorize it and add your personal flavor. We've found that talk of wine is intriguing to most guys whether they drink it or not. It shows a certain sophistication, intelligence and attitude that smart girls want to display and men want to explore.

All smart girls have the ability to be revered as a wine diva. It's as easy as memorizing key words, stories, events or even numbers. *Ugh,* you say. If that were so simple, you'd already be an expert. We agree. That's why we've developed a method of association to help you remember key wine trivia. Information imparted at the right time can impress the pants off anyone.

The Art of Association

We remember things by association. All pieces of information in our memory are linked to other pieces in one way or another. When you hear the word "body," you might be thinking about your loss (don't we wish!) or gain of five pounds lately. But as you know, the word "body" has other meanings. In wine parlance, "body" refers to the effect on the taster's palate of the wine's combination of alcohol and sugar. It may make sense, but it's difficult to remember. The reason it's difficult is there seems to be no obvious association between your weight loss/gain and the wine's body. But if you think of the sensation in your mouth when you taste the wine as the wine's "weight," you'll find a connection. Your body can be heavy or thin, and the wine's body can be heavy or thin.

To remember wine trivia and facts, create an association between two pieces of information, no matter how far-fetched. It doesn't have to make sense to anyone but you. If the association is clever and creative, it will be easier to remember. Linking pieces of information to a picture or theme in your mind or something silly, sexy or bizarre is even better because the visual makes it more vivid and easier to recall.

Associating with Women

We've linked some common wine terms with famous—and sometimes infamous—women to help you remember their meanings. It proves not only that associations are useful, but that women and wine definitely do mix.

Aging: The maturing process of wine to improve its taste. Aging is necessary for some wines to reach their full potential.

Association—**Grandma Moses:** Think of this self-taught painter who began painting for her own pleasure in her late seventies and whose artistic career matured steadily until her death at age 101.

Attack: The initial impact of a wine, usually perceived as a first "hit." If not strong or flavorful, the wine is considered "feeble."

Association—**Joan of Arc:** Joan led her troops in a victorious attack against the English in 1429. This first hit was so formidable that in subsequent encounters the English troops fled the battlefield.

Balance: A wine-tasting term that describes how well a wine's components (alcoholic strength, acidity, residual sugar and tannins) complement each other. When no single component stands out, the wine is considered well balanced.

Association—**Dixie Chicks:** The well-balanced music group combination of Emily Robison's banjo playing, Martie Maguire's fiddling and Natalie Maines's vocals have put this female contemporary country act at the top of the charts.

Blending: Combining different wines to achieve a product that is greater than the sum of its parts. The wines used for blending might be from different grape varieties, different regions or even different vintages.

Association—**Pocahontas:** Pocahontas helped unite two diverse groups, the Native Americans and the English, and encouraged communications between them, which helped foster future peace agreements.

Blind Tasting: A wine tasting where the identities of the wines are not known to the tasters. The purpose is to determine a wine's identity based on sense of smell and taste.

Association—**Helen Keller:** This American author and lecturer overcame the handicaps of blindness and deafness and used her other senses to learn to read and write.

Buttafuoco: A dry, light red wine from Italy's Lombardy region. It literally means "shooting fire."

Association—**Amy Fisher:** The teenage girl who shot the wife of her lover, Joey Buttafuoco.

Cane Cutting: The removal of the lower portion of the vine canopy.

Association—**Lorena Bobbitt:** The battered wife who took a butcher knife and removed her husband's penis while he was sleeping.

Finish: The aftertaste of the wine when the flavors or impressions linger. A distinctive, long finish is considered characteristic of a good wine.

Association—**Florence Griffith Joyner:** The exotic, Olympic gold-medal speed runner whose dazzling record-setting finishes and fashion statements are remembered in the world of women and sports.

Pigeage: The French term for the traditional stomping of grapes by foot.

Association—**Lucille Ball:** The episode of *I Love Lucy* with Lucille Ball stomping grapes by foot is enough to remember this wine term.

Racking: The practice of siphoning wine from one container to another, leaving sediment behind.

Association—**Imelda Marcos:** Wife of Philippine president and owner of hundreds of pairs of shoes, Imelda Marcos was accused of siphoning $352 million during the Marcoses' reign. She and her deposed husband left behind a country in economic ruin.

Terroir: French word for earth or soil, used to denote the land and all the other earthy attributes of a vineyard that are expressed in the wine.

Association—**Scarlett O'Hara:** "Do you mean to tell me, Katie Scarlett O'Hara, that Tara, that land doesn't mean anything to you? Why it's the only thing worth fighting for, worth dying for! Because it's the only thing that lasts."

Wining About Numbers

Remembering numbers is tough because they're difficult to associate. Our brains visualize pictures, not numbers. However, we've learned that smart girls associate numbers with two important things in our daily lives: our bank account balance and the number of calories we consumed at our last meal. No woman we know hasn't, at one time or other, counted calories and been able to recall the exact number in a Snickers Bar (280). Which is why it makes sense to use the calorie content of food to remember other numbers.

NUMBER	WINE TRIVIA	CALORIE ASSOCIATION NUMBER OF CALORIES in . . .
6	Number of glasses in one bottle of wine	One celery stalk
30	Number of glasses produced by one grape vine	One cup plain air-popped popcorn
48	Number of glasses contained in one case of wine	8-ounce can of V8 juice
177	Number of feet of longest flight of popping champagne cork	One plain bagel
295	Number of bottles of wine produced from one barrel	One chocolate-iced donut
600	Number of grapes used to produce one bottle of wine	McDonald's Super Size French Fries with ketchup
700	Number of wineries in CA in 1920	Jack in the Box Egg Rolls
952	Number of wineries in CA in 2002	Schlotzsky's Turkey Original Sandwich
49,000,000	Number of bubbles in bottle of champagne	Average number of calories consumed from birth to age sixty

WINE BAR:
Having a Wine-Lapse?

Every now and then even the sharpest of girls is at a loss for words. When this happens (and it's usually when some smart-ass tries to show off by asking an unanswerable question), just apply the same technique that male athletes use when interviewed after a big game.

Sports Announcer: Bubba, you made that great catch for the winning touchdown. What did the coach say to you when he sent you in with the play?

Bubba: Well, y'know, like we gave 110 percent, we put on our jocks, y'know, one strap at a time, and like, there's no "I" in team, y'know?

You get the drift. Don't even try to answer the question. A sentence said with authority, like, "I've always appreciated balance and body in wine," should suffice.

WINE-TUNING THE ART OF CONVERSATION

Telling a good story is part of being a diva and an admired conversationalist. A good story will have drama and suspense . . . or titillation and sex . . . or surprise and belly laughs. You wouldn't normally think of those elements in relation to wine. However, the stories we're about to tell you involving wine have them all. These behind-the-scenes events are truly tabloid fodder. This is the stuff that makes great conversation.

Use these tidbits at cocktail parties, as office chitchat, standing in line, as rest-room banter—or wherever you want to be a one-minute wine expert. Associating these tales with your favorite tabloid headlines will help you remember.

Murder. The wealthy owner of Tennessee's Monteagle Wine Cellars, Joe Marlow, was shot in the head as he was returning home with a bag of money from the winery. The February 2000 murder raised suspicions when the bag, containing thousands of dollars, was left intact at the scene. Charged with the bizarre crime was Marlow's seventy-five-year-old wife and employees of the winery. The winery's misfortunes continued when five months later it suffered $400,000 in damage in a fire. Charged with arson was the Marlows' former son-in-law.

Suicide. Margaux Hemingway was named for her grandfather's (Ernest Hemingway's) favorite wine. It is an expensive red Bordeaux called Château Margaux. This French wine is from a premiere Bordeaux château, in the same classification as Lafite- and Mouton-Rothschild. They are actually blends of a variety of grapes grown in vineyards that may be more than a mile apart. Margaux Hemingway, a well-known model and actress in the '70s and '80s, committed suicide in 1996 with an overdose of a barbiturate. Margaux was the oldest granddaughter of writer Ernest, who had used a shotgun to commit suicide thirty-five years earlier. She was the fifth person in her family to commit suicide. Ernest Hemingway's brother, sister and father also killed themselves.

Divorce. A divorced New York millionaire sued his ex-wife for custody of half of their two-thousand-bottle wine collection. Roger Yaseen was granted access to the couple's state-of-the-art wine cellar after his divorce from Janet in 1997. He wanted the divorce decree changed because he feared his wife was drinking his share of the wine. Janet countercharged that Roger poached some of the best bottles from the $500,000 collection for his second wedding reception.

Infidelity. A famed French cellar master, Robert Billion, was responsible for the production of the exclusive Champagne Salon

Le Mesnil, one of the Grandes Marques Champagnes. Mr. Billion's notoriety, though, was not limited to his Champagne expertise. His incessant philandering was well known, even to his wife, who in 1984 killed her husband with a pair of kitchen scissors. Mrs. Billion was acquitted and the Champagne house continued to ship her husband's Champagne years after his death.

Intimate Moments. The legend of the celebrated French actress Sarah Bernhardt bathing in a tub of Perrier-Jouët Champagne lives on throughout the world. Hotels, inns and B&Bs market this sexy tale to promote their rooms, baths, Jacuzzis and complimentary Champagne. Some go so far as to name menu items after the 1890s drama queen.

TOASTING WITH CONFIDENCE

The custom of toasting dates back to the ancient world. In the *Odyssey*, Ulysses drank to the health of Achilles. And in 200 B.C. Fabius Maximus declared that no man may drink before he had toasted Maximus's health. The term "toast" derives from a practice in the late seventeenth century of putting a piece of toast or crouton in a drink. The bread was believed either to improve the flavor of the drink or serve as a token of nourishment. The practice became commonplace in cultures worldwide and was combined with other customs.

Clinking of glasses began during the Christian era as a way to ward off the devil and make the wine safe to drink. There is also a saying that the clinking of a glass enriches the experience of drinking wine by stimulating your hearing along with the other four senses—sight, smell, touch and taste.

The art of proper toasting is straightforward, but it takes

preparation and practice. If executed properly, a toast can make any event a meaningful occasion. If done incorrectly, it can send even the most confident of girls to the rest room in mortification. Understanding the significance and etiquette of toasting is essential for all smart hostesses.

Here are some simple guidelines to make every toast a hit.

- Prepare your words in advance and rehearse them as if you were preparing for your Academy Award speech.
- Remember to KISS: Keep It Short, Stupid!
- Be positive. Smart girls don't misuse this platform with insults or foul language. And if it's a wedding couple you're toasting, do not bring up the past.
- Make sure you have some wine or champagne in your glass. Toasting with an empty glass is okay in an emergency, but *do not* use your water glass! It's considered bad luck.
- With glass in hand (but not raised), stand, and make eye contact with the person(s) to whom you are giving the toast.
- At the conclusion, raise your glass or clink your glass with your guest(s).

Smart girls are often the recipients of toasts. Some more guidelines:

- Remain seated when a toast is offered to you.
- Don't take a sip of your drink. It's considered self-congratulatory.
- In response to the toast, stand. No words are necessary beyond "thank you."

Toasts from the Past

A toast is a form of expression that can be used for any sentiment. So why not toast the wine we're drinking? Here are a few historical wine toasts to use the next time you want to raise a glass to your favorite drink.

Here's to Water, water divine—
It dews the grapes that give us wine.
(UNKNOWN)

Your words are my food, your breath my wine. You are everything to me.
(Sarah Bernhardt)

Wine improves with age—I like it more the older I get. (Unknown)

Friendship's the wine of life.
Let's drink of it and to it.
(UNKNOWN)

A meal without wine is like a day without sunshine. (Unknown)

Wine cheers the sad, revives the old, inspires the young, makes weariness forget his toil.
(Lord Byron)

Five qualities are wine's praise advancing:
Strong, beautiful, fragrant, cool and dancing.
(HELEN EXLEY)

A Toast to Your Future

Wine embodies every aspect of a woman's life—history, religion, health, love, family, work, play, sex, sports, beauty, fashion. It's serious business, yet it's outrageously fun. It's complicated, yet very basic—particularly when associated with your everyday experiences.

So, whatever you're doing right now—whether you're airborne with a glass of prestige cuvée in hand, reclining on the couch sipping some Sancerre, sunning on the beach slurping box wine from a paper cup, preparing for your dinner party by sampling tonight's Pinot Noir, or lounging in bed savoring your favorite Port—we toast you, wine divas of the world. Here's to your journey!

Cheers!

Pronunciation Guide for the Savvy Sister

Albariño	ahl-bah-REE-nyoh
Alsace	ahl-SASS
Amarone	ah-mah-ROH-neh
Asti	AH-stee
Auslese	OWS-lay-zuh
Banyuls	bah-NYUHLS
Barbaresco	bar-bah-RESS-koh
Barbera d'Alba	bar-BEHR-ah DAHL-bah
Barbera d'Asti	bar-BEHR-ah DAH-stee
Bardolino	bar-doh-LEE-noh
Barolo	bah-ROH-loh
Beaujolais	boh-zhuh-LAY
Beerenauslese	BAY-ruhn-OWS-lay-zuh
Blanc de blanc	BLAHNGK duh BLAHNGK
Blanc de noir	blahngk duh NWAHR
Blauburgunder	BLOW-ber-guhn-der
Blaufränkisch	blow-FREHN-kish

Bollinger	BOHL-in-jer
Bordeaux	bor-DOE
Botrytis cinerea	boh-TRY-tihs sihn-EHR-ee-uh
Bourgogne	boor-GON-yuh
Brouilly	broo-YEE
Brunello	broo-NELL-oh
di Montalcino	dee mawn-tahl-CHEE-noh
Brut	BROOT
Cabernet Franc	Ka-behr-NAY FRAHNGK
Cabernet Sauvignon	ka-behr-NAY SAW-vee-nyohn
Campania	kahm-PAH-nyah
Carmenère	kahr-meh-NEHR
Carneros	kahr-NEH-rohs
Cava	KAH-vah
Chablis	shah-BLEE
Champagne	sham-PAYN
Chardonnay	shar-doh-NAY
Château Cos	sha-TOH kaws
d'Estournel	dehss-toor-NEHL
Château d'Yquem	sha-TOH dee-KEHM
Château Gruaud-Larose	sha-TOH groo-oh lah-ROHZ
Château Haut-Bailly	sha-TOH oh-bah-YEE
Château Haut-Brion	sha-TOH oh-bree-OHN
Château Lafite-Rothschild	sha-TOH lah-FEET-rawt-SHEELD
Château Lagrange	sha-TOH la-GRAHNZH
Château Latour	sha-TOH lah-TOOR
Château Margaux	sha-TOH mahr-GOH
Château Mouton-Rothschild	sha-TOH moo-TAWN-rawt-SHEELD
Château Pétrus	shao-TOH pay-TROOS
Châteauneuf-du-Pape	sha-toh-nuhf-doo-PAHP
Chenin Blanc	shen-in BLAHNGK

Chianti	kee-AHN-tee
Chinon	shee-NOHN
Cinsault	SAN-soh
Clos de Vougeot	kloh duh voo-ZHOH
Cognac	KOHN-yak
Colheita	kuhl-YAY-tah
Condrieu	kawn-DREE-yuh
Copita	koh-PEE-tah
Corton-Charlemagne	kor-TAWN-shahr-luh-MAHN-yuh
Côte d'Or	koht DOR
Côte de Beaune	koht duh BOHN
Côte de Nuit	koht duh NWEE
Côte-Rôtie	koht roh-TEE
Côtes du Rhone	koht deu ROHN
Crianza	kree-AHN-zah
Cuvée	koo-VAY
Dolcetto	dohl-CHEHT-oh
Dosage	doh-SAHJ
Douro	DOO-roh
Doux	DOO
Eiswein	ICE-vine
Enology	ee-NAHL-uh-jee
Enophile	EE-nuh-file
Frizzante	freet-SAHN-teh
Fumé Blanc	FOO-may BLAHNGK
Gamay	ga-MAY
Gavi	GAH-vee
Gewürztraminer	guh-VURTS-trah-mee-ner
Grand cru classé	grahn kroo klah-SAY
Graves	GRAHV
Grenache	gruh-NAHSH
Grüner Veltliner	GROO-ner FELT-lee-ner
Halbtrocken	HAHLP-troe-ken

Hermitage	er-mee-TAHZH
Heurige	HOY-rih-guh
Kabinett	kah-bih-NEHT
Krug	KROOG
Lambrusco	lam-BROO-skoh
Languedoc-Roussillon	lahng-DAWK-roo-see-YAWN
Loire	LWAHR
Mâcon Villages	mah-KAWN vee-LAHZH
Madeira	muh-DEER-uh
Malbec	mahl-BEHK
Médoc	may-DAWK
Meritage	MEHR-ih-tihj
Merlot	mehr-LOH
Méthode	may-TOHD
Champenoise	shahm-peh-NWAHZ
Meunier	muh-NYAY
Meursault	mehr-SOH
Mis en Bouteille	mee zahn boo-TEH-yuh
Moët & Chandon	moh-EHT ay shahn-DAWN
Mosel	MOH-zuhl
Mourvèdre	moor-VEH-druh
Muscadet	meuhs-kah-DAY
Muscadine	MUHS-kuh-dihn
Muscat	MUHS-kat
Nebbiolo	neh-BYOH-loh
Nouveau	noo-VOH
Orvieto	ohr-VYAY-toh
Pauillac	poh-YAK
Penedes	pay-NAY-dahs
Perrier-Jouët	pehr-YAY-zhoo-AY
Petit Verdot	puh-TEE vehr-DOH
Petite Sirah	peh-TEET sih-RAH
Picpoul	PEEK-pool

Pinot Blanc	PEE-noh BLAHNGK
Pinot Grigio	PEE-noh GREE-zhoh
Pinot Gris	PEE-noh GREE
Pinot Noir	PEE-noh NWAHR
Pinotage	pee-noh-TAHJ
Piper-Heidsieck	PIPE-er-HIDE-sehk
Pomerol	paw-muh-RAWL
Pommard	paw-MAHR
Pouilly-Fuissé	poo-yee-fwee-SAY
Pouilly-Fumé	poo-yee-few-MAY
Premier cru	preh-MYAY KROO
Primitivo	pree-mee-TEE-voh
Prosecco	praw-SEH-koh
Quinta	KEEN-tah
Riesling	REEZ-ling
Rioja	ree-OH-hah
Riserva	ree-ZEHR-vah
Sancerre	sahn-SEHR
Sangiovese	san-joh-VAY-zeh
Sauternes	soh-TEHRN
Sauvignon Blanc	SAW-vee-nyohn BLAHNGK
Sec	SAHK
Sekt	ZEHKT
Semillon	seh-mee-YAWN
Semillon	SEH-meh-lon
Shiraz	shee-RAHZ
Soave	SWAH-veh
Sommelier	saw-muhl-YAY
Spätlese	SHPAYT-lay-zuh
Spumante	spoo-MAHN-tay
Syrah	see-RAH
Taittinger	taht-teen-ZHEHR
Tastevin	taht-VAHN

Tavel	ta-VEHL
Tempranillo	tem-prah-NEE-yoh
Terroir	tehr-WAHR
Tinto	TEEN-toh
Trocken	TROH-kuhn
Valpolicella	vahl-paw-lee-CHEHL-lah
Verdelho	vehr-DEHL-yoh
Verdicchio	vehr-DEEK-yoh
Veuve Cliquot	vurv klee-KOH
Ponsardin	pawn-sahr-DAN
Vin de pays	van duh pay-YEE
Vinho Verde	VEEN-yoh VEHR-deh
Vinifera	vihn-IF-uh-ruh
Vino Nobile	VEE-noh NAW-bee-lay
di Montepulciano	dee mawn-teh-pool-CHAH-noh
Viognier	vee-oh-NYAY
Vouvray	voo-VRAY
Weissburgunder	VISE-ber-guhn-der
Zinfandel	ZIHN-fuhn-dehl

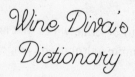

Wine Diva's Dictionary

acidity. Naturally occurring acids in grapes that are vital components for the life, vitality and balance of all wines.

aging. Maturing process of a wine to improve its taste.

alcohol. The major component in wine. Also known as ethyl alcohol.

appellation. The official geographical location where the grapes used in the wine are grown.

aroma. The smell of a wine.

astringent. The puckering sensation in the mouth attributable to the tannins and acids found in some wines.

austere. A tasting term that is used to describe young wines that have not yet developed a discernible aroma.

balance. A tasting term that describes how well a wine's components complement each other.

barrel. A container used to store or ferment wine.

big. A tasting term to describe wines that are full of flavor and with high levels of tannins, alcohol and grape flavor extracts.

bite. A result of good levels of acidity (especially in young wines).

bitter. Unpleasant taste that registers at the back of the tongue.

blanc de blanc. A white wine—most often sparkling—made exclusively from white grapes.

blanc de noir. A white or slightly tinted wine—usually sparkling—made exclusively from red grapes.

blend. The technique of mixing wines of different varieties, regions, barrels or vintages.

body. Perception of fullness or texture in the mouth due primarily to the wine's alcohol.

bottle aging. Allowing wine to acquire complexity, depth and texture in the bottle.

bouquet. The combination of flowery and fruity aromas that come from the alcohols and acids in a wine.

breathe. Allow air to mix with a wine to develop its flavor.

brut. Dry style of Champagne and sparkling wine.

capsule. The protective cover of tin, lead, aluminum or plastic placed over the top of a bottle of wine used to insulate the wine from outside influences.

cava. The Spanish term for sparkling wines made using the traditional champagne method.

character. A wine's features and style.

clarity. The appearance of wine that has no cloudiness.

clean. Wines that are straightforward and have no unpleasant odors or flavors.

cloudy. Opposite of clarity. Wine that is visually unclear.

complex. Nuances of flavors of a wine often achieved with aging.

cork. The spongy material from the bark of the cork tree used to seal wine bottles.

corked. Having the smell of wood "dry-rot" resulting from a defective cork.

crisp. Good acidity and taste without excessive sweetness.

cru. French term meaning "growth."

cuvée. Blend. In the production of Champagne, cuvée is the specific blend of still wines used as a base for Champagne.

decanting. Pouring wine from a bottle to a carafe or decanter.

depth. Full-bodied, intense and complex flavors.

disgorging. Removing sediment from a bottle of champagne following secondary fermentation.

dry. Opposite of sweet. All the sugar from the grapes has been converted to alcohol during fermentation.

earthy. Flavors derived from the soil where the grapes have been grown.

enology. The study of wine and winemaking. Also oenology.

extra dry. Classification for champagne that has a slight perception of sweetness.

fat. A big, soft and silky wine that fills the mouth.

fermentation. The process that turns grape juice into wine. The enzymes in the yeast convert sugar into alcohol and carbon dioxide.

fining. Clarifying young wine before bottling to remove impurities.

finish. The aftertaste or impression a wine leaves after it's swallowed.

fortified wine. Wine whose alcohol content is increased by adding brandy or neutral spirits.

fruity. The flavor or aroma of fruits in wine.

hard. Having an abundance of tannin or acidity.

ice wine. Extremely sweet wines made from grapes that have been frozen on the vines prior to harvest. Also called Eiswein.

late-harvest wine. Wine made from ripe grapes left on the vine for periods in excess of their normal picking times, resulting in an extreme concentration of sugar.

lees. The sediment of yeasts and small grape particles that settle in the barrel as wine develops.

maceration. Technique of fermenting uncrushed grapes under pressure to produce fresh, fruity wine.

magnum. A bottle holding 1.5 liters or the equivalent of two standard bottles.

Meritage. Name used for both red and white American wines that are produced by blending traditional Bordeaux grape varietals.

nutty. A fine, crisp flavor often found in Sherries and fine white wines.

oak. The flavor imparted to wine by barrel aging. It can be best described as a toasty or woodlike flavor. Sometimes a vanilla flavor will be imparted by fine oak.

oxidation. Exposure of wine to air, which causes chemical changes and deterioration.

pigeage. The French word for the traditional stomping of grapes by foot.

press. The piece of equipment used to gently separate grape juice from grape skins.

punt. The indentation at the base of a wine or champagne bottle, which reinforces the bottle's structure.

reserve. A term without a legal definition in the United States but often used to designate a special wine.

rich. Having well-balanced flavors and intrinsic power.

sec. A term, when applied to Champagne, that describes a relatively sweet wine. Used in the context of still wines, the term means "dry"—without any residual sugar.

secondary fermentation. The process of converting still wine into champagne that takes place in the bottle. In the production of still wines, the term is sometimes used in place of malolactic fermentation.

sommelier. French word for "wine waiter."

spumante. The Italian word for fully sparkling wines as opposed to those that are slightly sparkling, "frizzante."

tannin. Substance responsible for the astringent quality found in wine, especially red wines. Tannins form the basis for the long life of wines and, while they can be overpowering in young wines, with bottle aging they tend to become softer.

terroir. Literally, the "soil," the French term for the particular character (aromas and flavors) of a given vineyard, or even a small part of that vineyard.

thin. Lacking fullness, depth, complexity.

varietal. A wine named after the grape from which it is produced. In California, for instance, a wine labeled "Pinot Noir" must by law consist of at least 75 percent Pinot Noir grapes.

vilification. The process of making wine.

vineyard. The place where grapes are grown.

vintage. Harvest year of grapes and the resulting wines made from them. Ninety-five percent of the wine in a vintage-designated bottle must be from grapes harvested in that year.

viticulture. The practice (art, science and philosophy) of growing grape vines.

woody. In most wines this is an undesirable condition indicating that there is a taint of some type from defective wood or an overuse of new oak.

yeast. Naturally occurring, single-celled organisms found on the skins of grapes that are the primary promoters of fermentation. In the fermentation process, yeast turns sugar into alcohol and carbon dioxide.

Index

* * * * * * * * *

PORCH
PIRATE
LOVE

* * * * * * * * *

IRENE WOODBURY

CHAPTER ONE

Waddling into her cheerful green-and-yellow kitchen, balloon-size Kit Wells whipped up her daily s'mores protein shake. Into the blender she tossed vanilla Greek yogurt, pudding mix, a dash of almond milk, crushed ice, and a teaspoon of marshmallow extract. Graham cracker crumbs, whipped cream, and a half cup of chocolate chips were next.

With the blender whirring, the eight-months' pregnant blackjack dealer heard a chime on her phone. Her Ring.com door cam had detected activity at her front door. Must be UPS delivering the baby's crib, Kit figured. Into her phone she peered. A short, pudgy UPS delivery man in a brown shirt and pants was wheeling a hand-cart up her walkway and onto her front steps. On her small porch, he deposited a long, bulky box. Then he trotted back down the walkway, piled into his truck, and drove off.

Inside, Kit was pouring her mocha-colored shake into a tall glass. One sip in, she heard the Ring.com chime again. How strange, she thought. And then, glancing at her phone, she was horrified. A wiry porch pirate in a navy blue sweat suit and black knit cap had darted up her walkway, and was eyeing the just-delivered box suspiciously.

Plopping her shake in the sink, Kit grabbed her phone and took off. As she tore open the front door, the pirate was struggling down the walkway with the awkward box. Dashing out, she yelled, "Hey, come back here! That's my baby's crib!"

Head jerking, the pirate turned and saw the heavily pregnant, 22-year-old blonde lurching down the steps towards him.

But just then, as she pressed forward, Kit lost her balance and toppled onto the concrete. Sprawled on her side and writhing in pain, she clutched her heaving belly and cried, "Help, help, somebody please help me!"

The clear liquid now oozing down her legs was soaking the bottom of her tent-size denim jumper.

"My water must have broke!" she bleated. "No, no, it's too early. Goddamn porch pirate! What if the baby's head got hit?"

Dropping the box in the rock garden, the alarmed thief ran back to Kit.

"Holy shit, are you alright?" he gasped, leaning down.

"I, uh, don't know," she stammered. "My belly hurts. Oh my God, the baby's coming! I'm not due till next month. This is my first. I don't know what to do, call 911? I don't have time. You've got to get me to the hospital! Please, can you take me? Where's your car?"

"Over there," the unnerved pirate answered, pointing at a blue Ford Taurus parked on the street.

"Maybe you should try 911?" he added nervously, kneeling beside Kit, his eyes darting back and forth from her huge belly to her swollen face.

"There's no time!" she told him. "I need to get to Las Vegas General. I need to know how the baby is. Please, you've got to take me! You owe me—for stealing the crib and causing me to fall."

"Okay, Miss, okay," he said, putting his hands up. "I'm sorry you're hurt. I'll take you anywhere you want to go, just don't have the kid in my car. It's leather upholstery and I have zero experience with pregnant chicks about to pop. I'll get you to the hospital as fast as I can. Where do you want this box?"

"Put it inside, and get my purse off the hall table. I need my insurance card," Kit said, before letting out a fearsome yelp.

The ominous clear liquid was still trickling down her legs.

"The baby's moving," she groaned in agony, grasping her belly. "We've got to go—now!"

Jumping up, the pirate grabbed the box, lugged it up the steps, and dropped it inside the door. Spotting Kit's pink leather satchel on a nearby table, he tucked it under his arm and ran back outside. After picking Kit's phone off the concrete and tossing it in her purse, he stooped to carefully hoist her up. With his arm slung around her massive belly, they toddled to his car.

The motor was running and the passenger seat was piled high with boxes, no doubt a full day's haul. This guy was big leagues, Kit thought, and there was no time for rearranging.

After wedging the whimpering mom-to-be into the back seat—amidst more packages—they took off for the hospital. As they turned off Lantana Street and onto Sahara, a suddenly irate Kit threw up her hands.

"What is all this stuff?" she asked, looking around. "Who are you, and why are you stealing other peoples' things? My best friend in Indiana bought that crib for my baby, and you took it. What kind of lowlife would do something like that?"

From the front seat, the annoyed pirate gave his hugely pregnant passenger a piece of his mind.

"Look, Miss knocked-up, not that it's any of your business, but I got fired from my job. I can't collect unemployment, and I gotta eat and pay the rent. I didn't know what was in the box, or I never would have taken it. Just sayin'."

"Yeah, sure, whatever," Kit came back, "but I wouldn't be in labor right now if it wasn't for your thieving ways!"

"Hey, Miss whatever-your-name-is, get a grip. I'm trying to drive through mid-day Vegas traffic right now. Quit your bitching, or I'll drop you at the next corner right here on Sahara, and you can find another ride to the hospital."

Kit could tell this dude meant business, so she calmed down. Catching his eye in the rearview mirror, she said, "Okay, I'll stop with the comments, just keep the car moving."

"Can I ask what your name is, or would that piss you off, too?" she inquired moments later, as they stopped at a red light.

"My name's Danny," he answered, pulling his cap off to reveal a headful of light-brown curls. "What's yours?"

"Kit," she replied. "If you don't mind, I'm going to call the baby's father right now, so he can meet me at the hospital."

"Cool, go ahead, call your husband," Danny told her as he navigated down traffic-choked Sahara.

"He's not my husband," Kit shot back, twisting and squirming in the back seat. "He's my, uh, boyfriend. Well, not really, just someone I dated last summer. The pregnancy was a surprise for both of us."

"Okay, whatever," Danny said, nodding and smiling in the rear view mirror, "call your sperm donor."

"Ha ha, very funny, a porch pirate with a sense of humor. I really hit the jackpot, didn't I?" Kit exclaimed, fishing her cell out of her purse and rapidly clicking in a number.

On the other end, an unfamiliar female voice answered.

"I must have dialed wrong," Kit said, annoyed and perplexed. "Is this Mike Prescott's phone?"

"Yeah, this is Mikey's cell. I'm his personal assistant," the girl giggled on speaker phone.

"Where is he?" Kit said sharply. "I need to talk to him right now, this is an emergency."

"Take a chill pill, sweetheart," the female voice cracked. "He's sleeping beside me, and when he wakes up he'll be too busy to return your call!"

"Who is this?" Kit asked, irate and upset. "You sound like a regular on Jerry Springer."

"And you sound like a real bitch!" the girl snapped.

"Are you going to put Mike on, or not?" Kit asked.

"Not!" the little slut replied curtly before hanging up.

With shaking hands, Kit turned her cell off and dumped it back in her purse. Clutching her belly, she began rocking back and forth. Turning towards her, Danny saw tears streaming down the pale, swollen face of this pathetic pregnant chick gasping, moaning, and crying in the back seat of his car.

"Um, do you have a mom, or a sister or brother, or even a friend you can call?" he asked.

For a moment, Kit was silent as she dug through her purse for some tissues. Blotting her nose, she answered, between sniffles, "No, no, and no. My mom's down south somewhere with her husband and kids. The last time I saw her, I think I was two. Ditto for my dad. Who knows where he is? My grandparents raised me back in Indiana, but they're both dead. There are no brothers or sisters. I have friends out here, but they're all working."

Danny shook his head. His porch pirating forays had led to some strange predicaments and encounters over the years, but this one took the cake. Pumping the pedal even faster, he sped to the hospital.

Somehow, they made it.

After circling the block a few times, Danny finally found the emergency entrance. Down a long driveway his car barreled, and then screeched to a stop. An orderly in a white coat and pants hustled out the sliding-glass doors to meet them. Leaping out of the car, Danny ran to Kit's door and yanked it open.

"We need help!" he yelled. "She fell down some steps and landed on concrete. Her water broke, but the baby isn't due for another month. We think she's in labor. Can you get her to the new baby department, like now?"

Nodding, the orderly quickly motioned to a colleague inside for a wheelchair. Gently extracting the huge, moaning mom-to-be from the car, they placed her in it.

"What's your name?" they asked, wheeling her away.

"Kit Wells," she replied.

"Are you Mr. Wells?" they asked Danny.

"Um, no," he countered, "my name's Danny Potter."

"Are you her boyfriend?"

"No, again," Danny said.

"Well, are you the father of the baby?"

"Yes, yes, he's the father," Kit piped up, blotting her nose and staring at the orderlies. "Now take me inside, I think I just had a contraction!" Danny looked aghast, but said nothing as they guided the wheelchair through the sliding-glass doors.

While the car was driven off by a valet, Danny and Kit were swiftly moved to admissions, where a clerk asked what had happened. They told her that Kit was eight months' pregnant and had fallen. She then registered, provided insurance, and gave them her OB-GYN's name.

"Don't bother calling him," Kit added, with a dismissive flick of the wrist. "He just got married. He's in Cabo for two weeks. His office is closed."

"Oh dear, we are in bit of a pickle, aren't we?" the nurse commented. "No worries, we'll find you another doctor, stat."

Then she turned to Danny.

"Would you like to be in the delivery room?" she asked. "Have you two been through Lamaze classes?"

"Um no, I, uh, flunked out," Danny told her, shaking his head. "I have kind of a weak stomach, and I'm a little old-fashioned about these things." Then he patted Kit's arm and told her, "Don't worry, babe, I'll be out here waiting if you or anyone else needs me. Everything's going to be fine, you'll see."

Glancing up at him, Kit smiled weakly and nodded, still trying to comprehend the bizarre chain of events that had gotten her here. Then she was swiftly moved to a cubicle in the maternity ward.

CHAPTER TWO

In the hospital waiting room that April 2015 day, a dozen nervous, expectant dads were standing by anxiously for updates. After murmuring a vague hello and nodding at them, a confused, agitated Danny collapsed in a chair and slumped forward. With his head in his hands, he was trying to make sense of how he had suddenly morphed from a porch pirate caught in the act, to a dude rescuing a pregnant chick in a medical emergency.

Over the next few hours, Danny did all the things expectant dads typically do in the waiting room. He sipped cup after cup of stale coffee, chatted with other dad-dudes, scarfed down vending-machine snacks, watched sports on a TV bolted to the wall, and read old, withered newspapers. Occasionally, he got up and paced around the room amidst other jittery dads-to-be. And every time he spotted a nurse, he anxiously asked for updates on Kit and the baby.

"No news yet," they would reply, patting his arm. "Everything's fine, she's still in labor. We'll let you know as soon as the baby arrives."

Danny wouldn't even think of leaving the hospital until he knew that Kit and the baby were alright. It's the least he could do. After all, his stealing her baby's crib set in motion the accident that had caused Kit to go into early labor. If it weren't for him, she would have been home relaxing and enjoying the last month of her pregnancy, and he would have been off somewhere in Henderson or Summerlin, ripping off boxes from other porches and doorways.

Finally, six agonizing hours after he'd arrived at the hospital, a peppy brunette nurse strode into the waiting room and approached him.

"Congratulations, Mr. Potter, you have a healthy, six-pound-seven-ounce baby boy," she announced.

"Awesome, I'm over the moon!" Danny whooped. "We were hoping for a boy. How's his mom doing?"

"Good. She's a little tired. It was a long haul, and more challenging because he was slightly premature. But both mom and baby came through like champs, and are doing fine. Your son's in the nursery around the corner. You can hold him tomorrow. He's a handsome little guy, go take a look."

"Thanks, I can't wait to see him," a tired Danny told her with a smile, as he turned to high-five a few of the guys who'd been waiting with him. He was grateful and relieved that Kit and her baby had come through their medical ordeal alright. If all was well with her, it certainly made his life easier and less complicated.

After looking in on "his son," who seemed A-okay, Danny asked if he could see Kit.

"Sorry, she's sleeping right now and probably won't wake up till tomorrow morning. She's under sedation," a nurse replied.

A nodding Danny glanced at his watch. It was just after midnight.

Sighing, he told her, "I understand, I'm pretty wiped out, too. The baby looks great. I'll call Kit tomorrow."

"Sounds like a plan," the nurse smiled, as she turned and walked towards another anxious new dad.

Danny called Kit the next day, and the day after that, too. He cared about what happened to her and wanted to keep things civil, if only because of the strange, twisted way they had met. After all, Kit knew he was a porch pirate. She also knew his name, and had seen the packages in his car. She could still report him to the cops. He also realized, on some level, that Kit's relationship with her baby daddy was rocky. From what he had overheard in the car, the dude sounded like a real asshole. He felt sorry for her.

On the phone, Danny and Kit chatted briefly but pleasantly about the baby and how he was doing. She was recovering from the birth, but had apparently sprained her left wrist in the fall and was wearing a brace. Aside from that, she was doing well.

When Danny learned that Kit and the baby didn't have a ride home from the hospital, he offered to play chauffeur. Kit took him up on it.

Three days after the birth, Danny drove to Las Vegas General and took the elevator up to the maternity ward. It was noon. Relaxed and a bit tired, the puffy, still sore new mom was sitting on the bed in her room. Her long, blond hair was loose and flowing. She wore little make-up, and was dressed in baggy maternity jeans and a jaunty red-and-white polka-dot top that a friend had dropped off.

A cheerful, upbeat Kit showed Danny her new son's birth certificate. She had named him, Jasper Andrew Wells, in honor of the maternal grandfather who'd basically raised her. On the next line, displayed in dark-blue ink, Danny Potter was listed as the child's father! Dude did a double take. His jaw was on the floor. Never saw that coming.

Staring into his sky-blue eyes, Kit tilted her head and said sheepishly, "I hope you don't mind. Luckily, Potter's easy to spell. That is your name, right?"

"Right," a flustered Danny replied.

"I couldn't use Mike's name," Kit went on, tossing her hands up. "His dad's, um, a senator, and he wants to keep this quiet. You know, unwed mother gives birth to senator's first grandson doesn't work too well for some voters. And the nurses think he looks just like you, anyway, so what could I do?"

"It's okay, Kit," Danny said, although he was a bit taken aback. "I'm cool with it. You just took me by surprise. First time my name's ever been on one of these things," he added, glancing at the document.

With the desert sunlight streaming in to engulf them both, blond, blue-eyed Kit smiled and shook her head.

"Don't worry," she whispered, patting Danny's arm. "it's just a formality. You're not obligated to me or the baby."

As he nodded, a nurse entered the room and helped the still-weak, unsteady new mom into a wheelchair. A cooing Jasper, kicking his little arms and legs under a yellow blanket, was placed in Kit's arms. Out the door, they were wheeled to the elevator.

After checking out of the hospital, Danny and Kit stopped at a nearby Applebee's. With a pacifier dangling from his mouth, Jasper dozed peacefully in a corner of the red vinyl booth while Danny scarfed down a quesadilla burger and Kit munched on chicken tenders and fries.

From Applebee's, they drove to a Discount-Max Drug Store and picked up a cartful of essentials, including a plastic carrier with a soft, fleecy lining, for Jasper. In Danny's car, Kit rode in the back seat with the baby, who was cooing contentedly in the new carrier with sales tags still attached.

Back at Kit's apartment, Danny got her and the baby settled. He assembled the cherry wood crib—still packed in its box—that he had stolen a few days earlier, and Kit placed a wailing Jasper in it for his first nap. Then Danny left. As he hustled out the door, Kit wondered where he was going. Was there a hot date waiting, or did porch pirates work night shifts, too?

CHAPTER THREE

"So, how's the pregnancy going?" the father of the baby casually asked when he finally called Kit to check in. It was mid-May, and he was between meetings at his booming helicopter-tour company on the Strip. "Did you get the check I sent last week?"

"News-flash, Mike, the baby was born a month ago," Kit said tartly. "I fell down some steps in mid-April, and my water broke. Luckily we were both okay, but the birth was kind of tough. We spent three days in Las Vegas General."

"Oh, my God! Is it a boy or a girl?"

"A boy."

"I have a son! This is so cool," Mike exclaimed. "I can't wait to see him. Is he healthy? Does he have hair? How much did he weigh?"

"Six-pounds, seven-ounces, but he's gained some," Kit answered. "He's in great shape: light brown hair, blue eyes, about 22 inches long. Very handsome, just like his dad.

"His mom's doing okay, too. I had six hours of labor. It was a real marathon, with lots of pain and pushing, and I didn't know the doctor. But the baby's finally here, running my life and calling all the shots."

"Have you named him?" an excited Mike asked.

"Yes, I told you a few months ago, if it was a boy I'd name him Jasper Andrew, after my mom's dad. He was like a father to me when my parents got divorced and split. Grandma Rose was sort of nasty and cold, but Grandpa Jasper treated me like a princess. I always swore if I ever had a son, I'd name him after Grandpa."

"Jasper Andrew," Mike said in wonder. "Very traditional. I like it. This is unbelievable. I can't wait to see him! I wish you had called me."

"I tried," Kit shot back, "but some obnoxious tramp answered your cell and told me you were sleeping beside her. She didn't seem too interested in letting me talk to you, even after I told her it was an emergency. Not what you want to hear when your water breaks a month early, and you're in tears in the back seat of a car on the way to the hospital. And after that, I was kind of busy."

"Sounds like it's all good, Kit, but you're over-reacting about the girl," Mike scolded. "It's not like I'm cheating on you or anything. You know the drill. We had a thing last summer and you told me you were on birth control. Then you got pregnant. It's not my fault your birth control failed. And you wanted to keep the baby. I didn't. I thought you could give it up for adoption, but you didn't want to because you basically have no family here, or back in Indiana. So I agreed to help you financially because I thought it was the right thing to do."

"It was the right thing," Kit agreed, "plus you didn't want to upset your senator-father with another scandal, after the ugly details of your second divorce blew up in the papers," Kit added.

"Well, yeah, that's part of it," Mike admitted. "People like their senators' sons to be hard-working straight arrows. My dad's got high standards. Having a kid out of wedlock would offend his sense of morality and create a lot of gossip. His political enemies would use it against him in the next election."

"Whatever, Mike," Kit said, rolling her eyes. "Anyway, I got your check. Jasper's here anytime you want to see him. Afternoons are best, before naptime at four. Call first."

Two days later, Mike, a registered helicopter pilot who owned Heli-Vegas, an upstart charter firm that flew tourists around the Vegas Valley and Southwest, showed up. In his arms were a lush bouquet of yellow roses and a high-tech baby monitor. Kit was thrilled with both.

"He's got the Prescott chin and eyes," Mike noted with a smile, as he picked up the wriggling blond infant and cuddled him. Jasper cooed. He seemed to know his dad was in the house.

Kit melted when she saw Mike holding the baby. But moments later, as she plopped the flowers in a vase with water, she got a harsh reality check when Mike's cell rang. It was one of his girlfriends, checking in.

"Sure, sweetheart, I'll see you tonight," he purred seductively into the phone as the call wound down.

It was awkward and a bit painful for Kit, who wished the earth could just open up and swallow her right there. Would she ever get used to upsetting moments like these with her hunky baby-daddy?

Mike wasn't the only one making regular house calls at Kit's. Porch pirate Danny was still in her life. The two had had a strange, difficult first meeting, but they basically liked each other, and so, against all odds, they formed a friendship after Jasper's birth.

Every other week or so, Danny, who had a special bond with Kit's baby, would show up with bags of toys, clothes, and other presents for him. Once, he even lugged in a shiny new Graco high chair. He claimed all these bright, beautiful things were hand-me-downs from his cousin, Gigi, a new mom in Boulder City. But Kit sometimes wondered if most of it was loot from his porch-pirating ventures.

At one point the inevitable happened, and Danny hustled in with a large tote brimming with stuff while Mike was visiting. Kit introduced them, poured coffee, and the three made awkward chit-chat while Jasper dozed in his carrier.

Danny had brought designer crib sheets, blankets, and a slew of stuffed animals that day. There was also a jewel-encrusted watch for Kit, who gushed over the gifts.

"Where do you get all this baby stuff?" a perplexed Mike asked Danny. "Do you have a kid?"

"No," Danny replied. "It's all hand-me-downs from my cousin. Her son's a year older than Jasper."

"What do you do for a living?" was Mike's next question.

Danny rolled his eyes and responded, after a brief pause, "I, uh, dabble in merchandise acquisitions and product distribution."

"Cool," Mike said, nodding, while trying to figure out what the hell that meant and eyeing Danny suspiciously. What kind of game was this dude playing? He obviously was interested in Kit, and using all this baby stuff and jewelry as chick bait. Mike thought it was kind of sleazy and underhanded, and wished Kit could see through it, refuse the gifts, and send Danny packing. But she seemed to revel in the attention, and God knows she needed the stuff.

The afternoon breezed by pleasantly enough, but Mike did a double-take when Kit mentioned that Danny had assembled Jasper's crib. And then she let it slip that Danny was the one who had driven her to, and from, the hospital. Again, Mike couldn't help wondering, why? That sounded like something a boyfriend or husband would do.

By the time he left Kit's apartment, Mike couldn't get Danny, Jasper's crib, or that expensive watch out of his head. Who was this Danny Potter dude? How did he meet Kit? And, most important, were they sleeping together?

Mike knew Kit would never give him a straight answer on any of the above. So later that day, he called the person he always contacted when he had probing, undercover questions about someone: Harlan Ristow. This pricey, but reliable and discreet, private detective was often used by his dad in political situations. After relaying a few basic details, Mike asked Harlan to get the skinny on Danny.

A couple of days later, the pit-bull private eye called back with the lowdown. Daniel Waylon Potter was born in Sin City in 1988, grew up in rough-and-tumble North Las Vegas, and graduated from Cheyenne High School in 2006. That same year, he jetted off to Hawaii for a vacay with his pal-posse, and ended up staying in the Aloha State for a year. To get by, he tended bar in Waikiki, and drove an ambulance. When his dad died of a heart attack in 2007, his mom asked him to come home to help her and his two younger brothers.

Back in Vegas, Danny scored a job as a UPS delivery man. The unmarried dude's life was pretty routine and normal at that point. But all that changed big time in 2011. After four years with UPS, Danny was fired for reckless driving, accused of being drunk while causing a major accident with the van he was driving in mid-day traffic. And then Harlan unloaded an even bigger bombshell. Two misdemeanor burglary charges were filed against Danny in 2013-14. He apparently had become a porch pirate.

Mission accomplished. Mike now knew where the pricey gifts for Kit and the baby were coming from. Danny was ripping off homeowners right at their front door. From the designer diaper genie, to the deluxe bouncy chair, and Baby Einstein rattles, everything Danny had given Kit was probably stolen.

Mike didn't tell her right away because he knew she'd resent his calling a private eye. But the next time he saw her, he casually mentioned Danny.

"Has he been over lately?"

"Yes, he was here last week," she replied.

"Did he bring more things for Jasper?"

"Yeah, some cute toys, a stack of onesies, and a trinket or two for me," she answered coyly.

"Kit, I have to tell you something," Mike said, his voice dropping as he sat down on the couch beside her. "I was concerned about your relationship with Danny and him being around the baby, so I called a private detective my dad works with.

"What I found out blew me away. Danny's a porch pirate. He's been stealing stuff from doorways all over the Vegas Valley for years. There've been charges filed against him for reckless driving and misdemeanor burglary. He might even be in some kind of porch-thief cult. Did you know any of this?"

"Porch-thief cult? Whoa, Mike. That's so bizarre. But I don't want to talk about Danny right now," Kit said, angry and annoyed. "I want to talk about you. Why the hell would you invade my privacy by hiring a private investigator to check out his background? My relationship with Danny is none of your business. Back off, dude!"

"Well, if he's around my kid, it is my business," he shot back.

"You barely see Jasper, or me. Leave it alone, Mike! I can handle my own friendships."

"I don't want him bringing bags of clothes and toys over here," Mike doubled down. "It's stolen goods. I don't want my infant son wearing hot onesies, sleeping on hot baby sheets, or sucking on hot pacifiers. Keep that pirate creep away from Jasper!"

"Don't call Danny names!" Kit fumed. "I don't care what the private detective said, if Danny says the stuff is from his cousin, it is. And don't tell me what I can, or can't, do. Like you're a role model for good judgment and behavior. You're not my husband or father. I'll do whatever the hell I want!"

The next time Kit saw Danny, she felt strange taking yet another bag of baby stuff from him. But she didn't say a word about what Mike had told her. Why bother? She already knew he was a porch pirate. Maybe the stuff he was giving her was stolen, maybe it wasn't. It didn't matter. Either way, it was Danny being generous and trying to help her and the baby.

As for Mike, she believed he was jealous and wanted to get rid of Danny any way he could. But porch pirate or not, Kit knew that Danny was there for her and Jasper in a way that Mike would never be.

CHAPTER FOUR

Harlan's assessment of 27-year-old Danny Potter was spot on. After his firing from UPS, he had drifted into porch piracy with his boyhood friend and bro-from-another-mom, Cruz Morrissey.

Within weeks of ripping off their first box, the two had hit the big leagues of piracy with their unique blend of chutzpah, timing (the ability to grab a box and "clear a porch" in 20 seconds), and a certain dexterity that even a pro athlete would envy. Half the time they operated alone, the other half as a team, one grabbing the loot, the other clutching the wheel of the getaway car, with heart racing and motor running.

On the hunt in luxury high-rises like the Mojave Miraval on Paradise Road, the prowling duo were at their shameless best. One afternoon, clad in old UPS uniforms provided by Danny, they talked their way past the Miraval's security guard. Tearing down one floor after the other, Cruz scooped up packages lying outside gilt-edged front doors and dropped them through an open stairwell to Danny, who was also scouring hallways on lower levels.

Another time, at the Vegas Vistas Apartments on Howard Hughes Drive, security guards were in hot pursuit of the pirate-dudes, who were making a hasty getaway with armfuls of packages. In the main lobby, a panicky Cruz pulled the fire alarm as they rushed out the door. Bedlam broke out, as foam started spouting from the ceiling and sprinklers began wildly gushing. With the fire department on the way, the security guys abruptly turned back, letting Danny and Cruz bolt to the parking lot with the loot.

The spewing water was on their side that day, but that wasn't always the case. One mid-summer morning in 2013, as the sweat-suited banditos lifted boxes from a porch out on Willowstone Drive in Henderson, the automatic sprinkler system powered on, and the guys, along with their loot, got drenched. Laughing their asses off, they made it to the car, dumped the soggy boxes in back, and took off like bats out of hell down Sun Devil Drive.

Glitches with sprinklers, elaborate dog-poop traps, and close encounters with pepper, and bear sprays were everyday occurrences in the pirating world. Danny and Cruz had their share of setbacks, for sure. But more often, they successfully infiltrated apartment buildings, condo complexes, and front porches all over the Vegas Valley, and scooped up every package and box in sight.

Everything was fair game, from new treadmills and computers, to deluxe espresso-makers, designer jeans, sneakers, and gem-encrusted bracelets. Somehow, it all ended up in their getaway car.

Not to be outdone by rival pirates, the ruthless buccaneers even took to waterways when needed. One morning on Lake Las Vegas, they commandeered an idle kayak and paddled past a row of upscale marina properties. While Cruz sat afloat in the kayak, tethered to a pier, Danny raced across manicured lawns, snatching every box he saw. In this rich terrain, there was always the possibility of hitting the jackpot with a juicy jewelry parcel that would bring in thousands.

Anything they didn't sell was stored in garages and lockers, or given to family and friends, or, in ladies-dude Cruz's case, to the ever growing gaggle of girlfriends he attracted. Everything else got dumped in the nearest Goodwill bin. For the thriving thieves, porch piracy was a challenging, heart-thumping way to make a living. Any mere job would have seemed boring and tame by comparison.

Law enforcement was hard-pressed to control or stop what was going down on the streets of Las Vegas and its wealthier suburbs. Whether they were working tandem or solo, Danny and Cruz were determined, creative, and compulsive—a little bit James Bond finesse, a little bit Oliver Twist cunning. No fence was too high, no gate unbreachable, no porch unreachable.

It was a world of dizzying highs, but also lows. And lowest of all were the busts.

Danny had been booked a few times for misdemeanor burglary and reckless driving. He even got tossed in jail once for indecent exposure, after getting drenched in a torrent of sprinklers at a condo complex in Summerlin. When he peeled off his soaking wet clothes so he could run faster, he got caught, butt-naked, on a security camera. An eagle-eyed resident called the cops, and he ended up in the back seat of a squad car, wrapped in a blanket and tightly cuffed.

Cruz had his share of horror stories, too. Like the time he was bitten in the leg by a sharp-toothed German Shepherd that cornered him in the hallway of a Blue Diamond apartment complex. There was no way out, so he just stood there for 20 excruciating minutes, until the dog's owner finally showed up and led the foaming canine away.

Meanwhile, the owner's wife had called security, and guards nabbed a bloody Cruz, trying to cram a large, bulky box of golf clubs into the trunk of his car in the parking lot.

The desperado-dudes tried to learn from their mistakes. But it was hard, because you never knew what you were going to be up against the next day. A lot of it came down to luck, pure and simple. Sometimes the porch-pirate gods were with you, sometimes you were shit out of luck. And Danny was SOL big time the day he got busted in October 2015.

It was a typical warm, bright day in the Las Vegas Valley. Trucks and vans were zipping around, delivering all sorts of loot that any hungry pirate would covet. Danny was working the

Green Valley area, prime territory for high-end merchandise. Around 11 that morning, he spotted a UPS truck rushing down Mariposa Boulevard and turning sharply on Wayne Newton Drive. The truck hit the brakes at a large, Spanish-colonial house with terraced lawns and brick ramparts.

Nearby, behind a tall rockspray shrub, Danny, in dark sweats and a wool cap, was staked out in his blue sedan. In front of the house, the UPS guy unloaded three boxes from his van, and wheeled them up the walkway to the porch. As he rang the bell, Danny gaped at the boxes. He had no idea what was inside, but he was thrilled at the prospect of finding out.

There was no answer at the door, the boxes were left, and, moments later, the truck sped away. Lickety-split, Danny drove up the driveway. With the motor running, he bounded out of the car, sprinted up the steps to the porch, and grabbed everything that had been delivered. But then, almost instantly, a dog started barking Inside, and the front door flung open. Out jumped a bizarre, frightening sight: a fat, churlish man gripping a long, menacing hunting rifle.

Danny had just made it back down the steps with the loot when the bald ogre cocked his long gun and snarled, "Give me those boxes, you lowlife piece of scum!"

It was a pirate's worst nightmare.

Seeing no way out, Danny gave in fast and dropped all three boxes on the walkway.

"Now get your ass in that car and get the hell off my property," the human blimp bellowed, firing a shot, and taking off down the steps after Danny, with his surly black Doberman loping right behind.

Somehow Danny made it to his car, leapt in, and yanked the door shut. Outside, perched on hind legs, the irate canine clawed frantically at Danny's window. White foam was spewing from his sharp-toothed mouth. Right behind him, his owner waved the rifle and unleashed a volley of four-letter slurs.

In his blue sedan, a panicky Danny cranked the engine. Out of his mind with fear, he pulled the car forward, then threw it into reverse. Big mistake! He floored the gas pedal and the car bucked like a wild stallion. Then it shot backwards down the long, sloping lawn—and straight through a five-foot brick wall. Scattered across the lawn was a dead wake of shattered bricks, torn honeysuckle, and chunks of concrete.

But the bizarre drama had yet to reach its climax. Still gunning backwards, the Taurus plowed across the sidewalk and onto Wayne Newton Drive, a sleepy off-ramp for the rich and powerful that had never seen much action.

Suddenly, it was like Times Square. The minute Danny's car hit the street, it was broadsided by an oncoming Toyota 4-Runner. Within seconds, a green Subaru Forrester joined the fray from out of nowhere, smashing into the back of the yellow Toyota. With sounds of crashing glass and metal piercing the air, this bucolic country lane, largely shielded from the ills of urban life, had become the epicenter of a smoking, three-car pile-up.

The two stunned drivers, plus three passengers from the Toyota, and four from the Forrester, scrambled out of their vehicles and lurched angrily towards Danny, now crouched in his car with its mangled right side.

The pirate, minus a seatbelt because he'd been trying to escape the rifle and dog, had been violently throttled in his seat. Onlookers were cursing the bedraggled box bandit, now in shock, with sharp pain ripping through his back and neck. Just then the enraged homeowner, still gripping his rifle, waddled across his mashed lawn and over the crushed brick wall to Danny's car.

Red-faced and livid, he wrenched open the door and dragged the dazed pirate out. Slamming him against the car, he pointed his long gun at Danny's midsection and exclaimed with glee, "Put your hands up, you punk-ass thief, the cops are coming!"

Luckily, the raging Doberman had been dragged inside the house and was no longer on the scene.

21

Within minutes, two Vegas Metro squad cars showed up. A couple of ambulances, lights flashing and sirens blaring, also sped to the scene. EMTs were soon assisting the Toyota and Forrester passengers, who'd sustained a volley of injuries, from concussions and whiplash, to cuts and burns. Two Triple A trucks arrived to tow away the mangled cars.

"This goddamn porch gangster tried to steal my son's new laptop and printer. Then he crashed through my wall. Take him downtown and book him!" the owner of the house ranted at the cops.

The officers grabbed a frazzled Danny, reeling with pain, and patted him down for guns or knives. Grimacing, he mumbled, "my back hurts," while being cuffed. One of the officers shot back, "you've got way bigger problems to worry about," and shoved him in the back of a squad car. With his head down, he was driven to the station, while his car was towed to the Clark County impound lot.

Danny was quickly booked for reckless driving and vehicular assault, a felony, as well as misdemeanor burglary for the array of loot stashed in his car.

That night, Kit's jaw was on the floor as she watched local TV news coverage of Danny being led away by police. She was torn up and heart-broken over the friend she had met just six months before. Then the phone rang.

"Are you watching channel 5?" Mike barked.

"Yes," Kit answered.

"I told you this dude was trouble," Mike gloated. "I hate to tell you this, Kit, but I think the pirate's headed for prison. He caused a major accident, people got hurt, and there were stolen goods in his car."

"I don't know about the stolen stuff, or how the crash could have happened," Kit sputtered. "Danny's a great driver. I hope he's okay. I'm sure he has his side of the story."

Mike rolled his eyes.

"Kit, you are so naïve when it comes to this asshole porch thief. Get him out of your life—now—before he does something to hurt you or Jasper."

Shaking her head, an upset Kit blurted, "Sorry, Mike, I can't talk anymore, Jasper needs me," and hung up.

Danny spent the next two weeks vegetating in a bleak, windowless Clark County jail cell. Kit went to see him a few times. The visits were brief, tense, and closely monitored by rough-hewn armed guards.

Danny was sad and subdued, not at all like his old cocky self, and so was Kit. The only time the orange-jump-suited prisoner cracked a smile was when Kit pulled up photos of Jasper on her phone.

A slick, no-nonsense, court-appointed lawyer met with Danny in his jail cell. During their 30-minute visit, the two decided he would plead guilty to vehicular assault, a felony.

Two weeks later, Danny's trial in a city court went off like clockwork, with a tough judge, an even tougher prosecutor, and Danny and his lawyer present. Danny's mom, Bonnie, was also there. She cried softly when her son stood up and murmured, "guilty," to the judge's query of how he would plead.

To no one's surprise, Danny was hit with an 18-month sentence in the Nevada Regional Corrections Center, a medium-security prison in Carson City. His penalty wasn't the maximum for a felony of such consequence, but close to it.

That night, Danny's mom called Kit. Bonnie confided that Danny was crazy about her and Jasper, and that he had asked her to call and let her know how the trial had gone. Bonnie was stumbling through this ordeal basically alone, since Danny's dad, who'd been a poker dealer at Flamingo, had died in 2007 of a heart attack.

"Thank God Waylon isn't here to see what's happening to Danny," she told Kit. "He lived and breathed for that boy. This would have killed him.

"I've got two younger sons to think of," Bonnie added. "They're both gutted by this. They look up to Danny and want to be just like him. How do I explain this to them?"

For her part, Kit was powerless to answer.

"I'm so sorry for what's happening to your family," she finally responded. "Jasper and I will miss Danny. He was really good to us."

"He was really good to all of us," Bonnie agreed. "That's the problem. We were all enabling him. We pretty much knew he was stealing the stuff he gave us, but we said nothing. We just let him keep doing it.

"Everything in my kitchen came from Danny: the blender, the toaster, the air fryer, even the designer can-opener," her voice trailed off. "And my other sons got expensive sneakers, electronics, and clothes. Danny was always giving things to people. From the time he was little, that's the way he was. Maybe he thought we wouldn't love him if he didn't show up with an armful of presents."

"That's sad," Kit said wistfully. "I hope he didn't think that about Jasper and me."

"No worries," Bonnie told her. "I don't think so. He really cares about you and that son of yours, and talks about you all the time. You're the only one he told me to call about this court stuff."

"Um, what will happen to Danny's apartment on Oakey, now that he's going to be gone for 18 months?" Kit wondered.

"I talked to the manager today," Bonnie replied. "He's letting us out of the lease and we're putting his stuff in storage. When Danny comes back, he can stay with me till he gets his act together and finds a job. Then he can move into another place.

"Listen, honey," Bonnie went on. "I'll give you a ring if there's any news. Otherwise, the boys and I will drive to Carson City once a month to see Danny. You're welcome to tag along, but I think he would be upset if you saw him in that jumpsuit. Orange never was his best color.

"This whole thing's kind of a kick in the ass for all of us. I hope 18 months in lock-up will knock some sense into that boy, and he'll straighten out when he comes back."

"That would be great," Kit agreed. "Danny's smart and he's got a personality that lights up a room. He could get a job on the Strip making good money. He just needs someone to give him a chance."

"Right on, sweetheart," Bonnie said. And then, after hesitating for an instant, she added, "You know, he never was the same after he got fired from UPS. He always said it was a set-up by the boss's skanky wife, Coney, who was having sex with some of the drivers in the vans.

"Danny walked in on a steamy scene one day, and after that she wanted to get rid of him. He told me she paid one of the mechanics to mess with his brakes, and that was what caused the big bust-up on Charleston that got him fired."

"Oh, my God," Kit murmured. "Danny never told me."

"He doesn't like to talk about it because there's nothing anyone can do about it now. It messed with his head big time and turned him into a porch pirate. And hanging out with Cruz Morrissey didn't help. That boy was a bad influence on Danny from the day they met in kindergarten. Cruz better get a grip and change his ways, or he'll end up in a prison cell, too.

"Every time I see his mom, Carmen, at Von's, she runs and hides in frozen foods. She doesn't want to face me because she knows her son ruined my son's life. I totally get it. What mother wants to say, 'My son, the porch pirate?'"

CHAPTER FIVE

In his dreary prison cell, thoughts of Kit were all that kept Danny going. He missed her, and wondered what she was doing and if she was seeing anyone. A beautiful girl like that, 22 years old and alone, with a six-month old baby, needed someone. It seemed a no-brainer to him that one of those gambler-dudes at Caesar's would take notice and fall for her big time. This thought haunted Danny's days and nights. But he wasn't about to reach out. He was too ashamed, too disgusted with himself, and too enraged that he'd ended up in this goddamn hellhole.

When he wasn't fantasizing about Kit, Danny reflected back on the other babes he'd known. And there had been many. Though he'd never actually been in love, quite a few females had been crazy about him. And why not? He was sweet, fun to be with, full of surprises, and an exciting, attentive lover. Not a guy you would ever be bored with. He was also good-looking, about 5'11", with sandy-brown hair and blue eyes. Thin, but with a strong chest and arms from lifting all those heavy boxes and running to the car with them.

Kit wasn't able to see him very well that first day. He was all covered up in sweats and a slouchy knit hat. And then things got so crazy at the hospital, she barely noticed him. But the day he arrived to take her home, she was surprised to look up from her bed and see this hunky guy standing before her in jeans and a purple and gray knit shirt. Wow, she thought, the porch pirate's kind of cute, and he's got swag. Who knew?

They became part of each other's lives over the months. But now, with Danny in lock-up, Kit felt sad and alone. Then again, her life in Vegas had always been kind of lonely.

She'd arrived in 2011, just six months after graduating from Taylor High School in Kokomo. Her childhood there had been dicey and troubled. She was born in 1993 to a downtrodden teenage couple, who'd endured all the tensions and humiliations of a classic shotgun wedding just weeks before her birth. Two years of nonstop bickering and financial struggles followed, culminating in a nasty divorce.

Kit's fair-haired mom, Lori, soon took off with a fertilizer salesman for South Carolina, where the two ultimately married and raised a family. Her tall, lanky dad, Darryl, hightailed it to Chicago, where he scored a gig playing piano in a jazz group. Both of them were just 20 years old, and anxious to move on after their disastrous marriage. As a result, when they left Kokomo, they basically turned their backs on everything, and everyone, there.

That included their two-year-old daughter, Kittredge Destry Wells, who got dumped on her maternal grandparents' doorstep. In all fairness, the couple did the best they could, but it didn't last long. When Kit was just eight, her beloved Grandpa Jasper was hit by a freight train while rescuing Kit's puppy from some railroad tracks near their apartment. Seven years later, the colder, nastier Grandma Rose perished in a fiery car crash caused by a drunk driver in downtown Kokomo.

With both grandparents gone, 15-year-old Kit felt like the lone survivor of a plane crash. And then things got worse. There wasn't a single relative willing to take her in. She was one step from foster care when the family of her best friend, Rainey Pearce, stepped up and gave her a place to stay.

Down Marchland Avenue Kit moved, from her grandparents' bleak, weather-worn apartment building to the Pearce's two-story, gabled-frame house. There she slept on the couch, did her share of cooking and cleaning, and somehow made it through high school.

By graduation, both Kit and Rainey were restless souls, bored with Indiana's bland normality and longing for the open road. That meant Las Vegas, a place they had visited with classmates and been thrilled with. The girls were convinced Sin City would provide the golden opportunities for glamour and success that Kokomo lacked.

On a cold, dismal day in January 2011, Kit and Rainey crammed a rusty old Toyota with a dozen stuffed suitcases and boxes, and took off in the middle of a blizzard for Sin City. Six grueling but exhilarating days later, they made it.

On a bright, mid-week morning, they pulled up to the famous, "Welcome to Fabulous Las Vegas," sign and parked the car. After sauntering to the iconic red-white-and-blue landmark looming before them, they turned to savor the warmth of the desert sun on their pale, Midwestern faces. As a newlywed couple posed nearby with a beefy Elvis impersonator, Kit and Rainey snapped a slew of selfies to share with friends back in Indiana.

The cash-poor but excited girls—Kit, slim, 5'6", and blond-haired with blue eyes, and Rainey, shorter and pudgier, with chestnut hair and dark eyes—quickly found work on the Strip. In the cavernous Excalibur kitchen, they chopped vegetables, made pies, and assembled salads for the casino's buffet. Their hours were crazy, the pay meager, but it was fun and frantic and they got free meals. With both chipping in, they could easily afford the rent on their small, one-bedroom apartment behind The Egg & I on Sahara Avenue.

It helped that they had each other to turn to as they adjusted to their 24/7 lives in Sin City. Unfortunately, Rainey's relocation lasted only a year. At that point, her high school boyfriend, Justin Pickett, who'd dumped her in junior year for one of her friends, charged into Vegas in a red pickup and swept her off her feet with a diamond ring and a marriage proposal.

Rainey swooned 'yes,' and two weeks later, with a teary-eyed Kit looking on, the couple tied the knot at the Desert Bells Wedding Chapel on the south end of the Strip.

After a short honeymoon in cold, rainy Seattle, the newly-weds drove back to Vegas, packed Rainey's stuff, and loaded it in Justin's truck. Then off to Kokomo they sped to begin their own version of happily ever after.

When Rainey left town in February 2012, Kit felt lost. But by then, she'd scored a better job waitressing at a steak house in MGM Grand. The tips were generous, the hours regular. She was able to pay the rent on the apartment and take courses at a reputable gaming school on Flamingo Road. There she learned enough to get hired as a Kitty Kat Babe blackjack dealer at Caesar's, a few days after her 21ST birthday.

And then along came Mike Prescott. Meeting the dynamic son of Senator Bill Prescott and his high-society wife, Gwen, had been a seismic event in Kit's young life. When the six-foot, green-eyed, blond heli-pilot strode into the Kitty Kat Lounge one night in jeans, dark boots, and a brown leather flight jacket, Kit was dazzled. And Mike couldn't take his eyes off the gorgeous, blond blackjack dealer rocking a peacock-blue sequined bikini, silver bustier, black fishnets, and four-inch heels. Surrounded by ringing slots and raucous craps tables, hearts fluttered, and phone numbers were exchanged.

All through that luminous summer of 2014, they dated. Mike bought Kit expensive gifts, and showed her around his iconic hometown. It was nonstop fun and games, and the sex was sizzling, accompanied by a tenderness that Kit mistook for love. But just four months in, she found out she was pregnant, and Mike started distancing himself. There were echoes of her parents' confused, twisted young lives.

Mike's indifference and aloofness after Kit revealed her pregnancy hurt like hell.

"Do you want to keep it?" he had asked early on, over a quick breakfast at a diner in Paris.

"Yes," she replied without hesitation. "I want this baby. The circumstances aren't the greatest, but still, it's a flesh-and-blood relative, and I haven't known many of those."

"I get what you're saying," Mike conceded. "But I have to be honest. I'm 32 and just got divorced for a second time. I don't want to get married again, or be bogged down with some big parental commitment. I thought you were on the pill. How could this happen?"

"My hours are so weird, I guess I lost track and slipped up," Kit said sheepishly. "I'm sorry, I know the timing is off. But boy or girl, I want this baby. Will you at least help me financially?"

"Yes, I will," Mike agreed. "But, please, please, you can't let anyone know I'm the father. My dad is up for re-election in 2016, and things are tough enough. The last thing he needs is the scandal of a Prescott grandson born out of wedlock. That would not be very cool."

"Oh, Mike, screw the politics," Kit shot back with a dismissive flick of the wrist. "This is a flesh-and-blood-human-being we're talking about. He or she will need a mom and a dad. Grandparents would be nice, too, but I guess that's not going to happen."

"Kit, let's just take this one step at a time," Mike told her, patting her arm across the table. "Stay healthy, do the Kitty Kat Babe thing as long as you can, and get through your pregnancy. Then we'll see what happens after the baby's born."

Kit didn't hear from Mike for another three weeks, which nearly killed her. At that point, he explained it was late summer and he was busy flying hordes of tourists all over the Vegas Valley. She believed him, up to a point. But she also thought he was trying to avoid her.

Five months into her pregnancy, Kit was still working at Caesar's. But even in a lowcut silver-sequined maternity dress and flats, it was hard for the twenty-pounds-heavier mom-to-be to stand behind a blackjack table eight hours a day. Her feet and ankles were swollen, she was always exhausted, and had to run to the loo constantly.

By her seventh month, Kit's symptoms had intensified. She was bloated, tired, cranky, and often nauseous all through her shift. Finally, she went on early maternity leave.

A month later, porch pirate Danny sprinted into her life and shook things up big time. Talk about meeting cute.

CHAPTER SIX

It was the summer of 2016, and business was booming at the Kitty Kat Lounge. To keep up with demand and bring in even more fans and gamers, management was clamoring for new promotional videos.

After some fast brain-storming, the powers that be at Caesar's settled on a novel idea to use in-house talent, rather than professional showgirls or models, for the new ad campaign. This meant that Kit, and her Kitty Kat cohorts, would go to L.A. for a long, all-expenses-paid weekend to film the glitzy new spots in a Hollywood studio. In addition to expenses, each babe would receive a hefty, $5,000 bonus.

Kit, who had finally gotten her pre-pregnancy body back, jumped at the offer. Her only concern was Jasper. She was hoping he could stay with his regular babysitter, a sweet, grandmotherly neighbor named Mrs. Brambles, for the long weekend. But right before the trip, an accident up north intervened, when Mrs. Brambles' frail, older sister in Winnemucca fell and broke her arm. Mrs. B felt compelled to go to her. Contrite and regretful, she called Kit and told her she wouldn't be able to take Jasper.

Kit tried a few other sitters, but no one was available. In desperation, she called Mike. At first he balked, telling her it was short notice and would interfere with his work schedule and social life. But Kit persisted, and Mike finally agreed to take his 15-month-old son for the four-day weekend.

While an excited Kit packed a large suitcase for L.A., she also crammed a jumbo-size mommy bag with bottles, bibs, teething rings, diapers, snacks, and pacifiers for Jasper. A small suitcase of baby outfits was also packed, and long lists of detailed instructions were drawn up for Mike.

Despite Kit's careful preparations, she was nervous when Mike arrived to pick up the baby and whisk him away in his pale gray lounger-carrier. As he lumbered out the door with it, the large tote was slung over his broad shoulder, the small suitcase clutched in his other hand.

Kit and a dozen stoked, stacked babes flew to L.A. early on a Friday, and checked into luxurious suites at the Beverly Hills Hilton on chic, upscale Roxbury Drive.

For a single-mom who worked long hours, got by on little sleep, and never had any time for herself or friends, every minute was bliss.

Glamour-puss pamper sessions with Beverly Hills' finest hair, make-up, and costume wizards began each day. These were followed by long, grueling hours on the set, with lots of tricky dance moves and repetitive takes. But afterwards, the babes would slither into slinky cocktail dresses and go out for long, lively dinners with the Caesar's advertising team and hunky camera crew.

A few of the guys were interested in Kit, but she was too busy focusing on the project to pay much attention. All the hard work paid off. Kit's weekend in L.A. was a huge success. The marketing honchos at Caesar's were thrilled with the flashy new ads featuring the gorgeous, talented babes. In L.A., all of them were stars.

Meanwhile, in Vegas, Jasper's first three nights at Mike's condo went off without a hitch. But Monday night, not so much. While the baby slept nestled in his cushy lounger in the living room, Mike was entertaining a playmate du jour in his bedroom. Her name was Amber Taupin. The buxom brunette was a topless dancer in the raunchy Vegas Rocks revue at Planet Hollywood.

Their lusty sex romp wound down sometime around midnight. Hours of deep sleep ensued for both. Early on Tuesday morning, Mike and Amber indulged in a raucous, sensual shower. Then he got dressed and hustled to the living room to check on Jasper.

But the baby's lounger was gone—and so was he!

Lying askew on a nearby coffee table was a blunt, short note scrawled in red on the back of an old take-out food receipt. It read, "the kid is safe, you will get a call."

Shocked and reeling, a vague, subdued Mike folded the note and put it in his pocket. Telling Amber the baby's mom had picked him up earlier, he acted as normal as possible while sipping coffee and nibbling toast with her in the breakfast nook. The confused, bewildered showgirl was then sent home in a cab.

A devastated Mike left for work, but his heart wasn't in it. Still, he had to go. He was the owner of Heli-Vegas, it was midsummer, and there were a dozen Grand Canyon tours scheduled for that day. Amidst a flurry of meetings and phone calls, he kept watch over his cell like a hawk.

Back at his condo that Tuesday night, Kit's call came in around 6 PM. Tired but elated, she was back from L.A., and anxious to pick up Jasper.

"Um, Kit, please don't freak out," Mike said, trying to prepare her for the gut-wrenching news, "but Jasper's not here."

"Well, where is he?" she shot back, alarmed and confused.

"I, uh, don't know," Mike said softly. "There was a girl here with me last night," he went on. "We were asleep when someone broke in, in the middle of the night, and took him.

"This morning, the girl joined me in the shower. Then I came out to the living room to change and feed Jasper. But his lounger was gone—and so was he. There was a short note from the kidnapper."

"A note? What did it say?" Kit blurted, her voice and temper rising.

"Just that he would be safe, and they would call."

"Well, have they?" she asked.

"Um, no, not yet." Mike replied.

After a gasp, Kit started screaming and crying.

"Where's my baby?" she wailed. "I want my son! Mike, I trusted you with him, and you said you would keep him safe. Who was this girl you were with? Does she know anything about what happened?"

"Not really," Mike said. "It was Amber Taupin from Vegas Rocks. I told her some bogus story about why the baby wasn't here this morning, and sent her home in a cab. She seemed pretty confused."

"Yeah, me too!" Kit fumed. "Have you called the cops?"

"I don't want to do that. Then it will be public knowledge he's my son. My dad's election is this November. We have to sit tight and wait to hear from the kidnapper."

"Sit tight and wait? No way! I want my baby," Kit shrieked. "The hell with your father's election. Call the cops right now. Get Jasper back. What if they do something to him? What if they hurt him—or kill him? I want him back—now!"

"Kit, please try to stay calm. We have to do things on their terms," Mike said firmly. "We can't get the cops involved or the kidnappers might panic and hurt him. Just wait, we'll hear from them. They'll demand ransom. I'll pay it, whatever it is. I have money from the sale of two condos in Miami last year. Don't worry, we'll get him back."

"I never should have left him with you, but Mrs. Brambles was in Winnemucca with her sister and I didn't know what else to do. I had to go to L.A. I should have taken him with me and hired a nanny at the hotel.

"There are girls running in and out of your condo at all hours. It's party central over there, and now look what's happened. Your life will be nonstop hell if anything happens to my son!"

35

"He's our son, Kit, and threatening me won't help," Mike shot back. "I'm sorry this happened. We're both victims. Please, can you come over? Do you think you can drive? You've got to get a grip and make it out here."

"I don't know," Kit answered. "How can I drive like this? I'll kill myself and someone else."

"Take a drink, or a pill, or something," Mike told her. "Pull yourself together, get in your car, and come over. We can help each other through this. I'm off work for the next few days, so I can totally focus on getting Jasper back."

With her hands shaking on the steering wheel, a livid, unhinged Kit somehow made the 30-minute drive to Mike's condo in Henderson.

At the door, he held her, but she was rigid and cold. Mike had made them drinks. As they sat on the couch and sipped, they waited to hear from the kidnapper. Every minute was agony. At that point, Jasper had been missing almost 24 hours.

Finally, around 10 PM, Mike's cell rang. Grabbing it frantically, he yelled, "Hello, Hello, Hello."

In a strange, low voice that was neither male nor female because a voice disguiser was being used, the kidnapper said, "Your son is fine."

"Where is he? Who is this? When can we get him back?" Mike demanded.

There was a pause on the other end.

"Your son is fine," the voice repeated.

"$75,000 gets him back. No negotiating. Put the money in a leather satchel, in hundreds and twenties. Drop it in locker number 10 at Circus Circus, under the Los Bozos roller coaster. Use the combination 4369 to lock the door. You have 48 hours to deliver, or you'll never see him again. After the money is collected and counted, he'll be dropped off. No cops. No family. No friends. No games. His life is on the line. Just do it."

"Okay, okay, $75,000 in $100s and $20s. Locker number

10, Los Bozos roller coaster, code 4369. I'll get you your money," Mike stammered. "We want to hear his voice. Can we, please, just hear his voice?"

A few seconds later, the familiar sound of Jasper's soft cooing could be heard on the phone.

Kit grabbed Mike's arm when she heard it.

"Jasper," she screamed into the phone. "Mommy's here. Mommy will get you back soon! Mommy loves you, sweet boy. Please give him his bottles!"

As the kidnapper's phone abruptly clicked off, Mike and Kit collapsed on the couch. She was crying, he was trying to comfort her.

"Don't worry, babe," Mike told her, "I'll get the money and take it to Circus Circus tomorrow. We'll get Jasper back soon, I promise."

Whimpering and nodding, Kit blotted her nose with a Kleenex, and the two terrified parents clung together.

CHAPTER SEVEN

So, who had kidnapped Jasper?

A dumped, former lover of Mike's, of course.

Jolene Fisher was her name. She had found Mike in bed with another girl the night she took Jasper. It was 3 AM on a Tuesday and the sexy showgirl, dressed in a lightweight trench coat over a skimpy, purple lace mini-dress, hadn't expected to find the hunky pilot at home. She thought he was flying a charter to Santa Fe that night.

Jolene's intention had been to sneak into Mike's condo, with a key that he had given her while they were dating, and snoop around. She wanted to find dirt on Mike, so she could blackmail him as payback for the way he had used her for sex for two months, and then callously tossed her aside like a dirty wash-cloth.

After finding him in bed with someone else, a jealous, enraged Jolene had tip-toed back to the living room, where she spotted the baby sleeping peacefully. Mike had never mentioned a baby to her. Was this a secret love child he'd had with the girl he was now in bed with, she wondered?

And then, impulsively, she grabbed the plastic handle of the lounger the tiny tot was sleeping in, slung the nearby tote stuffed with baby food, bottles, and diapers over her shoulder, and snuck out of Mike's condo.

In the quiet, early-morning darkness, she wedged the lounger into the passenger seat of her car and hopped in the driver's seat. All was quiet till she started the engine, and the baby, swathed in a blue cotton onesie, woke up crying. As his piercing screams rocked Jolene's green Honda Accord, she reached into the tote, grabbed a bottle filled with apple juice, and propped it in his tiny, plump hands.

"Here, little dude, drink this," she whispered. He instantly quieted down, and she got on the road.

The destination: her sister's place in Indian Springs. The Fisher girls had grown up in this tiny Nevada desert town known for its artesian spring water and the Creech Air Force Base.

Twenty-seven-year-old Tammy was three years older than Jolene, and the polar opposite. While Jolene was a glamorous, seductive, cunning showgirl, Tammy was a rough-hewn, laid-back desert rat. Her thin, straggly hair was shoulder-length and mousey-brown. Plaid flannel shirts, denim overalls, and fleece jackets were her wardrobe go-to's. The queen-size hellcat told it like it was, took few showers, and didn't interact with the opposite, or even the same, sex, very often.

When the parents of the train wreck siblings relocated to Tonopah in 2012, Jolene had run off to Vegas to begin her showgirl career, and Tammy had stayed behind, hunkering down in the red-brick, ranch-style house they had grown up in.

At first, she wasted all her time and money in the small but pungent Indian Springs Casino. When it closed down in 2014, Tammy was lost.

In need of a reason to get up in the morning, she got a job stocking shelves at the Dollar Depot store on Grouse Street. Unfortunately, it lasted only a few months. Tammy repeatedly got caught letting homeless people steal dog food off the shelves for their hungry animals. After a loud, bitter confrontation with the store manager in front of customers and co-workers, she was fired.

Since then, she'd hung out mostly at home, scarfing down ample meals and snacks while watching old movies and Jerry Springer reruns with her scruffy German Shepherd, Granby. She rarely left the house, and why would she? It was a binge of comfort-clutter. Piled on every table and stacked in every closet and cupboard were cookware sets and dishes, egg poachers, mounds of dirty clothes, vacuum cleaners, exercise gizmos, and cases of gourmet dog food. From every shelf, counter, and dresser, large red and pink heart-shaped boxes of Swiss chocolates beckoned. And looming over it all, in every corner, were stuffed bald eagles with glaring gold eyes.

Reams of credit card bills for the relentless Internet purchases poured in every month. But Tammy never batted an eye. She had plenty of dough stashed away from a generous trust fund set up by long-gone forebears who'd struck it big in the Silver State's gold mines.

Little sister Jolene didn't drive the 45 miles from Vegas to her sister's home very often, but when she did, she made snide comments about Tammy's compulsive hoarding, weight, sanitary habits, and reclusive nature. Big sis felt that nothing she ever did was good enough for Jolene, and she resented the hell out of it. Tammy considered Jolene a pampered, platinum-blond princess who'd been spoiled and indulged all her life, while she had sat alone in a corner, fat, forlorn, and ignored.

The sisters were at each others' throats constantly. Yes, they argued a lot, but when it came to money, they often found common ground. And so, on the way to Tammy's house in the wee, small hours that morning, Jolene called her.

"Don't go to sleep, Tam," she urged. "I'm coming over and I'm not alone!"

"Another new boyfriend to rub in my face?" Tammy asked.

"No, nothing like that. I've got a business deal I need to run by you," Jolene told her. "We could both make a bundle, I'm on my way."

Tammy was intrigued. She figured she had nothing to lose since she normally went to bed at 5 AM anyway. So she said, "Okay, come on down."

When Jolene arrived a half-hour later, she lugged in a dozing, 15-month-old baby strapped in a pale gray lounger and a tote brimming with diapers and bottles. Tammy took one look at the cute, blond bundle, and her heart melted.

"Whose baby is this?" she asked.

"I think it's Mike Prescott's," Jolene said gleefully. "I just swiped him from Mike's condo in Henderson."

"Hell's bells!" Tammy exclaimed. "Why would you do that?" she asked, clearing space on the living room couch so the twisted sisters could sit with the carrier perched between them. As the baby slept, Granby parked himself at Tammy's feet, nestled his moist snout in her lap, and stared up at her.

In a hushed, excited tone, Jolene explained that she had kidnapped the baby as a way to exact revenge for Mike's shoddy treatment of her.

"$75,000 should be enough ransom," she told Tammy. "I think Mike will pay it because the kid's probably a love child of his that nobody knows about. To keep it secret, he'll pony up the cash. I know how this dude thinks, and I've seen his bank statements up close and personal."

"Girl, you are a badass!" Tammy declared, high-fiving her sister. "So where do I come in? How much do I get?"

"You take care of the kid for a couple of days, while I'm back on the Strip going to rehearsals and dancing in Bitch Goddesses. After a day or two, I'll get the cash from the locker, come out here, and take the kid back. I'll split the $75,000 with you, half and half. But you can't say a word to anyone."

"Winner winner, chicken dinner!" Tammy yelped. "My lips are sealed. Who am I going to tell, the UPS driver? What's the precious one's name?"

"I don't know, and who gives a fuck?" Jolene cracked.

"Girl, you are one tough bitch. If Mama and Daddy heard you cursing like that, you'd get your mouth washed out with Lysol!" Tammy prattled as she reached across the coffee table for a pink, heart-shaped box of chocolates and tore off the cellophane.

41

Jolene smiled.

"Mama and Daddy are so busy with bingo games and church picnics, they don't know which end is up," she said, shaking her head. "Now hand over those chocolates, girl, and go heat up a bottle. The kid must be hungry after the long drive."

After Jolene left that morning, Tammy, who had zero experience with babies, started bonding with the blue-eyed tot, and fell hard for him. She briefly fantasized about calling him Jango and keeping him forever.

But all that changed over the next few days, as Tammy faced a torrent of dirty diapers, soiled onesies, bottles and nipples that constantly needed cleaning, and a barrage of baby food jars. Her nights sucked, too. They were long and often sleepless, as she tried to deal with a cranky, scared 15-month-old who missed his mama, and somehow knew his world had been turned upside down.

Mid-day Wednesday, a desperate Tammy called Jolene's cell and left a rambling message.

"The kid won't stop crying!" she rasped. "I gave him a bottle and he threw it on the floor. The dirty diapers are piling up. More boxes of Pampers are coming from Baby Zone, and a case of baby food. He spits everything out or throws it on the wall. It's like he knows something's up. You better get your ass down here and take him, Jo. Find another babysitter. I can't handle this shit much longer."

Jolene got the message, and all the others that followed. But she was too busy with Bitch Goddess rehearsals, plus her own rocking social life, to pay much attention. Instead, she throttled on, knowing that Tammy would somehow cope till she could get to the locker and collect the ransom.

CHAPTER EIGHT

First thing Wednesday morning, Mike made a withdrawal of $75,000 from an account at Suncoast Bank. A drop in the bucket for him, really. After selling two condos in Miami the year before, he had hundreds of thousands of dollars stashed there.

Once the ransom was changed into $100s and $20s, and stuffed in a leather satchel, he lugged it to locker number 10 under the Los Bozos roller coaster at Circus Circus. Using the kidnapper's four-digit code, he plopped the bag inside and locked the door.

Meanwhile, at Mike's condo, a distraught, frazzled Kit was pacing the floor and climbing the walls. She tried to rest, but couldn't sleep. She tried to eat, but the very thought of food revolted her. On and off she cried, day and night.

After dropping the money at Circus Circus, Mike drove straight home, where he and Kit waited for some sign that the $75,000 had been picked up and Jasper would be dropped off.

But then a glitch occurred—on the kidnapper's end—that threatened the whole deal.

Mike had delivered the ransom to the locker, mid-morning on Wednesday. But Jolene got caught up at work, plus she wanted to prolong the agony of a missing baby for her ex as long as possible. So she didn't pick up the money till Friday afternoon.

In her black lace shorts, pink tank top, and leopard-print sandals, she then sped to Indian Springs to divvy up the cash with Tammy, pick up the kid, and return to Vegas for her 10 PM show.

But problems arose big time in Indian Springs when Jolene barged in her sister's door, and an uppity Tammy got in her face.

"Where've you been, girl? I've left a ton of messages the past three days," she howled. "The kid's driving me bat shit crazy! I wanted you to come out here and get him. Why didn't you call me back?"

"Sorry you're pissed, Tam. I've been busy with rehearsals and shows," Jolene explained in the dingy hallway. "But I'm here now and I've got the ransom money, so let's rock on and seal the deal."

"Seal what deal?" Tammy ranted, throwing her hands up. "Your stupid-ass deal sucks! I've been watching the kid for three-and-a-half days. It's been a shit-show of dirty bottles, stinky diapers, and baby food thrown all over my kitchen. He screams at night and cries all day. I've barely slept in days. Meanwhile, you're off in Vegas getting facials and manicures and shaking your little booty for all those perverts at Luxor. Not fair any way you cut it, Jo. So bottom line, I get $40,000 of the ransom, you get the rest."

"What the fuck?" Jolene snapped, setting a cold Mountain Dew on a table heaped with unopened boxes. "I'm the one who put my ass on the line, took the kid from Mike's condo, and drove him out here. You get half, I get half. Now where is he? I've got to get back to Vegas for my show at 10."

"Sorry, Jo," Tammy countered. "I know you're used to getting your way. But this time big sis is calling the shots. I'll take $40,000, you get $35,000."

"Tammy, you've always been six sandwiches short of a picnic, but this time you've gone too far. We'll divvy up the ransom 50/50. Now hand over the kid!" Jolene demanded.

"Give me my $40,000 and I'll turn him over," Tammy countered.

"Ain't gonna happen," Jolene doubled down. Then she took off, rampaging through the house, searching for the baby. But there was no sign of him.

The panicky showgirl then bolted out to the backyard. In the 105-degree heat, she searched Tammy's car and a hulking dumpster at the edge of the yard, next to a putrid tool shack. When she heard Granby barking wildly near the wood shed, she suddenly remembered that Tammy had always hidden there as a child when she was sulking over something.

Jolene ran to the shed, with Tammy at her heels trying to stop her. In the tiny cabin, the kidnapped baby was wailing as Granby barked loudly and clawed at the door. The sisters struggled in the underbrush, shoving and scratching at each other. But Jolene was finally able to knock Tammy to the ground, unlatch the door, and wrench it open. There the tow-headed tot lay, screaming and flailing in his soiled lounger, perched atop a stack of rotting firewood.

Grabbing the plastic handle, Jolene turned and darted back through the barren, brown yard. Close behind was Tammy, still demanding her $40,000. At Jolene's car, the irate, frightened baby alternately cried and whimpered as she set his lounger down for a moment and turned to face Tammy.

"For being a greedy bitch and trying to out-ransom me, you get $25,000, I get $50,000," she barked. "Take it or leave it."

"I'm leaving it!" Tammy hollered, stomping her foot. "If you don't fork over at least half the $75,000, I'm calling the Vegas cops tomorrow and telling them you kidnapped Mike Prescott's kid."

Jolene was livid.

"And I'll tell them you were an accessory!" she fired back. "I brought you into this deal because I thought you could use the extra cash, and I wanted us to do something fun together as sisters. Now you're threatening to turn me in to the cops? That's so fucked up.

"You can have $30,000, bitch, but I'll never cut you in on another deal. As business partners, we're finished, done, over."

"Yeah, yeah, whatever, Jolene. I'll take it in hundreds," Tammy said, smirking.

After anchoring the baby lounger in the passenger seat of her car, Jolene went to her trunk. Jerking it open, she grabbed the leather bag and counted out Tammy's cut.

"Here," she hissed, tossing packs of $100 bills at Tammy that bounced off her and landed in the dirt.

Then Jolene hopped in her car. Beside her, the baby was crying, sobbing really. If this kept up, she'd never make the 45 miles back to Vegas. She needed to fix him a bottle, and she needed to do it now. Locking him in the car, she ran inside. After finding the mommy tote—hidden in the oven, of all places—she fished out a bottle and dumped some milk in it. Slinging the tote over her shoulder, she grabbed a heart-shaped box of chocolates and a cold Mountain Dew from the fridge and raced out to her car.

A frazzled Jolene propped the bottle in the baby's plump white arms. Grasping it, he began sucking hungrily and quieted down. Then she started the car.

"Lowlife, kidnapping whore!" Tammy taunted over and over as Jolene revved the engine.

"Run inside and binge-watch Jerry Springer," little 'sis yelled, powering her window down. "I have to get back to the real world."

Jerking the car in reverse, Jolene floored it. In a torrent of thick desert dust, she backed out of the driveway and skidded onto Horsetail Road. Down I-95 she tore, back to Vegas.

By 7:30, she and the baby were hustling into her flat. After a diaper change, she quickly spooned some pureed chicken breast, green beans, and vanilla pudding into him. Then she filled his bottle with Half and Half and set it in his outstretched white arms. After turning on a night light and a noise machine that mimicked soft ocean waves, she left.

With the baby sleeping alone in the living room of her downtown Vegas apartment, Jolene rushed to the Strip to do warm-up exercises at Luxor before her 10 PM Bitch Goddesses' show. There was a cast party at the Cat House afterwards that she had to attend.

By 6 AM, she was dragging her tired ass through the door of her apartment to retrieve a still-dozing Jasper.

An hour later, as Mike and Kit lapsed in and out of a fitful sleep that balmy Saturday morning, Mike's cell rang.

"Money received," the voice-disguised caller stated. "The kid is on your doorstep."

There was a click, and then stark silence.

Racing to the door, Mike and Kit ripped it open. There, huddled in his lounger in a dirty white onesie with blue bunnies on it, was Jasper! Dropping his bottle, he emitted a small yelp of happiness when he saw his parents.

They quickly pulled the lounger inside. Kit picked her baby up, held him in her arms, and covered his plump face with kisses. Standing beside her was a beaming Mike. Between them, the two held Jasper and cried with joy. Then Mike made pancakes, and they all took a nap.

That afternoon, a still shaken Kit drove Jasper back home to their apartment on Lantana Street. She was due at the Kitty Kat Lounge that night, and Mrs. Brambles had returned from Winnemucca, so everything appeared normal, at least on the surface.

In her car, Kit felt nervous being away from Mike for the first time in days. She was grateful that the two of them had grown closer, as co-parents and friends, during the kidnapping. But she was also furious that it had happened in the first place, and totally blamed her womanizer ex.

Neither Mike nor Kit ever said a word to anyone about what had happened. They were both too scared and too traumatized, and they didn't want the kidnapping to become public. They just wanted to put it behind them, and somehow move forward.

As for the Fisher sisters, at the end of the day they got away with this atrocious crime. Taking the money and running, Jolene made a down payment on a luxury condo in Summerlin, and moved on with another guy. And Tammy adopted a slew of abused and abandoned animals, and had small homes and pens built for them on her property. She also made a hefty donation to the local animal shelter.

It took a while for life to return to normal for Mike and Kit. As soon as he could, Mike got his locks changed, and both parents vowed to watch over their son more closely. But the thought that the kidnapper was still out there somewhere, lurking around, made them both nervous. What they dreaded most was that he or she would take Jasper again and demand more money.

Kit tried to not worry about it, but it wasn't easy. Having a baby with Mike Prescott, son of Senator Bill Prescott of Nevada, turned out to be a lot more difficult and complicated than she ever could have imagined.

CHAPTER NINE

It finally happened. Mike got a last-minute cancellation on one of his Grand Canyon tour flights, and called Kit to offer her the seat.

Early the next morning, in jeans, a teal V-neck top, and a blue velvet jacket, she drove to the Heli-Vegas building on the south end of the Strip. It was already 75 degrees that mid-October Tuesday. After parking her silver Chevy Malibu in the lot, she trekked to Mike's office. Over coffee and pastry, the two chatted about Jasper, who was safely ensconced with Mrs. Brambles, and the day ahead. This would be Kit's first visit to the Canyon, and she was stoked.

At 8:30, with Mike at the controls, five passengers—two just-married couples in afterglow, plus Kit—took off from the helipad. Rotors like thin, noisy dragonfly wings lifted the green-and-yellow striped chopper up, up and away into the gossamer blue sky. At an altitude of 12,500 feet, it churned forward briskly at 160 mph.

After a chilly, 90-minute flight through skies dotted with pale gray clouds, they landed at Grand Canyon Village Airport. When they could finally tear themselves away from the jaw-dropping views, they headed to El Tovar, a ruggedly handsome hotel modeled after a European hunting lodge. Between forkfuls of big, puffy John Wayne omelets (one or two of his movies were filmed nearby) in the sprawling but rustic dining room, they ventured out to the deck to gaze a mile deep into the stunningly beautiful Grand Canyon.

Stretching before them for hundreds of miles were 17 million years' worth of layered limestone, sandstone, granite, and shale. A visual feast compressed into grayish-green, beige, and copper-colored canyons, pyramids, plateaus, and peaks. Majestic splendor beckoning in every direction.

Amped up by the food and scenery, the group hiked down Bright Angel Trail towards the bottom of the Canyon. At some point, one of the new brides sidled over to Kit and asked if she and Mike were dating.

"Um, no, not really," Kit shrugged. And then, after a brief pause, she added, "We're friendly exes co-parenting an adorable son."

"Oh, that's nice," the petite brunette, in a burgundy tunic and khakis, replied politely. She seemed perplexed, but let it go. Momentarily shifting her eyes from the colorful barrage of canyon surrounding them, Kit checked out the sparkling princess-cut diamond on her tour-mate's finger. It had to be at least two carats. She suddenly felt wistful, sad, and even a bit envious. Maybe there was something to be said for going the traditional route.

Later, over tacos and tuna melts at El Tovar, the group listened attentively as tour-guide Mike revealed his vast knowledge of the canyon, and threw in some colorful anecdotes just for fun. Then they snapped more photos and took another, less strenuous hike. By the time everyone reboarded the chopper, a magnificent sunset was underway.

The flight back to the Strip was smooth and flawless. While everyone gazed out the windows, riveted, Kit's eyes were trained on dashing heli-pilot Mike. She was impressed with his flying skills—and him—and glad she had come on this day-long outing.

Back on the Strip, the night was young, so Mike and Kit piled into his black Lexus and drove to Paris. Making their way to the center of the casino, they took the glass elevator to the elegant, romantic Eiffel Tower restaurant on the 11th floor. While taking in panoramic views of the Vegas Valley and Bellagio fountain show, the former lovers dined on filet mignon prepared by a chef from Provence, and sipped a rich Bordeaux that had been flown in from Paris.

The mood was light and flirty as Mike and Kit chatted about the day, and their lives. At one point Jasper's kidnapping, three months before, came up. Both of them shuddered, and then quickly moved on to something more pleasant.

Afterwards, Mike had one thing on his mind, and it wasn't after-dinner drinks at Drai's.

"You look so beautiful," he whispered in Kit's ear as they sat close in the front seat of his car. "Why don't you come back to my place and spend the night? We haven't been together in over a year. Let's see if the magic is still there. I think about you all the time, and miss what we had. I can't make any promises, but tonight will rock your world!"

Kit took a deep breath and gazed at the blond, green-eyed dreamboat decked out in jeans, a black knit shirt, and a leather flight jacket. Sitting close to him, drawing in the mingled scent of leather and after-shave, she felt turned on. But she was also uncertain.

"How can I trust you?" she asked, tossing her hands up. "A couple of your girlfriends called today while we were at the canyon. You're a classic chick magnet. I can't handle all that competition."

"What competition? You don't have any competition," Mike cracked. "You're in a league all your own, sweetheart. Forget them. I certainly have!"

Pulling her close, he kissed her sweetly, then more deeply. It got very intense fast. She was panting, her knees were weak, her stomach lurching like she was on a roller coaster. It felt good, but bad, but good. When she could finally think straight, she reached for her purse.

"Let me call Mrs. Brambles," she whispered.

Mike knew the drill.

"Sure, babe, go ahead," he said softly.

The matronly grandma picked up on the third ring and told Kit that Jasper was already asleep that tranquil Tuesday night. There was no problem letting him stay till the next morning.

And so, to Mike's condo they sped through the inky, black night. Staring over at him in the driver's seat, Kit felt warm, safe, and breathless with excitement. She spent that night wrapped in Mike's arms, making love amid passionate sighs, just like the old days. No commitments, but the sex was hot.

The next morning, Mike was already in the shower when Kit woke up. Wandering into the steam-filled bathroom, she joined him for some soapy fun and games. Then she dried her long blond locks and redressed in her jeans and teal V-neck top. In Mike's cozy, sky-blue breakfast nook, they tucked into the house special: scrambled eggs and toast, with freshly squeezed OJ and coffee.

"I should go pick up Jasper," a concerned Kit suddenly said, taking a final sip of coffee and setting a slice of toast on her plate. "He must be wondering where I am."

"Love that pint-size dude! Wish I were going with you," Mike chirped. "But it's cool. I have to go to work. We have six tours scheduled for today, two this morning for Bryce Canyon, and four, later, for the Grand Canyon.

"Come on, baby mama, I'll drive you back to Heli-Vegas, so you can get your car."

"Cool, baby daddy," Kit laughed, nuzzling him and reaching for his hand as they strolled out of his condo.

CHAPTER TEN

That mid-week morning, Kit drove home from Heli-Vegas on cloud 9. She couldn't believe she had spent the night making love with Mike and sleeping beside him. It brought back lusty, romantic memories of their affair in the summer of 2014.

Still, this was the same guy who was in bed with some tramp while Kit was giving birth to their son—and sleeping with another slut while a kidnapper took Jasper from the next room. Kit strongly suspected the culprit had been an enraged ex of Mike's, which made the whole nightmare even more agonizing and appalling.

Despite all of the above, she tried to remain in afterglow and savor these happy, magical hours. But her troubling backstory with Mike continued to haunt her. Was having sex with him the best thing she could have done, and also the worst? Did it mean the same thing to both of them? How could she trust him after all he had done?

Kit was elated and excited, but full of questions and concerns as she pressed the doorbell at Mrs. Brambles'. While making polite chit-chat with the plump, white-haired widow, she gathered up Jasper and all his things.

Back in their cozy flat, two floors up, Kit laid the 18-month-old in his crib, then headed to the kitchen to make coffee and think things through.

It was all about Mike, of course. Should she try to get back together with him? Were they back together already, or was last night just casual sex for him? Kit honestly didn't know. She only knew there was a third person involved here: Jasper. He had a right to have a relationship with his father. He'd had Danny for the first six months of his life, then Danny went to prison. He'd been gone for a year now, and would be back soon. But whether or not Danny would still want to have a relationship with Kit and Jasper was anyone's guess. Maybe lock-up would change him and make him want to turn away from everything, and everyone, associated with his pre-prison life? Maybe he would want to move out of Vegas and make a fresh start somewhere else?

As Jasper's father, Mike was the one Kit felt she should try to have a relationship with. She had to give Mike another chance in the hopes it would get them back together, and the three of them could be a family. Maybe they could even give Jasper a sibling or two down the road. If their future babies turned out anything like him, that would be amazing.

Kit briefly fantasized about a wedding with the senator's dynamic, dreamboat son. Would it be a large, lavish affair covered by all the papers? How would his parents react to meeting her? And how would they take the news that they had a grandson?

Kit didn't have a clue. Maybe the Prescotts would embrace Jasper and make him part of their lives. Or maybe they would be ashamed of him, since he was born out of wedlock to a lowly blackjack dealer at Caesar's, and choose to ignore him. Maybe they would turn their backs on Kit, too. Maybe her marrying Mike would cause a rift, and create a dividing line of Prescott family members for, and against, it.

A worst-case scenario, for sure. But why get all carried away with negative thoughts? Kit knew that would get her nowhere. She needed to keep an open mind and take things one step at a time. First, think in terms of having a great love affair with the man of her dreams, handsome, successful heli-pilot Mike, and then get to the finish line and worry about the details.

Again, Kit's mind drifted to romantic fantasies of marrying Mike. What would their wedding be like, she wondered? Surely his parents would pay for everything, and invite all their high-society friends. And Kit would squeeze in a few guests of her own: some Kitty Kat Babe cohorts, perhaps, and a couple of close friends from Indiana, like Justin and Rainey. No family, of course. There was none. Just Jasper. Jasper was Kit's everything. That's why marriage to Mike would solve all her problems and make the pieces fall into place. She wanted more babies, a big family of her own. How long would she have to wait?

Kit's mind was reeling with images of white lace gowns, multi-tiered cakes, and lush, velvet-ribboned bouquets of lilies of the valley with ivory-colored roses. But she was getting way ahead of herself. Thirty-three-year-old, twice-divorced Mike Prescott was in no way, shape, or form, marriage material. He may have had multiple orgasms with Kit the night before, and enjoyed every minute, but he had no intention of getting back together with her, let alone marrying her. He was having way too much fun playing the field. Dinner and sex with Kit once in a while would be sufficient. He didn't need the rest.

After their dreamy day and night, Kit waited and waited to hear from Mike. She so wanted to pick up the phone and dial his cell. But she couldn't do it. He would perceive her as a desperate baby mama who needed him too much. And then he would feel trapped and try to distance himself. That would hurt Kit, and Jasper, too.

So Kit sat tight and held on. She got up every day, worked out, took care of the baby, shopped for diapers, formula, and food, and went to work, all the while waiting, waiting, waiting.

Finally, three weeks later, the call came. Mike was upbeat and casual. He wanted to know when he could stop by to see Jasper.

Kit suggested Tuesday, her day off, the following week, and he agreed.

That day he arrived, suave and strapping as always, and wrote a check for baby expenses. Scooping Jasper up, he bounced him on his broad shoulders. The baby giggled, and Mike beamed. Eventually Mike and Kit loaded Jasper into his high chair and fed him jars of pureed turkey and butternut squash, and then put the roly-poly chatter-box down for a nap.

In the hallway of Kit's apartment, her smile faded as she faced Mike down.

"Where do things stand between us?" she asked, tossing her hands up.

"What things?" Mike shot back.

"Um, we slept together three weeks ago, didn't we? And I didn't hear from you till you called to schedule a visit with Jasper. Now you're here, and it's all about him. What about me?"

"What about you?" Mike asked, staring at her, perplexed and annoyed.

"Do we have some kind of relationship, or not? I'm confused. Are we back together?" she asked.

"Well, babe, if you have to ask that question, the answer's pretty obvious," a cruel, cavalier Mike chuckled. "Sorry if you're under the impression we're back together because we went to the Grand Canyon and spent the night at my condo afterwards.

"I think I've made it crystal clear over the past year: I'm 33 and I've been through two marriages that went bust. I don't want any kind of commitment or relationship holding me down. I want to be free to have lots of experiences with lots of different girls."

"And I'm just one of the many?" Kit shot back, hurt and outraged.

"That's kind of blunt," he retorted. "You're my baby mama, so that makes you special. I value our friendship, and if it veers into a sexual thing once in a while, well, we're both adults and we can handle it. Why turn it into something it isn't? That kind of deception and delusion will hurt both of us, and Jasper, too.

"Let's keep things casual, and see where it goes. We can get together once in a while and enjoy each other, but that doesn't mean we can't spend time with other people and enjoy them, too."

"How many others have you enjoyed over the past three weeks?" Kit demanded, her temper boiling. "I need to know what kind of numbers we're talking here."

"Oh, come on, Kit," the buff heli-pilot sneered, rolling his eyes. "Do you really expect me to get that specific with you? That's ridiculous, so high school. What difference does it make? A few, a half-dozen, a dozen, one a day. What the hell, I don't know. Let's just say there've been more than a few, and less than a dozen."

"Get out," Kit told him. "Get out now. We won't be sleeping together again. Let's just keep it at co-parenting Jasper. You're an asshole. No woman should have to put up with this kind of shit."

"Oh, I think quite a few are happy with the terms I offer: good times, great sex, no strings or complications, and no annoying confrontations like this. Just endless fun and pleasure."

At that moment, Kit finally realized she wasn't in Kokomo anymore.

"Mike, get out and leave me alone," she ordered, pointing at the door. "I wish I had never gone to the Grand Canyon with you. I wish we had never had dinner at Eiffel Tower, or spent the night at your condo.

"Call me the next time you want to see Jasper and drop off a check, okay? Now, go. The baby's asleep, and if we start screaming and yelling it'll wake him up. He gets very cranky."

"If you change your mind, let me know," Mike said, heading for the door. "Don't burn any bridges, babe."

"Hand me the matches, Mike," Kit hissed. "Now get out and leave me alone!"

She opened the door, and out he went.

Then she fell on the couch and cried her eyes out for being such a fool and sleeping with him, and then coming home and having all those ridiculous fantasies of a storybook wedding, and life, with him. What an idiot, she thought, as she burst into another round of tears.

The saddest part, of course, was that Kit truly loved Mike. She was wildly attracted to him, and liked and admired him as a person. But what an asshole.

They say that time heals all wounds. Well, sort of. The pain over Mike stayed with Kit for a long time. Her childhood had been a sad patchwork quilt of love, rejection, and confusion. She desperately wanted to grow up and find the kind of romance, stability, and joy she had read about in fairy tales. But so far, it had eluded her.

At least she had Jasper. He was the light of her life. She wished she could just tell Mike to go to hell and never see him again. But with Jasper in their lives, that was impossible. For now, at least, she could avoid Mike and have Mrs. Brambles preside over his monthly visits instead of her. And the checks could be mailed, or deposited directly into her bank account. Kit would figure out a way to deal with it.

Still, the pain and sadness lingered. Yes, Kit was beautiful, and many men desired her. But she wanted Mike, the father of her baby. She longed for the family life she had never known as a child. That was the way it was, and nothing could change it.

The persistent glumness over Mike lifted a bit during the holidays. Watching Jasper's excitement as he celebrated his second Christmas was a feast of warm and fuzzy moments for Kit.

In mid-December 2016, she sauntered into Bonnie Potter's house in North Las Vegas with an armful of presents for her and Danny's younger brothers. As they sat on the couch sipping eggnog near the tinsel-drenched tree, Kit asked how Danny was doing in prison.

"As well as can be expected," Bonnie sighed, looking around, embarrassed and flustered. "He has a few odd jobs, like making leather wallets, cleaning the rec center, and chopping veggies for the chow hall. But he's bored out of his mind, and lonely, too. He has a few friends, but you can't trust anyone in there. It's pretty rough, and the food is nasty. Danny complains constantly about the Spam, fake eggs, baloney, and stale bread.

"I cook his favorite dishes sometimes, and take them up there. But the guards do aggressive pat downs on the pot roast—and me. I get upset because my other two boys are standing there, watching, and they don't like what's going on. If Danny knew, he'd have a fit. They call it the Nevada Regional Corrections' Center. So when does the corrections' part kick in? Just sayin'.

"But back to you, Kit. Danny asks about you every visit. He's counting the days and nights till he gets released. I just hope he's learned his lesson and will never go back."

Kit nodded.

"Jasper and I both miss him," she said wistfully. "Do you think Danny will still live in Vegas when he gets out?"

"It's hard to say, sweetheart, but I think so," the attractive, fiftyish blonde replied. "Here's hoping he'll be sitting here with us next Christmas."

Both ladies raised their glasses to that.

CHAPTER ELEVEN

Who wants to stand behind a blackjack table, 40 hours a week, smiling and looking sexy in a skimpy costume and four-inch heels, while dealing cards and stacking chips?

Nobody.

Life as a Kitty Kat Babe was often a grand and glorious grind. But the work was steady, the tips rocked, and the girls all kind of got along, so Kit hung in there.

And then, in April 2017, there was a wonderful surprise. As Kit stood poised in her sequins and stilettos, artfully shuffling a deck of cards, she looked up and saw a familiar face across the table.

Danny Potter was back in town!

Just the dude she needed to see.

Kit's heart leapt and then turned soft and marshmallowy. For a few seconds, she just stood there, frozen in place with the cards in her hands as the whole casino seemed to come to a standstill.

The former porch pirate, who'd been released the day before, had bulked up a bit in the pen, but still looked trim and buff In jeans and a black V-neck sweater. A suave contrast to the navy-blue sweat suit and knit cap he'd worn two years before while stealing Jasper's crib.

With his baby blues drinking in every inch of Kit, a warm, sweet smile crept across Danny's face. In her peacock-blue sequin bikini and silver bustier, she oozed glamour and sex appeal. Re-calling the baggy denim jumper she'd worn over her huge belly the day they met, and how limp and greasy her dishwater-blond hair had been, Danny couldn't help thinking: you've come a long way, babe.

"Hey, Kit," he called out, tilting his head flirtatiously, "I'm back, and you're looking hotter than ever!"

"Oh, thanks," she purred, laughing softly while glancing around at her four players, who were suddenly all ears.

"You're looking pretty amazing, too," she managed to reply in a high, thin voice. "Are you playing at my table?"

"Yeah, hit me," Danny cracked.

With her heart fluttering, Kit dealt the cards and the game began.

Who knew Danny was such a good player?

As the stacks of chips in front of him grew taller, Kit glanced over and saw a pair of pristine, tanned arms encircling his waist from behind. Danny spun around, and a twenty-something brunette with long, gleaming brown hair and dark, flashing eyes, was smiling up at him. Laughing, he put his arm around her and pulled her close.

"Kit, this is my friend, Tina," he said casually from across the table, "we're taking off in a few, okay?"

"Cool, I'll deal you out," Kit nodded.

As she stared at the striking young girl in black jeans and a low-cut, red-beaded top, her heart sank. Was this awkward scene the reunion she had been looking forward to for 18 months?

As Danny gathered his chips, Kit piped up, "Um, I'm having a birthday party for Jasper at two o'clock on Saturday. Just some friends, and a bunch of toddlers. If you want to stop by, we'd love to have you. You know where we live."

"Cool, I'll be there. Can't wait to see the little man," Danny shot back, wrapping his arm around Tina. Kit couldn't help staring as the duo turned and wove their way through the crowded casino. Noticing how distracted their dealer was, her players were becoming annoyed. It was time for Kit to get her mind back on the game, pronto.

When her shift ended, Kit lingered in the Kitty Kat dressing room, moping over Danny. He'd come back from prison after 18 months, and shown up at the Kitty Kat Lounge—with a date of all things. A pretty chick who was obviously into him. What the hell?

Kit was happy he was back, but why was she so glum about the other girl? There were lots of reasons. It was a delicate time for her, with all the Mike issues, the constant hassles of her married boss threatening to fire her if she didn't sleep with him, and the customers hitting on her every night. Kit felt lonely, but under siege. She couldn't wait till Saturday. She was hoping Danny would show up, and they could talk and laugh like the old days. She was hoping he'd be happy to see Jasper, and that Jasper would remember this dude whose name was on his birth certificate, and who was like a dad to him his first six months.

Saturday finally arrived. It was a typical April day in the desert: 85 degrees and sunny. Kit wanted Jasper's second birthday to be a rollicking romp because he was at the age where it would make a real impression. So she traipsed to the party store for silly balloons and hats, and drove to the High Roller Bakery to pick up a large, yellow sheet cake with white icing and Happy Birthday, Jasper, scrawled across it in blue frosting. Lodged in the center were two tall, thick candles for the birthday-boy to blow out.

By 2 PM, a handful of Kitty Kat babes had arrived with their amped-up toddlers. Everyone brought presents wrapped in festive paper. Mrs. Brambles even showed up with her three rambunctious grandsons, Frank, Dean, and Sammy.

Around 3 PM the doorbell rang, and in sauntered Danny with a lime-green dinosaur glider-toy that had orange and yellow rocks painted on it. Squealing with delight, Jasper hugged Danny and made a beeline for the irresistible new toy. After tearing a big blue bow off, he climbed all over it. A smiling, indulgent Kit grabbed her camera and started snapping.

For three chaotic hours, the rowdy party galloped on. And then, one by one, all the guests departed, except Danny, who'd co-hosted with Kit. As for the birthday boy, after too much cake, too many presents, and too much excitement, he'd had a meltdown around 4:30. Kit finally calmed him down, carried him to her room, and nestled him in his crib. Within seconds, he was out.

Closing the door quietly, Kit tip-toed back to the living room, where Danny was picking party hats and punctured balloons off the carpet. As she thanked him for his help, he plopped down on the couch, and Kit did the same.

"How 'bout a glass of wine?" she asked, taking a deep breath.

"Hit me," Danny told her.

Kit returned from the kitchen with two glasses of Chablis, and they both kicked back and took a sip.

"Nice party, awesome cake. We didn't get stuff like that in lock-up. On your birthday, you were lucky if you got a stale cupcake from the commissary," Danny cracked, removing his glittery party hat and setting it on the coffee table. He was dressed in leather boots, jeans, and a cobalt-blue shirt that brought out his eyes.

And then, changing the subject, he added, "Jasper's a really cool kid, you've done a great job with him."

"Thanks," Kit murmured, smiling. "Best thing that ever happened to me. But it hasn't been all stuffed animals and vanilla pudding. There's been some dark stuff, too."

"Oh, yeah, like what?" Danny asked, tilting his head and gazing at her.

Kit hesitated.

"I don't know if I should get into this or not," she said softly. "I try to not think about it, but last summer Jasper was kidnapped from Mike's condo. I had left him there for four days so I could go to L.A. to do some commercials for Caesar's.

"Mike was in bed with one of his slut-mates, and sometime in the middle of the night, someone broke in and took Jasper from the living room, where he was sleeping.

"The next day, they called Mike and demanded $75,000 ransom. He paid it, thank God, and we got Jasper back. Those three days were a nightmare for all of us."

"That is so bizarre," Danny said, shaking his head. "Do you have any idea who took him?"

"Not really," Kit replied, "but I would double down on a royal match that it was an ex-girlfriend of Mike's. When I told him that's what I thought, he totally blew it off. But he's dated lots of badass showgirls, and sometimes gives them keys to his condo. After a few weeks, he usually gets bored and moves on without saying a word. Most of them go quietly, but some get really pissed and want revenge. I think that's what went down."

"Makes sense," Danny nodded. "But nothing has happened since then, right?"

"Right," Kit nodded. "I sure as hell don't leave Jasper with Mike, and I really watch over him. But it's been a scary time.

"The kidnapping was so draining," she went on. "I didn't sleep for a week. Jasper seemed okay, like he didn't know anything was wrong. But I'm sure it affected him. He was only 15 months at the time."

"Poor kid," Danny said, shaking his head. "Your baby daddy is a real piece of work. Sounds like it was his fault, one-hundred percent. What a douche-bag. He can't blame you in any way. You've been a poster-child for perfect momhood from day one," Danny reassured her.

"Thanks, you're sweet. I agree, baby daddy is the culprit," Kit affirmed, laughing softly.

It was a sound Danny loved, and she looked so pretty, all aglow in a short, blue-eyelet sundress and silver-leather sandals, with her golden locks tumbling loosely over her shoulders. He didn't think it was possible, but Kit looked even more beautiful than before he'd left for prison.

"I think we could both use some more wine," she said, getting up and heading for the kitchen.

Back in the living room, she poured refills for both of them and set the bottle on the coffee table. It was covered with a mess of crumpled wrapping paper, bows, and plastic plates and forks smeared with cake frosting.

Ignoring the disarray, Danny sipped his Chablis and turned to Kit.

"Speaking of your ex," he said, "I thought he'd be here today."

"Um, no, I think he's partying in Mexico with one of his girlfriends," Kit told him with a dismissive flick of the wrist. "I can't keep track. Was it Sheena, Tiffany, or Tabitha? Or maybe all three? I try to stay out of Mike's love life."

"What about your love life?" Danny inquired with a cute smile. "How's that going?"

Kit took a deep breath. She felt shy and awkward, but what the hell? She was going to go for it and spill the truth, more or less.

"Not so great," she admitted, tossing her hands up. "My married boss is all over me, and it's getting kind of scary. I hope he doesn't fire me for not sleeping with him. Plus there are a lot of guys coming on to me because they're turned on by my job, costume, and stilettos. None of them give a damn about me as a person. They just want to have sex with a Kitty Kat Babe, so they can tell their raunchy, disgusting friends, and then dump me and move on to someone else. It's kind of a hard gig to meet someone in. True love doesn't happen very often for Kitty Kat Babes."

"Sorry to hear that, but I'm glad you don't have a boyfriend. I've missed you," Danny confessed. "The days in lock-up were long, the nights even longer. It was a nonstop shit-show of horrible food, deranged guards and inmates, bullshit jobs, and being treated like an animal that doesn't deserve happiness or respect or anything good. What can I say?"

"Oh, Danny, I'm sorry you went through all that. I would have come to visit, but your mom told me you didn't want me there."

"That's right," Danny admitted. "I didn't want to see your pretty face on the other side of that Plexiglass. It would have been grim, plus the guards would have gone all horndog and tried to hit on you. I didn't want to put you through that."

Nodding, Kit took another sip of wine. After a brief pause, Danny went on.

"I guess I totally fucked up with the porch pirating," he conceded, shaking his head. "I'm sorry it all went down the way it did in Green Valley. Eighteen-months in a medium-security prison was a high price to pay. It sucked big time, but I learned my lesson."

"No more porch pirating for you?" Kit asked.

"No more pirating for me," Danny agreed. "That's all in the past. I'm going in a different direction now, with a real job."

"Really?" Kit said excitedly. "Where? Doing what?"

"Sin City Skydiving, over on Industrial Road," he replied with a smile. "I went to high school with the owner. He always told me there'd be a job waiting if I wanted one. I'm going to manage 25 people. Should be interesting. Taken any indoor skydives lately?"

Kit laughed.

"Um, no, can't say I have. But I have a feeling that's all about to change. When do you start?"

"Next week," Danny said. "I was over there today. It's really cool. You're good to go anytime for a comp dive."

"I'm afraid of heights," Kit chuckled. "How high do you jump from?"

"Sixty feet," Danny replied, "in a 120 mph wind tunnel. Ass-kicking stuff, like you're in free fall. Jasper would love it, but they don't allow kids under three. The whole scene rocks. Come by sometime and I'll show you around."

"I'll think about it," Kit answered coyly, taking another sip of wine.

"But maybe there are other adventures we could explore right here," Danny teased, staring at her. "I told you I missed you, but you never said you missed me. Did you?"

What a flirt, Kit thought.

"Yeah, Danny, a lot. You're one in a million. From porch pirate to prison to indoor skydiving. You're one badass dude!"

They both laughed.

Seizing the moment, Kit asked, "So, who was that girl you were with the other night? She seemed really into you."

"Oh, that was Tina Morrissey, my friend Cruz's little sister. I've known her all my life. We used to be tight, but now we're just friends—without benefits."

"It looked like more than that," Kit remarked, tilting her head.

"Well, it isn't," Danny countered. "She was just glad to see me out of lock-up and back on the Strip. She's a dancer in the Dirty Dolls show at Bally's. There are plenty of dudes panting after her. I'm just another big brother. I'm close to the whole family. You'll have to meet Cruz sometime."

"Your mom told me a little about him," Kit chirped. "She said he's been a bad influence on you since kindergarten."

"Oh, you know Mom. Everyone's a bad influence on me. That's just the way she rolls."

They both laughed lightly, sipped more wine, and set their glasses down. Turning to each other, Danny reached for Kit's hand. After slowly kissing it, he did the same to her mouth, but more fully, softly, and deeply. A sense of warmth, joy, and excitement overtook them both. And why not? It was late on a Saturday afternoon, a cool jazz tape was playing, and outside a spring rain was falling. Glad to be in each other's lives again, the two snuggled on the couch and got closer.

CHAPTER TWELVE

And just like that, the friendship between Danny and Kit blossomed into a romance.

They had always liked each other, and then they were forced apart for 18 months. Now they were back together and hellbent on making up for lost time.

It wasn't easy. Kit worked from 10 PM to 7 AM; Danny, from 10 AM to 6 PM. So, they were on opposite ends of the clock. But that didn't stop them. A few nights a week, Danny would show up at Caesar's around 7 PM to take Kit to dinner at Spago before her shift. As they munched on pizza or pasta, they would chat about Danny's adventures that day at the skydiving emporium. It was refreshing to spend time alone, away from Jasper, who tended to whine a lot and demand all of Kit's attention.

Both of them arranged their schedules so they would have Tuesdays and Wednesdays off. On those days, while Mrs. Brambles watched Jasper, Danny and Kit would indulge in the kind of fun, touristy activities they'd missed out on over the years. It was an endless merry-go-round of mostly outdoorsy stuff, which they both craved since they'd spent so much time recently in a casino, a prison, or taking care of a baby.

Off they'd go for hiking or horseback-riding in Red Rock Canyon, kayaking on the Colorado River, hot-air ballooning over the Mojave, or zip-lining across downtown Vegas. They also caught every Cirque du Soleil show, and chowed down in top-rate eateries on the Strip. French, Italian, Mexican, you name it, they ate it. After the horrors of prison food, Danny couldn't get enough, and ditto for Kit on her own home cooking.

There was lots of hand-holding under the table, and kissing over it, as Danny and Kit fell head over heels for Vegas—and each other.

It was the maiden voyage for both. Kit had never experienced a great love. Her infatuation with Mike had been a hot, joyful affair—until it careened into an unplanned pregnancy just four months in. Back in Kokomo, Kit's high school crushes had been idle fancies that evaporated into thin air, or shattered for the flimsiest of reasons. Ditto for Danny. He'd had his share of silly flings and casual affairs, but nothing serious or long-term. Now things were different, as Cupid took aim with his bow and arrow and pierced through the hearts of both lovebirds.

Falling in love took Danny and Kit by surprise. But why? They should have known something was up the day they met, when Danny wedged eight-months' pregnant Kit into the back seat of his car and whisked her to the hospital. Within minutes they were bantering and bickering, while checking each other out in the rear-view mirror. And then, when they got to the hospital and the orderly asked if Danny was the baby's father, without hesitating, Kit said yes. What was up with that?

More major hints of a cosmic connection: Danny didn't object when he found out Kit had listed him as the father on her baby's birth certificate. And he jumped at the chance to drive her and Jasper home from the hospital. Then he started showing up at her apartment every other week with bags of baby stuff.

Tender feelings had obviously been flickering in the hearts of both since day one. It just took a while, and an 18-month forced separation, for the flicker to erupt into a full-fledged flame.

As she embarked on this slightly ridiculous, but totally essential, affair, Kit felt guilty about leaving Jasper with Mrs. Brambles so much. But the mild-mannered widow didn't mind, as long as her three young grandsons were there anyway. She often told Kit, "No worries, 'hon. It's just one more bottle to warm, one more diaper to change, and one more baby to put down between play sessions at the park."

Still, Kit was nervous about leaving Jasper with anyone after the kidnapping the previous summer. But she totally trusted Mrs. Brambles, and gave her a beeper so that she could contact her at a moment's notice. Kit had also asked Mike for more money on her monthly checks, so she could give Mrs. B a hefty raise.

Speaking of Mike, when he found out Danny was back from prison and Kit was having an affair with him, he went ballistic. The nerve of the guy. He didn't want Kit himself, except as an occasional sex partner and adoring baby mama, but he resented the hell out of her being with someone else.

When Kit knew Mike would be visiting Jasper before work, she made sure Danny hadn't stayed over the night before. She didn't want her new boyfriend anywhere near her apartment when Mike was around. She feared a fight would erupt, and Danny would get into trouble again with the cops.

Of course, when Mike did come by, he and Kit got into fierce arguments over Danny. During one of their most toxic face-offs, Mike bellowed, "I don't want that porch thief anywhere near my son. He just got out of prison. I don't consider him safe."

"He's safer than you!" an outraged Kit yelled.

"The guy was stealing from people," Mike ranted. "What do you think he is, some kind of folk hero or Robin-Hood-dude who steals from the rich and gives to the poor? Hell no, Kit! He's a common crook, a criminal. Why do you think they put him in prison? Who knows if, or when, he'll go back to pirating? You can't trust him."

"Shut up, Mike. It's you I can't trust!"

"But he's the one with the police record, not me," Mike fumed, throwing his hands up.

"Leave me alone!" Kit shouted. "Danny makes me happy. He's had some problems, but that's all in the past. He would never cheat on me the way you did. Who are you to judge him?"

"You're still naïve little Kit from Kokomo, aren't you?" Mike sneered. "Go ahead, make me the bad guy, insult me all you want, and keep seeing him. But if he starts pirating again, it's game over for you two. I'll report him to the cops—and make sure he goes to prison for a lot longer than 18 months this time."

"Mike you're a conceited, self-centered ass," Kit raged. "You're jealous of my relationship with Danny because it's real and pure, something you never had in your life.

"Don't worry, Danny has a good job at Sin City Skydiving," she went on. "He's not stealing anything from anyone. He probably makes more money than you do!"

"I doubt that," Mike replied smugly, rolling his eyes.

And so it went. This fight more or less repeated each time Mike came by. Luckily, he only showed up every few weeks.

CHAPTER THIRTEEN

All through that golden spring and summer of 2017, Danny and Kit's giddy binge of sun, sex, and sparkle throttled on. And why not? They were young, in love, and in Vegas.

On holidays and birthdays, the couple briefly emerged from their intimacy bubble to spend time with Danny's family. They also got to know each other's friends. Danny was dazzled by the talented, badass-glam Kitty Kat Babes. And Kit found his pal-posse interesting, too, but a bit rough around the edges.

Case in point: Cruz Morrissey, a lanky, raven-haired Irish-Mexican dude always in jeans and Harley Davidson tees. Danny and he were both born in 1988, and both had grown up in North Las Vegas, where their bromance stretched all the way back to kindergarten.

But Cruz's influence on Danny went way beyond the sandbox, grade school lunchroom, and Binion's poker pit. He was also the one who'd lured him into porch pirating after he got fired from UPS.

"Bro, you're crazy," Danny had told him one hot summer day in 2012. "I used to deliver this stuff for UPS. Why would I want to rip it off?"

Cruz had nodded vaguely. But the cunning, charming porch bandit knew how to draw his friend in. They ended up pulling off a few scores just for fun, with Cruz grabbing the loot while Danny played getaway driver.

Danny was surprised at what a kick it was. Within weeks, they were pirating full-time, and Danny was making more money than he ever had. Every day was like Christmas for the desperado-dudes.

At some point they started doing solo hits, too. Danny was obviously working alone that April day in 2015 when he spotted the long, bulky box on Kit's small porch. Six months later, he was on his own again when the calamitous bust on Wayne Newton Drive unfolded, landing him in lock-up.

After his release, he'd returned to Vegas and started a lush new life that included a one-of-a-kind love affair with Kit, and an ass-kicking gig at Sin City Skydiving.

But then along came Cruz—again.

Sounding desperate and alarmed, the troubled pirate-thief called Danny four months after his release and issued a come-on.

"Let's hook up at Sinbad's, maybe around midnight," Cruz had said in a low, urgent tone. "I need a favor, something I can't get into over the phone." Of course Danny agreed, even though he didn't have a clue what his friend wanted.

Later that night, the badass buccaneers, in jeans and colorful cotton shirts with snaps instead of buttons, were hunched over a corner table in their macho hang-out at MGM Grand.

"Potter, I totally fucked up," a pale, unshaven Cruz confessed. "I'm in deep shit with the loan sharks. While you were off making license plates at that country club in Carson City, I was playing way too much Texas Hold'em at Binion's. Before I knew it, I was in the hole for $50,000. I thought I could win it back, but no way with these pros. They play dirty, win dirty, cheat dirty, and then threaten dirty.

"They called me today and told me to get them their $50,000 in 30 days, or face the consequences. Meaning they'll kill, or maim, me or my mom, or Tina. That's the way they roll. if they don't get their money, my ass is in a sling."

A feeling of dread cut through Danny as he stared across the table at his scared-shitless, distraught pal. Taking a gulp of cold Sam Adams, he leaned in and asked, "What's the plan, dude? How are you going to get the bread?"

"Best way I can think of is doing big time porch hits like we used to, and then hawking the stuff on the Internet," Cruz told him. "But I can't do it alone. I need my old getaway driver. We can hit all those houses again in Blue Diamond, Henderson, Green Valley, and Summerlin—where the rich folks hang out.

"What the hell else can I do, rob a bank?" he went on, throwing his hands up. "Porch pirating is the only game in town for this kind of cash in 30 days. You'll get a cut, for sure. Can I count you in, Potter? Come on, 'bro, my life is on the line here. I don't want them messing with my mom or sister."

Plopping his mug down, an agitated Danny bowed his head and ran his hands through his thick brown curls.

"Sorry Cruz, no can do," he said softly when he lifted his head and stared across the table. "Kit made me promise my pirating days were over. She would dump me in a New York minute if I got into this game again. You're gonna have to find other talent. There's no way I can risk losing Kit. She rocks my world like no other chick. I just did hard time for burglary and reckless driving. I don't ever want to see the inside of a prison cell again.

"Plus, I scored this cool management gig at the skydiving palace on Industrial Road. They would fire my ass on the spot if I got in trouble again. No dice, Cruz. Deal me out."

"You don't understand!" an angry, desperate Cruz came back, pounding the table. "This is the big leagues of loan sharks. We're talking Marcum brothers here, Otis and Cade. These Mob pricks have connections all over town. They can have my house torched tonight. They can kill me, my mom, or sister, without anyone ever knowing. I can't take a chance like that. I've got to get the money. If you don't help me, how will you live with yourself if something happens to me or my family?"

"Back off, dude!" a flustered Danny said, getting in Cruz's face. "I've only been out four months, and my life is the coolest it's ever been. The last thing I need is this porch pirate shit."

"I hear you, but this is a fucking emergency. It's just for one month," Cruz steamrolled on. "What's the big deal, Potter? We used to do this stuff every day. We were the Butch Cassidy and Sundance Kid of porch pirating. Remember all those big time hits at the marina? There were some huge hauls in Henderson and Spring Valley, too.

"You'll get a cut, 'bro, and the whole time Kit will be prancing around the Kitty Kat Lounge in her shiny blue bikini, dealing blackjack and smiling at all those assholes panting after her. She won't know a thing about what's going down with us. How could she?

"As soon as we hit $50,000, we'll quit and go straight. Call it an early retirement. You have my word."

Closing his eyes, Danny shook his head in agony. The last thing he wanted was to be lured back into the pirating game. But he cared about Cruz, and he knew how rough the Marcum brothers played. So he gulped some more beer and mulled things over.

"Fifty-thousand in thirty days, and then it's over, right?" Danny asked, looking Cruz in the eye.

"You got it, dude, those are the terms," Cruz replied, staring into Danny's bloodshot baby blues.

As a buxom, blond cocktail wench in a glittering gold mini-dress tottered to their table with more beers, an exasperated Danny blurted, "I'll do it," and nodded awkwardly.

"But the hours might be kind of screwy because of the job and Kit, okay? And forget about giving me a cut. You take it all. You need it more.

"In a day or two, maybe we can drive out to case Green Valley," he went on. "The place is wall to wall with mansions, big porches, wide driveways. It's a pirate's dream, or, in my case, nightmare. That's where I got busted two years ago."

"That's all in the past, dude," Cruz said. "It's a new day. No more handcuffs or grungy jail cells for us.

"We'll work Green Valley, but hit Lake Las Vegas and Henderson, too. Those households won't know which end is up. We're gonna do it, dude. We're gonna get the $50,000, pay those fuck-tards off, and then we'll be living high on the hog at Caesar's, chowing down on prime rib and hanging out in the Kitty Kat Lounge with all those hot kitten-pussies. We'll pay the Marcums off, tell them to go fuck themselves, and all live happily ever after."

High-fiving Cruz, Danny chided, "You're a total pain in the ass, 'bro!"

He meant it as a compliment, of course. Gazing across the table, he was marveling at Cruz. Even back at Cheyenne High, he'd had a way with words. But that wouldn't help him now.

As for Danny, he was buoyant on the outside, but cringing on the inside. What had he gotten himself into? And how was he going to keep all this from Kit?

CHAPTER FOURTEEN

Over the next few days, Danny and Cruz pulled off a couple dozen scores. The guys would follow UPS and FedEx trucks, wait for the goods to be delivered, then grab the boxes before anyone could open the front door, or the cleaning lady, milkman, or paper boy showed up.

These early morning grab-and-runs went off without a hitch. And the hauls were lucrative: state-of-the-art air-fryers with all the bells and whistles, deluxe espresso-makers, designer sneakers and watches, computers, high-tech vacuum cleaners, expensive clothes. There were even some luxury jewelry ensembles and shiny new bikes from Italy and Japan.

Within two weeks, the money was rolling in. Before they knew it, the pirate-dudes had stolen, and then re-sold, $20,000 worth of stuff. But that was still far short of the goal.

Then everything changed in a heartbeat one hot summer night, as Kit waited in Danny's car for him to run inside his mom's house to get his phone before they went to dinner.

Leaning over to change a music tape, she accidentally bumped the garage door opener.

Up the heavy door slowly lumbered. Stacked against a wall were dozens of boxes and packages. Kit was riveted. Heart racing, she leapt from the car, tore inside, and pulled down a few.

All the address labels had been ripped off or blacked out. Why? What could possibly be in these boxes? Was Danny back to pirating? How? When? He had a good job, and everything was going great. How could he do this?

"Danny!" Kit screamed.

He quickly ran out.

"Once a porch pirate, always a porch pirate!" she shrieked, pointing at the mountain of cardboard.

"Kit, calm down!" Danny exclaimed, throwing his hands up, "that's Christmas stuff for my mom, brothers, and you and Jasper. You know I like to shop early, and I'm making up for last year. It's not pirate loot."

"Oh, really? So, tell me, what's in this box, this one right here," she demanded, lugging a bulky parcel down and dropping it at Danny's feet. "You tell me, then we'll open it together to see what's inside."

"Kit, that's not fair. I can't remember what's in every single box. Give me a break."

"No, you give me a break! Tell me what's in this box," Kit doubled down, pointing at it.

"Um, I think there are designer sneakers for Jessie in that one."

When Danny opened the box and it was a life-size baby doll for some poor little girl who would never see it, Kit shot back, "Wrong, dude!"

Then she insisted they try another one.

"Here," she said, grabbing a heavy white box marked, "fragile," and pulling it down. "What's in this?"

"Um, I think that's a designer coffee-maker for Mom. You know, her Mr. Coffee sucks," Danny answered.

"Wrong again!" Kit cried when he opened it and it was a food processor.

"Well, she needs one of those, too," Danny said sheepishly. And then, annoyed and angry that Kit was putting him through this ridiculous game, Danny cracked, "What the hell? A box is a box, they all look alike."

"These aren't gifts for your family and me and Jasper, are they?" Kit fumed, getting in his face. "This is all stolen stuff.

You're pirating again, aren't you? You promised me you would go straight when you got out of prison."

"I swear, I tried to keep that promise," Danny told her, "but Cruz got into trouble big time while I was in lock-up. He racked up major poker debts, and the loan sharks are threatening to kill him, or his mom or sister, if he doesn't come up with $50,000.

"He begged me to do some pirating with him, so we could sell the stuff and make the money in 30 days. That's the deadline those fuck-tard loan sharks gave him. Thirty days, or people go missing, or die."

"Poker debts? Death threats from loan sharks? Not what I signed up for!" Kit cried. "This is way too much for me to handle. I'm just a single mom trying to raise a kid in Vegas and keep my head above water. I don't need this shit in my life. I don't want to be around criminal activity—yours, Cruz's, or anyone else's. What about Jasper? I'm trying to give him a normal, stable life.

"This porch pirate stuff is so fucked up," she ranted. "Mike told me he would report you to the cops if you got into it again. I told him it would never happen, but I guess I was wrong."

"It's just for 30 days, till we get the $50,000," a flustered Danny countered, staring in Kit's eyes while gripping her forearms.

"Cruz is like a brother to me. What was I supposed to do, tell him I couldn't help, or that he should go out and rob a 7-Eleven? I had to drive getaway for him. He swore he'd go straight—with the gambling and the pirating—once he pays the sharks off. I believe him."

"Well, then you're as stupid as he is," Kit fired back, "the dumb and dumber of porch pirating!

"Danny, please, I can't be with you right now," she added, shaking her head. "I want to go home. Maybe we should stop seeing each other for a while? I need some time to think things through, plus I don't want to be around you if you're stealing stuff. I don't want any part of this.

"Jasper shouldn't be around it either," Kit went on, glaring at the tall mound of boxes. "I never knew my own father, and I want something better for him. I want Jasper to have a good, strong man in his life. Someone he can look up to and respect, not a shady dude who steals stuff off peoples' porches and sells it on the Internet."

"Kit, don't bring Jasper into this! You know I love that kid like he's my own."

"Yeah, I know," Kit conceded. "But when he gets older and sees what you're doing, it will confuse him and make him wonder if that's the right way, or the best way, or the only way to go through life."

"Okay, okay, I hear you," Danny said, agitated and upset. "I'll stop the pirating right now. Just don't tell your psycho-dude ex what's going on. Cruz and I have enough to deal with. We don't need Metro breathing down our necks, too."

"I won't say anything to Mike," Kit told him. "Now, please, take me home. I want to be alone for a while."

"What do you mean for a while? How long is a while?" Danny asked, alarmed.

"I don't know, I just don't know. I've got to figure things out," Kit said, her voice trailing off.

He didn't want to, but Danny drove Kit home. He tried to come in, but she wouldn't let him. When he tried to kiss her, she backed away, fished the key out of her purse, and darted inside the same door she had burst out of the day he stole her baby's crib.

Danny just stood there, stunned and hurt. On the other side of the door, Kit was crying as she lurched towards the couch and collapsed on it.

First thing the next morning, a depressed, sleepless Danny called Cruz and told him he couldn't continue with the pirating.

"Kit saw the boxes in my garage and freaked," he said. "She blew up and kind of broke up with me. We didn't spend the night together. She's at her place, and I don't know if I should call her or leave her alone. I'm totally lost here, dude. I honestly don't know what the fuck to do."

"Come on Potter," the cunning, charming Cruz cajoled. "Chicks come and go, but we're 'bros for life. I gotta have you in the driver's seat to do some scores today near downtown. It's condos and apartments, so the getaway is tight and fast. I need you, dude."

"Sorry, no can do," a subdued Danny replied. "And Kit is not some chick who will come and go. I love her. And the kid is very cool. I can't do it, Cruz. I'm already in over my head with this chick. I can't risk pissing her off any more than she already is."

"Dude, I can't believe you're letting some broad come between us," a dejected Cruz said.

"You're not the one who just spent 18 months in lock-up, are you?" Danny shot back. "There's Kit, and there's prison. Two big fucking reasons this is over. Sorry, man, you can find another partner and rock on."

"Whatever," Cruz said, "Think about it, and let me know. We just need another $30,000, and then we're good to go."

"There's nothing to think about. It ain't gonna happen," Danny said, "Try Dalton Gates. He's done some pirating. He's an amateur, but a pro like you could show him the ropes fast. He'd jump at an opportunity like this.

"I'll borrow my brother's pickup this weekend," Danny added, "and move the boxes from my garage to yours. You need to turn this shit over fast."

"What the fuck?" a disgusted Cruz said, taking a deep breath and rolling his eyes. "I don't want Dalton Gates. He's a big, slow, dumb-ass loser. But I need someone—now. If he's all I can get, I'll take it," he mumbled before hanging up.

Later that morning, Cruz called Dalton, and he was all over it. He was a good kid, but young, inexperienced, oversize, and slow. He drove a faded, battered 2000 red Nissan Sentra with a snug trunk. But after he and Cruz pushed the back seats down, there was plenty of room.

Eighteen-year-old Dalton was eager to drive getaway and score some cash. But unfortunately, things didn't go well. One week in, Cruz was lifting some boxes from a porch on Palomino Drive in Mesquite, when the homeowner spotted him on his door cam, ran out, and gave chase.

Cruz bolted across the lawn to the red Sentra in the driveway, where Dalton was waiting. But just as Cruz heaved the boxes in back and jumped in the passenger seat, Dalton's car stalled. With Cruz screaming over and over, "Move this fucking car, dude! Move it! Move it!" Dalton pumped the gas pedal frantically. But his battered old Sentra wouldn't turn over.

"It's dead!" he yelled at Cruz.

Seconds later, the red-faced homeowner and his son were all over the car, pounding on the windows.

"Goddam porch pirates," they raged. "Give us our stuff. Hand over those boxes, you little fucks!"

Leaping out, Cruz and Dalton sprinted for the street. But the homeowner and his son chased them down, and soon all four were tussling and wrestling in the middle of Palomino Drive.

A neighbor called the cops. Lights flashing and sirens blaring, two Metro cars sped to the scene. It took four officers to break up the brawl.

"Lock these bastards up and throw away the key!" the bloody, disheveled homeowner barked at the cops, as they helped him and his son off the ground.

Meanwhile, a bruised, bloody Cruz and Dalton were hurled against a squad car, roughly patted down, and cuffed. The officers recovered at least a dozen boxes of stolen goods from their trunk.

Into the back of a squad car, both pirates were loaded. For the next week, they cooled their heels in a cramped, dirty jail cell downtown. The charges: misdemeanor burglary and disorderly conduct.

Cruz was irate and unhinged—with Dalton and the cops. But at least the loan sharks couldn't get to him in jail.

CHAPTER FIFTEEN

The day after Cruz got out of jail, lowlife gangsters Otis and Cade Marcum got ahold of him on his cell.

"Tomorrow is payday," Otis taunted. "Be at the pick-axe shack on Ramrod Road at noon. If you're a no-show, we'll find you, and it won't be pretty."

Cruz started to tell them he only had half the money, but the line went dead. Then he called Danny.

"I just got out of jail and the 30 days are up," he blurted, agitated and upset. "I only have half the money. Should I take the $25,000 to Searchlight tomorrow?"

"Yeah," Danny answered after a pause. "Tell them you need more time to get the other half."

"These crude fucks don't understand the meaning of 'more time,'" Cruz retorted. "I feel like taking off for Mexico or Miami. Just blow the hell out of here and start a whole new life somewhere else."

Not what Danny wanted to hear.

"You could never come back," he said glumly, after a brief pause. "They'll find you and kill you, wherever you go. Plus, if you leave town, they'll go after your mom or Tina. Running away is not the answer, dude. You need to talk to these pricks and see if they'll give you two more weeks."

"Yeah, I guess you're right," an agitated, subdued Cruz murmured. "I'll drive to Searchlight tomorrow, take the $25,000, and wear a bullet proof vest in case they try to gun me down."

"You're scaring the hell out of me," Danny confided. "Do you want me to come with you?"

"No, that would be a shit-show, for sure," Cruz told him. "I'll call you and tell you how it goes."

The next morning, after a long, sleepless night, Cruz drove down a winding, rutted highway to Searchlight, a sleepy old mining town 60 miles south of Vegas. Nervous and hitting 75 most of the way, he was welcomed to the dusty desert hamlet with a $100 speeding ticket. What a bummer.

It was early and he was restless, so he meandered into Terrible's casino and blew a wad of greenbacks on slots and video poker. When the sound of his rumbling stomach became louder than the one-armed bandit's bells and whistles, he got up and trekked to Terrible's Road House, one of the town's top eateries. There Cruz treated himself to a High Desert Special: a sausage-with-sauteed-onion medley delicately baked in a corn muffin, with a side of scrambled eggs, and the whole plate smothered in country gravy. The dish lived up to advance billing, and then some.

While he chowed down in a brown vinyl booth, a green-eyed waif-waitress in a yellow-and-white checked uniform flirted with the hunky dude in black jeans and a hoodie. She couldn't help it. There was something so sexy about the way the sun was streaming in and flitting through his glossy dark locks, which were cut short on top and layered shaggily down both sides. And the coffee-colored eyes and lightly tanned skin…

"Heading to Laughlin?" she purred, tilting her head as she poured another cup of joe.

"Yeah," Cruz nodded, smiling slightly. "Time to chill with some pals and hit the poker tables."

"Well, have fun high roller," she chirped, flashing her pearly whites. "Stop in on your way back, or give me a call sometime."

Then she handed him a check with her name, number, and a heart, all scrawled in red, on the back. He left a big tip.

By 11 AM, Cruz was back in his car. After filling the tank at Terrible's, he made his way out to Ramrod Road, five miles from the casino. He had been here before, so he knew the drill. It was in the middle of nowhere, allegedly near the Marcums' rambling, steel-bunker compound.

Surrounding him was a bleak muddle of desert landscape. Distended cactus, grizzled evergreens, and gnarly sage brush, all jutting out of brown, barren earth. Nothing, really, but an ugly version of it. In the distant horizon were endless mountains in the same dreary shade as the country gravy that had smothered Cruz's High Desert Special.

He pulled up to the pick-axe shack, a rotted, ramshackle hovel, with a door barely hanging on its rusty hinges, around 11:45. The Marcums weren't there yet, so he was alone for the moment in this forlorn setting.

Pressing on the door lightly, it opened with an eerie creak. There was a rickety old table inside, and some battered, three-legged chairs. A filthy dog dish was shoved in a corner near a withered roll of toilet paper. And an old stone cross dangled from a wall. The dirt-and-wood-plank floor was covered with torn, decaying newspapers.

A feeling of doom and gloom swept over Cruz as he wandered back outside and sat in his car to wait for the sharks. They finally pulled up in a black Toyota pickup.

That early fall day, the Marcums were dressed in grimy jeans and leather jackets with the sleeves cut off, exposing their brawny, grossly tattooed arms. Cruz gazed back and forth at their ruddy cheeks and dirty, disheveled sandy-brown hair. Both were in their mid-to-late-thirties, the sons and grandsons of miners, card sharks, and mobsters. And that was just the men. Who knew the dismal, dysfunctional back stories of the women they'd sprung from?

Into the shack, the three shuffled. With shards of sunlight streaming through the cracks in the wooden-plank walls, Cade stood behind the table and barked, "Where's the $50,000?"

"I, uh, ran into some problems and couldn't get it all," Cruz stammered, "but there's $25,000 in this bag."

He handed over a red nylon backpack.

"Otis, count this," Cade ordered, tossing the bulging bag at him.

As Otis shuffled through the rubber-banded packs of bills, Cade told Cruz, "You have 24 hours to get the other $25,000. I don't care what you have to do, rob a bank, steal it from your mother, play poker all night, sell your ass to a high roller. That ain't my problem. The bottom line is, I want the other $25,000 in 24 hours. That's a little over a thousand an hour.

"Get me my money, punk, and come back here tomorrow at one. Failure to comply equals game over, and you, or your mom, or that hot little sister of yours will suffer the consequences."

Cruz gulped and nodded.

"I'll, uh, get the money," he murmured.

"Now get the fuck out," Cade snarled. "What kind of asshole shows up for a meeting with half the money?"

Fearing he would be shot right then and there, Cruz was weak in the knees and barely able to walk. Outside the shack, he staggered to his white SUV, climbed in, started it, and aimlessly drove away.

Dazed and in a state of crippling anxiety, he could barely make out the gully-scarred, one-lane road. He wondered what he was going to do. Get a loan for $25,000 by tomorrow? How could he? Where would he? His credit sucked all over town. It was impossible to get the money in 24 hours. Moments later, in the middle of the Mojave, he pulled over, hurtled out of his SUV, and spilled his guts on a small mound of rocks and tin from an old campfire.

Back in Vegas that night, Cruz was again wracked with thoughts of leaving town. Just jumping in his car and taking off for L.A., or Florida, or even Tijuana. If he couldn't meet the sharks' demands, he decided he wouldn't return to Searchlight the next day. That would be suicide. Instead, he would hide out on the Strip and go on a bender: drink himself into a coma, veg out in front of a video poker terminal for hours, and find a girl to have mind-blowing sex with. Then, in the next few days, he would go home to fetch his mom and sister, drive them to a glitzy Strip resort, and check them in for a week or two. They could shop, play slots, go to spas. He wouldn't tell them what was going on. He would just say it was a gift and pay for it all with credit cards.

The 24-hour loan shark deadline came and went, and Cruz did not go to Searchlight. Instead, he drove to the Strip and spent the day boozing and playing poker at Mirage. Later, he went home with the shapely cocktail wench who'd been serving his drinks all day.

The next morning, he was back at home when Danny called to check in. Cruz poured out the details of his grim meeting with the Marcums, and how he had missed the new 24-hour deadline for the other $25,000.

Danny felt guilty that he hadn't finished the 30 days of pirating to help Cruz get the $50,000. He knew Cruz was frantic and at the brink. Feeling sorry for him, and knowing how much his buddy loved indoor skydiving, he urged him to drop by Sin City Skydiving for a comp dive or two, to get his mind off things. They could talk afterwards, and maybe grab a burger at Shake Shack. Cruz jumped at his friend's offer.

CHAPTER SIXTEEN

After parking his white SUV in the Sin City Skydiving parking lot, Cruz hustled inside. Danny greeted him with a macho semi-hug, and proudly showed him around the imposing, steel-and-glass emporium, flanked by a slew of sleazy strip joints on Industrial Road.

A stoked Cruz then suited up for his comp dive. As he tightened the strap on his gray metallic helmet, he realized he wouldn't be making the daredevil plunge alone. A nondescript loner with disheveled dark hair, dull brown eyes, and a medium build, had shown up at the ticket cage. After paying his fee, he insisted on doing a tandem dive. Taken aback, Danny weighed the options and decided that Cruz and the stranger were of similar height and weight, so he would hook them together.

After both were zipped into skin-tight Spandex flying suits—Cruz's in yellow, the other diver's in blue—they watched a brief infomercial about what to expect on their tandem leap. Then the pair, making idle small talk, rode a glass elevator to the launch platform. There they were connected with a six-foot cable and catapulted into the wind tunnel for their two-minute descent, from 60 feet up, at 120 miles per hour.

But one minute in, things went horribly wrong. The diver in blue suddenly pulled a small, 9-millimeter pistol from a side-flap in his helmet. Jerking towards Cruz, he yelled, "Game over, you loser. Now die!" and pulled the trigger.

Pop, pop, pop.

Three shots rang out, one after the other. Two of the bullets tore into Cruz's chest, one into his abdomen. A shock of piercing red blood gushed from his mouth, with more spurting from all three bullet holes. The grisly sight was made even more ghastly by the wind in the tunnel wildly splattering the blood up and down the glass enclosure.

As customers and spectators screamed and shielded their eyes, chaos erupted at the skydiving palace. Realizing that one of the divers had been shot, the wind tunnel operator recoiled in horror and hit the emergency switch. The wind abruptly stopped and Cruz, now a dead weight in freefall, dropped to the ground, with the shooter landing beside him.

Jumping off the floor, the gunman ripped off the tandem cable and butted through the enclosure with his helmeted head, leaving behind a thousand pieces of shattered glass. Out an exit door he raced to the parking lot, where a black SUV was waiting with a getaway driver.

Danny, who'd been watching from the sidelines, leapt from his chair and rushed to Cruz. After removing his helmet, he gently lifted his friend's bloody torso onto his lap and pleaded, over and over, "Hang on, 'bro, you're gonna make it, just hang in there, Cruz, please." But his efforts to stop the profuse bleeding and revive his friend failed. Cruz never regained consciousness, and a sobbing Danny was soon covered with his friend's blood.

Someone called the paramedics, who arrived in 10 minutes. Dazed and devastated, Danny was still hovering over Cruz, who was pronounced dead at the scene. As a pale, grim Danny watched, his body was removed by EMTs, and later transferred to the Clark County Morgue.

Vegas Metro had arrived soon after the EMTs. When Danny saw two cops making a beeline for him, his heart sank. Right off, they started firing questions, and Danny told them what he knew. In a low monotone, he explained that Cruz had racked up huge poker debts over the summer, and the loan sharks had demanded payback while making death threats. Cruz had not been able to cover the amount they wanted, so this hideous public shooting was retribution.

Danny didn't mention the names of the sharks—he didn't want to become their next target. He simply said that a hit man sent by them must have been tailing Cruz, and followed him to the skydiving emporium. There he booked a tandem dive with his intended target, and then killed him.

Danny provided a brief description of the hit man and turned over his credit card receipt, which was most likely bogus. The cops, who were aware that Cruz had spent a week in jail recently, and Danny had been released from prison six months before, told Danny to come to the station the next morning to answer more questions.

After dealing with them, Danny had to face his bosses, who were completely blindsided by the gruesome killing. Squirming in his bloody shirt and pants, Danny revealed what he knew about Cruz's gambling debts and the threats against him. His bosses were shocked and appalled, and especially worried how this outrageous crime would affect their company's image and bottom line.

A short statement was prepared for Danny to read on local news. While waiting for the camera crew, Danny cleaned up a bit, changed his clothes, and threw the bloody ones out. He then retreated to his office, closed the door, and sat slumped at his desk, nauseous and frozen with shock. He couldn't get the image of Cruz's bloody face and glazed eyes out of his head.

Cruz's mom and sister were also on his mind. They needed to be called, and the sooner the better. Danny didn't want Carmen to find out about her son's lurid death on TV news. Two or three times he picked up the phone, but the killing had been so gut-wrenching, he couldn't bring himself to dial her number. Finally, he reached out to his own mom instead. After breaking the shocking news, he asked her to contact Carmen Morrissey.

Bonnie didn't want to make the traumatic call either, but for Danny's sake, she did.

Once Danny had taped the TV statement, he was free to leave work. The mood was tense and uncertain as he walked out of SCS and headed for his red SUV. In the parking lot, he looked around warily for anyone or anything that might be connected to the shooting.

It was 3 PM on a bright, mid-week day, and Danny didn't want to go home. He couldn't face his mom, or deal with Cruz's either. Sick to his stomach and emotionally drained, he drove to MGM Grand, where he threw back some drinks and choked down a BLT at Sinbad's. Then he hit the casino for a video-poker-and-booze binge that careened into the next morning. For hours he felt numb and lost, and that's exactly what he wanted.

While Danny was hiding out in the casino, Cruz's brazen murder made the lead story on local TV news at 10.

"This was a private incident," a somber Danny stated in the video he'd taped earlier, "a revenge act brutally carried out one block from the Strip. Our deepest sympathies are with the Morrissey family. Sin City Skydiving wants the public to know our facility is safe, but we're adding extra security to reassure our customers."

A minute later, Mike, who was watching at home, grabbed his cell and called Kit.

"Are you watching Channel 5?" he asked.

"Yes," she murmured.

"Did you see Danny talking about the shooting?"

"He was just on, before the commercial," she replied softly.

"I hate to be repetitive," Mike said in a tone dripping with arrogance, "but you need to stay away from this dude, and keep Jasper away from him, too. This guy's trouble with a capital T, one step from big time crime."

"Danny's my friend, and this is none of your business!" Kit snapped. "I hear Jasper crying. I have to go. Bye."

Then she hung up.

But she was in tears. Crying for Cruz, for Danny, and for herself. She knew that Cruz's killing was an act of retribution from the loan sharks, and that it probably wouldn't have happened if she hadn't demanded that Danny stop pirating with Cruz.

So, where did that leave her relationship with Danny? Torn apart and damaged beyond repair, she feared. How would he ever forgive her?

CHAPTER SEVENTEEN

A few days, and sleepless nights, later, Kit finally got up the nerve to go see Danny at his mom's house in North Las Vegas. One of his younger brothers answered the door and told her to wait in the living room.

Danny's mom toddled in to say hello and brought Kit a cup of coffee. Both of them were sad and bleary-eyed. Sitting on the sofa, they had an awkward 15-minute chat that was accompanied by quite a few downward glances and sad head shakes. Neither had been a huge fan of Cruz's, but they certainly didn't wish him a cruel and violent death.

Bonnie then led Kit through the silent house to the family room, where a disheveled Danny stood up and mumbled, "Hey, Kit."

"I'm so sorry about what happened to Cruz," she said, nervous and flustered. "I saw it on the news."

Danny nodded. His eyes were red and puffy. Like everyone else, he was enshrouded in head-to-toe black. A silent Bonnie then shuffled back to the kitchen, where Cruz's two younger brothers were.

Tina was with Danny in the family room. Before he got up to greet Kit, they'd been sitting on a beige leather couch comforting each other. Gazing at her, Kit suddenly felt jealous and awkward, as if she was intruding.

"Um, Tina, why don't you go see my mom in the kitchen," Danny suggested.

Nodding silently, she left the room.

As they sat down on the couch, Danny said to Kit, "I'm kind of surprised you're here. After that bizarre scene with the boxes in the garage, I didn't think I'd ever see you again."

"Oh, I'm sorry. I was really upset. It was just so shocking, the last thing I expected to see behind that door," Kit said, her voice trailing off. "How are you doing?"

"I'm so out of it, I don't know what to think or feel," Danny told her. "Cruz is gone, gunned down in cold blood at Sin City Skydiving. My bosses are shocked shitless. They knew Cruz and me were tight. They asked if I had anything to do with it, or if I had any idea it was going to happen. I told them no, but that I knew it was a possibility.

"Cruz told me over and over he was being threatened, but I never thought they would pump bullets into him during an indoor skydive. What kind of animals are those fuck-tards in Searchlight?"

Wide-eyed and taken aback by his angry, distraught tone, Kit stared at Danny.

"This whole thing sounds like something out of a horror movie," she said softly, clutching his arm. "I'm sorry you had to watch your friend die like that." And then, shaking her head and glancing down, she added, "Speaking of your bosses, do you, uh, think you're going to be fired?"

"I don't know," Danny replied. "I asked for a week off to think things through. I don't know what my next move, or theirs, will be."

Still holding Danny's arm, Kit blurted, "I feel terrible about what happened, and sort of responsible. You don't blame me for Cruz's death, do you?"

After a brief pause, Danny answered, "I told you why he needed the money. I swore I'd stop pirating as soon as we got the $50,000, but you kept pressuring me. You threatened to cut me out of your life unless I stopped, so I did. And look what happened? Cruz couldn't get the money, so those asshole loan sharks killed him. His mom is totally gutted, and so is Tina. They're both scared they'll be killed next. It's a totally fucked up scene, and in a way I do blame you."

Sitting beside Danny, Kit burst into tears. He made a lame attempt to take back what he had said, but she was too hurt to hear a word. When she could finally speak, she asked about Tina.

"Why is she here? Is she your, uh, girlfriend now?"

"No, Kit, it's not like that. Cruz was her brother, so I'm helping her through this, and he was like family to me, so she's helping me. We need each other right now."

Taking a deep breath, Kit nodded. There was a tap on the door and it opened quietly.

"Danny," Tina said in a voice barely above a whisper, "my mom's here. She wants to see you."

"I should go," Kit stammered, crushed and confused as she got up off the couch. "I'm so sorry about Cruz," she repeated, kissing Danny on the cheek. Nodding somberly, he showed her to the door.

"Thanks for coming by," he said, as she walked out to her car. Then he turned to go back and join the others.

Kit was in tears as she drove home. Danny had seemed so cold and distant. She had no idea where they stood now.

The next morning Danny got a call from his boss, who informed him they felt he wasn't right for the job, and they were terminating him. A severance check would be mailed. He was disappointed, but hardly surprised. They knew he had just gotten out of prison when they hired him, so they were wary from the start. But Cruz's killing was more than they could handle.

And so Danny got fired from another job.

Of course, he felt like a loser. It didn't help that his relationship with Kit was rocky and strained, and he had just witnessed a close friend's violent death.

Not knowing where to turn, or how to cope with this trifecta of miseries, a sad, overwhelmed Danny hashed things over and decided to leave town. The events of the past few days had been too jarring and traumatic to process. Needing to hit the reset button big time, he would go to Reno.

Later that week, after an eight-hour drive north on I-95, Danny arrived in "the biggest little city in the world." That hot, mid-October day in 2017, he checked into the vintage-glitzy Silver Legacy on Virginia Street, in the center of the action.

For the first couple of weeks, the troubled, exhausted dude slept a lot, wandered around town aimlessly, and played poker every night. With lady luck finally on his side, he won several thousand dollars, enough to cover his room and poker bets for at least a month.

So Danny was getting by in Reno. But his days and nights were dominated by thoughts of Kit. He felt sad that he had let her down in so many ways, from the day they met when he stole her unborn baby's crib. Does it get any lower than that? And then, over the next three years, their relationship had careened from uncertainty, to happiness, to confusion and despair. Would it all have turned out differently if Danny had just kept the promises he'd made after getting out of prison?

Cruz was also on his mind: what a short life he'd lived and how messed up it had been. Danny didn't want to end up like that, so he decided to do something productive in Reno. After all, the money he was pulling in as a poker ace wouldn't last forever. So he took a chance and tried his hand at dealing, like his dad had done for decades at the Flamingo in Vegas. Danny soon discovered he had a real talent for the game, too.

Six weeks after Danny arrived in Reno, he moved into a furnished, one-bedroom flat in the sprawling, brown-brick Appaloosa Apartments on Nevada Street near downtown.

His next few months were spent dealing poker to a constant stream of Reno characters, and tourists from all over the world. He was doing okay, productive and functioning. But that didn't mean he wasn't lonely and lost at times. He missed Kit, and still had nightmares and flashbacks about Cruz's grisly death in the wind tunnel. Staying busy helped, and frivolous flings with cocktail waitresses and showgirls didn't hurt. But Kit and Jasper were never far from his thoughts.

Every week Danny checked in with his mom and brothers, but they knew nothing about Kit. At times, he was gripped by pangs of jealousy. He wondered if she was dating anyone, if her married boss was still trying to get into her pants, or if she had gotten back together with that obnoxious baby-daddy of hers.

CHAPTER EIGHTEEN

Back in Vegas, Kit had her share of heartache and regrets, too. But at the end of the day, she hadn't been able to cope with Danny's craziness. After his release from prison, he'd landed a good job. Still, Cruz had lured him back into porch piracy. Yes, death threats from loan sharks are always a compelling reason. But bottom line, the outlaw lifestyle didn't fly with Kit. It scared the hell out of her and made her run for the exit.

Would Danny ever settle down and be a mature, responsible adult? Kit didn't know, but she had her own future, and Jasper's, to think of. Still, Danny was on her mind a lot. She was constantly weighing his good points and bad, trying to decide whether he was worth another spin on the love-go-round, or not.

On the down side, he was an unpredictable, compulsive, ex-con box bandit, with a posse of scummy friends and stacks of stolen goods hanging out in his garage.

On the up side, Kit loved him, and probably had from the day they met. There was something so magical, quixotic, and magnetic about Danny. He was also exciting in bed, an amazing kisser, and great to look at, a hunka hunka burnin' porch pirate.

Kit often thought back to the day they met, and was impressed by the way he had dealt with her pregnancy crisis. How many guys would have panicked when she fell and her water broke, and just jumped in their car and taken off?

Not Danny. He was a decent dude with a heart of gold. Plus, he was quick on his feet and smart. And there was an appealing authenticity to him. For a guy who made a career out of stealing things, he was a very honest human being. It was an odd combination: a porch pirate with personal integrity. Would Kit ever meet anyone like Danny again? She doubted it.

While trying to forget him, she dated around. But nothing serious evolved. Her relationships with guys were a tangled, frustrating muddle. Just like her Kitty Kat cohorts, Kit was constantly navigating through a sea of unsuitable dudes. An endless array of dicey, unsavory potential boyfriends and mates, from grifters, druggies, and deadbeats, to compulsive gamblers, womanizers, boozers, perverts, and psychos.

And then there were the dudes with double lives, who were happily married to their high school sweethearts back in Baltimore or Cleveland. They were so convinced that what happened in Vegas would stay in Vegas, they thought they could get away with whatever it was they were trying to pull off. For every encounter with one of those, Kit felt like she needed to consult a private detective, a doctor, a psychologist, and maybe even a lawyer. In Vegas, going out on a date sometimes took a village. What the hell?

Sadly, the men in Kit's life over the past few years had been wrong for her on so many levels. At the top of the list was Danny, a great guy who couldn't down hold a job, or kick his porch pirate habit. And then there was baby daddy Mike. A conceited ass and proud playboy, for sure, but at least his checks arrived on time. Kit's married boss was a lying, cheating, manipulative creep who was constantly trying to get her into the sack. And raunchy, scary casino rats from all over the world were hitting on her every night of the week.

In between all of the above, Kit attempted a few decent, pleasant, casual relationships. The guys were nice, stable, reliable types. Let's just say they looked good on paper, but most of them she wasn't attracted to. And when she was attracted, something always kept her from getting too involved, or saying the "L" word.

The porch pirate, of course.

Four-hundred-thirty-eight miles north, he was also trying to move on with his life. Bored with the poker-dealing gig after only a couple of months, Danny started searching for something more substantial and fulfilling.

While checking out a help-wanted board in a Silver Legacy coffee shop one day, he spotted an ad for ambulance drivers that piqued his interest. He had been trained as one while living in Hawaii in 2006, and loved it, the speed, the drama, the constant adrenaline rush. His pirate days had only honed and sharpened his motoring skills in high-stress situations. He thought back to the day he drove Kit to the hospital. It had been oddly satisfying, and made him feel needed and important.

After making some calls and doing research, Danny decided to pursue the formal training needed to become an ambulance driver in Nevada. The first certification he completed was emergency vehicle operator. Then came a first aid course and one in CPR. The final step was the National Ambulance Driver Competency exam. After passing, Danny was fully certified.

He had held down the poker dealing gig the entire time he'd trained, and was grateful to his bosses for the flexible hours. Six months after arriving in Reno, Danny started applying for positions as an ambulance driver. With his upbeat personality and can-do attitude, he aced his job interviews. Despite his troubled background and dicey driving record, he soon scored a job with Reno Ambulance Corps, a private company serving all the hospitals in the Reno-Tahoe area.

From day one, Danny excelled at his new job. He was still a part-time poker dealer, but his ambulance driving soon became his primary occupation. He loved the uncertainty and split-second challenges, as well as the tension and human-interest angle In each medical drama that confronted him.

Back in Vegas, Kit continued to wonder if she and Danny should attempt a do-over of their ill-fated love affair. She knew it was risky, and also unrealistic since Danny now lived in Reno. But why let that stop her?

Calling Danny's mom was Kit's first step. Bonnie was delighted to hear from her, and proudly prattled on about her son's dynamic new career. Hoping to get the lovebirds back together, she also dropped major hints on how and when Kit could find her son in the poker pit at the Silver Legacy.

Thrilled to learn that Danny was thriving, Kit wanted to reach out to him. But how? Should she call him, or go see him? She finally decided to drive to Reno and surprise him at the casino. Of course, she was terrified. What if he was dating some showgirl or cocktail waitress and Kit made a complete fool of herself?

Bonnie had mentioned that Danny didn't have a girlfriend. But maybe he did, and Bonnie wasn't aware of it? As usual, Kit was confused. But she needed to find out, one way or the other, if there was still a chance for her and Danny. She was tired of wallowing in doubt and indecision, and determined to take action.

CHAPTER NINETEEN

On a Friday morning in July 2018, nine months after Danny left town, Kit climbed in her silver Chevy Malibu and began the eight-hour drive to Reno. It was already 105 degrees, a typical mid-summer day in the desert. Kit's long, golden locks were pulled back in a sleek ponytail. Her make-up was minimal. She wore pink shorts, a floral-print tee, a baseball cap, and sunglasses. Comfort and cuteness, Mojave style.

Down I-95 Kit sped, till she reached Beatty. There she turned off, filled the tank, and stopped at the iconic Death Valley Nut & Candy Shop. After wandering down aisles stocked with saltwater taffy, licorice, gummies, hard candies, and fudge, she veered to the dairy bar and bought a double-scoop pineapple-coconut ice cream cone.

It was hot, and she was craving something cold and creamy. Strolling across the parking lot with her luscious treat, she plopped down on a shaded bench in front of the Stagecoach Hotel. Licking away, she was consumed with thoughts of Danny. Would he even want to see or talk to her? Or was he still so bitter and angry about what had happened to Cruz that he wanted no further contact?

Anxious and uncertain, she considered turning back for Vegas. But something compelled her to go on. Call it desperation. She had to know, one way or the other, if she had any future with Danny, or was it time to move on?

Back in the car, Kit's desert odyssey continued. Goldfield

was the next town in this endless stretch of brownness and bleakness. Then came Tonopah. Kit got gas again, and hit the Burger King for a Whopper and fries. The onslaught of food and relentless heat made her groggy. Cranking up the A-C, she throttled on to Hawthorne, another sleepy mountain town nestled in the shadows of the Sierra Nevadas.

Walker Lake was the next scenic highlight. And then, suddenly, Kit was in Fallon. She had been driving for seven hours. One more, and she would hit Reno.

At 7:00, as the sun was setting in luminous gold and orange bands beyond the mountains, Kit pulled into Reno. It was her first visit to this hardscrabble frontier town with the Truckee River churning through it. She didn't know what to make of a city that had evolved and thrived from industries as diverse as mining, railroads, gambling, divorce, and tourism.

Cruising down bustling Virginia Street, Kit gazed around. The sprawling metropolis oozed a vintage western vibe. At the Silver Legacy, she parked in the underground garage and quickly registered. In her room she unpacked lightly, and called her friend, Ginny, a Kitty Kat Babe with two kids of her own who was watching Jasper back in Vegas.

All was well, so Kit moved on. After a quick cat nap, she fluffed her hair, freshened her make-up, and slithered into a sexy, black silk halter-dress. A warm, juicy roast beef sandwich in the coffee shop came next. The food calmed her down a bit, but Kit was still nervous and jittery, so she played some slots before sauntering to the poker pit.

It was after 10 PM, and there Danny was, handsome as ever, dealing a hand of poker after a hard day on the ambulance beat. Kit's heart was pounding as she watched him interacting with the players at his table.

At 11 PM, he finally looked up, and was blown away to see her. Despite the heat and long drive, Kit looked stunning in the black dress that hugged her curves in all the right places. Her long, blond hair was loose and tumbling over her pale shoulders, her make-up light and fresh. She looked feminine and sweet, but also sexy.

Tossing her locks flirtatiously, she called out, "Hey dude, deal me in," and laughed. Melting at the sound of Kit's voice, Danny responded, "Anytime, beautiful," and jumped up to kiss her.

"I think I just hit the jackpot, guys," Danny cracked, scanning the table of horndog poker-dudes leering at Kit.

"Sweetheart, can you wait just a few minutes," he asked, "and we'll have a drink."

"I'll be over here," Kit smiled, veering to an I Dream of Jeannie slot, where she amused herself for the next 10 minutes. Then she and Danny headed to the casino bar.

After kissing her again and ordering two ginger ales, he playfully asked, "So, what brings you to Reno?"

"I drove up here to see a dude I used to date in Sin City," she replied coyly.

"Anyone I know?" Danny teased, tilting his head.

They both laughed. Then he got a grip and said, "This is so cool. I'm glad you came up. I've missed you and the little man, too. How is he? Where is he?"

"Jasper's great," Kit gushed. "We've missed you, too. He's back in Vegas with a Kitty Kat friend of mine. She has five-year-old twins, a boy and a girl, so he's having a blast."

"They're all playing a hot game of blackjack by now, I'm sure," Danny cracked. Then he asked, "Where are you staying, and for how long?"

"I have a room upstairs," she answered in a breathy little voice, batting her baby blues. "Just for a few days. I'm leaving on Tuesday."

"Well, that should give us time to, uh, get reacquainted," Danny murmured.

Kit laughed nervously. She suddenly felt a bit hot. Putting his glass down, Danny reached over and kissed her again, this time more intensely. Weak at the knees and breathless at the bar, the two snuggled even closer.

"What's your room number?" Danny asked, wrapping his arm around her.

"485," Kit whispered in his ear.

"I'll come up at six, when my shift is over," Danny said softly.

"I'll be waiting," Kit purred.

They kissed again. Then Danny reluctantly returned to the poker pit, and Kit slinked upstairs to the fourth floor.

CHAPTER TWENTY

The minute Danny's shift ended, he took the express elevator to four. Hustling down the hall to room 485, he tapped lightly on the door. A sleepy-eyed, groggy Kit, clad in a pink lace teddy and short satin robe, opened it. Danny stepped inside, and just like that they were in each other's arms, kissing, tumbling onto the king-size bed, rolling around, and tearing each other's clothes off. More kissing followed, and then they made love, with moans of ecstasy and cries of passion pouring from both. All that morning they were blissfully entangled, and then, finally, there were a couple of hours of sleep.

Mid-day, the two finally emerged from Kit's room and removed the "Do Not Disturb" sign. Holding hands, they strolled through the casino to the garage, where they hopped in Danny's red Ford Explorer. A short drive later, they were at one of his favorite hang-outs, the raucous Peg's Glorified Ham n Eggs on Mae Anne Avenue.

Kit, who was decked out in a short, red spaghetti-strap dress and flirty polka-dot sandals, nibbled an enchilada omelet. Lover-dude Danny, in black jeans and a gray Silver Legacy tee, devoured huevos rancheros smothered in hot sauce and a short stack of pancakes.

Over the table, they laughed, kissed, held hands, and caught up. Clearly they both missed the good old days in Vegas, and each other. After breakfast, Kit sipped coffee and whipped out her phone so Danny could see more photos and videos of Jasper.

He lit up when he spotted the rambunctious toddler tearing around on a shiny blue tricycle.

That afternoon Kit checked out of the hotel, and into Danny's apartment. He took a few days off from the poker pit, and the two made love, watched old movies, and hung out at his favorite eateries, between ambulance runs. The sex was hot, sweet, and romantic. Between the sheets, and the kisses, they laughed a lot. Every morning when the two woke up beside each other, love-happy grins were splashed across their faces.

As Danny and Kit dove head-first into this second chance at love, their troubled past in Vegas seemed to melt away. Forgive, forget, and focus on the present became their mantra, as they enjoyed the hell out of Reno and each other.

It worked. That torrid, romantic weekend exceeded all Kit's expectations. Danny had grown into the kind of man she had always hoped he could be: fun and exciting, but also mature and responsible. And Danny was grateful that Kit still wanted him, and could get beyond everything that had gone down in Vegas.

Fast forward five months to December 2018. After many thrilling trips back and forth from Vegas, Danny asked Kit to move to Reno.

"Are you sure we're ready for this?" was her first response, as they sipped coffee and nibbled toast one morning at his breakfast bar. "It's a big step, you know, and I love Vegas, my apartment, and the Kitty Kat gig."

Then, after thinking it over for a minute, she admitted, "The drive back and forth is pretty tiring, and I miss you all the time, too. But Jasper and I take up a lot of space. We wouldn't want to crowd you out of your man-cave."

"No worries, Kit," Danny assured her. "I'm so over the man-cave thing. A man-woman cave sounds like a lot more fun. It would be so cool and cozy. You could move some of your stuff in here, and we'll store the rest in a locker in Pleasant Valley. We can set up a bed in the living room for Jasper. There's plenty of space for all of us. Later on, we'll get something bigger and more permanent."

"Um, that's a lot of we's. It sounds tempting, but I'll have to think about it," Kit told him, nestling her arm around him on the stool beside hers, as she leaned over to kiss him.

"I love you, you love me, and we both love Jasper. What's to think about?" a hurt Danny retorted, tossing his hands up. "We should be together. The way things are now, we're just wasting time. Life will be easier and better if we're all together. You can get a good job up here, and find someone in this building to watch Jasper. I'll teach you how to deal poker. You'll make more money than you ever did with blackjack."

Kit liked what she was hearing, but she still needed some time. Back in Vegas, she carefully mulled things over. A few days later, she dialed Danny's cell and announced, "Call the moving van—Jasper and I are Reno-bound!"

"Awesome!" Danny shot back. "This is so cool. You'll love it up here, babe. It's Vegas, without the chaos and craziness. Are you sure about this? You're not going to change your mind and break my poor country-boy heart, are you?"

"Not a chance!" Kit told him, laughing. And then her voice dropped. "Without you," she admitted, "life in Vegas is empty and sad. Home is where you are, babe. This move is just what Jasper and I need. It will be a fresh start for all of us. Plus, the schools up there look good and the job market's hot."

"Now you're talking!" an ecstatic Danny exclaimed. "I'll come down and help you pack. Just give your boss two weeks' notice, and tell your landlord you're leaving. It will all go smoothly, you'll see. If there are any glitches, I'll be there."

"Sounds like a plan," Kit gushed. "I can't wait, and Jasper's stoked, too. Let the packing begin!"

The next day she notified her landlord she was leaving, and gave two-weeks' notice at work. Then she called Mike.

"You're going to quit Kitty Kat Babes to move to Reno to be with the porch pirate?" he asked incredulously.

"Mike, please, Danny has a good job as an ambulance driver, plus he works part-time as a poker dealer. He's loved and respected up there. He hasn't done any pirating for over a year."

"Still, the guy did 18 months in prison," Mike countered. "He's a scam artist. How can you trust him? Face reality, Kit, this dude's not for you. And what about Jasper? How will he adjust to this change? You're taking my son to a city that's over 400 miles from here, and I'm supposed to stand by quietly and say nothing?"

"You only see him once a month, so why is this such a big deal?" an exasperated Kit asked.

"I'm warning you," Mike said petulantly. "If you move to Reno with Jasper, I'll stop the support checks."

"And I'm warning you," Kit vowed, "if you cut me off, I'll call the Las Vegas Review-Journal and tell them my son is Senator Prescott's grandson. We can do a DNA test to prove it. Is that what you want?"

"Don't threaten me," Mike snapped.

"Don't threaten me!" Kit countered. "Take a chill pill, dude, and deal with it. I'm moving to Reno. When we get settled, I'll send our new address so you can mail the checks."

"Kit, you better think this through. Don't let that ex-con manipulate you, or pressure you into doing something you'll regret later. This move is major."

"I have thought it through, Mike, and he's not pressuring me. End of discussion."

And so, the move steamrolled ahead in early 2019. Danny was thrilled to have Kit and Jasper with him in his one-bedroom flat. Within weeks, Kit had scored a job at Sassy Sally's Saloon in Circus Circus as a poker princess, thanks to the dealer training she'd gotten from Danny. Her new costume was a short, tight, red-lace dress, topped off with a silver-and-red sequin cowgirl hat. In early 2019, Reno was bursting with tourists and conventioneers, and Kit's tips rocked.

CHAPTER TWENTY-ONE

On Valentine's Day, Danny and Kit treated Jasper to a special breakfast at Peg's. In their blue-vinyl booth, the besotted couple, clad in jeans and pink and red V-neck sweaters, tucked into chile rellenos and eggs doused with ranchero sauce.

Squirming beside them was Jasper, cuteness overload in an orange turtleneck bedecked with hearts, and khakis. On a plate in front of him was a large, smilie-face pancake, drenched with butter and syrup. When Kit turned to cut it into bite-size pieces, Danny reached into the inner pocket of his jacket and pulled out a tiny, black velvet box. With no one watching, he slid it into a ceramic crock holding creamers and sugar packets.

A few minutes later, he asked the waitress for more coffee. When Kit reached into the crock for a creamer, her probing fingers encountered a small, hard object.

"What's this?" she asked, head tilted as she plucked the box out.

"I have no idea," Danny replied with a grin that could have lit up the Vegas Strip.

With Jasper squealing over and over, "Mommy, is that a toy?" Kit opened the box. Inside was a classic, round-cut, one-carat diamond ring, set in white gold. Even in crowded, noisy Peg's, people were staring. Wrapping his arm around a teary-eyed Kit, Danny kissed her.

"Sweetheart, you've made me the happiest dude on planet earth," he declared, taking her hand. "Without you, the rest of my life would totally suck. Will you be my valentine, and marry me, too?"

Kit was laughing and crying at the same time. A befuddled Jasper was staring at both of them, and so was everyone else at Peg's.

"Yes, and yes," Kit gasped. "You check all my boxes, Danny Potter. I can't live without you, either!"

As the giddy couple kissed and cooed, diners in nearby booths applauded. Free coffee was served to all. With Jasper perched on Kit's lap, total strangers paraded by the table to congratulate the newly engaged couple and catch a glimpse of the stunning ring on Kit's finger. Typical Reno, she thought, gazing around.

For the next couple of months, the newly engaged couple and Jasper lived happily in Danny's cozy, third-floor apartment. Everything around them seemed dipped and coated in a thick, gauzy haze of joy, from the gold-colored drapes in the living room, to the blue comforter with stars on it on Danny's bed, to the yellow-and-gray dishes he'd picked up for $20 at a garage sale in Somersett.

With both of them doing well at their jobs and hoping to expand their family once they were married, Danny and Kit bought a rambling, three-bedroom house in sedate Sparks, just outside of Reno.

Kit was ecstatic, but everything was happening so fast. She had moved to Reno in January. Danny proposed in February. They bought the house in March. And now their wedding was scheduled for April 20, 2019, exactly four years after they had met, which would also be Jasper's fourth birthday.

In a whirlwind of wedding preparations, Kit mailed invitations to 75 friends in Vegas and Reno. She was uncertain about whether or not to send one to Mike, but decided to go ahead. A few days later, he called.

"I got your invitation, Kit. Thanks," he said, pleasantly enough. But then his voice dropped.

"I can't believe you're walking down the aisle with that low-life porch thief," he said bluntly. "Don't you think you're rushing things? You just moved up there two months ago. You're not pregnant again, are you?"

"Not that it's any of your business, but no, I'm not pregnant!" Kit fumed. "How rude and obnoxious can you be?"

"Sorry if that question offends you," Mike answered in a voice dripping with insincerity, "but given our history, I think it's fair."

"Go to hell, Mike!" Kit said, on the verge of hanging up on him.

"Calm down, Kit, no offense intended. I just found it strange and a little worrisome that you would jump into marriage so soon after moving up there."

"How sweet of you to be concerned," Kit replied sarcastically, "but, no, I don't think we're rushing things. We want to be together, Danny's a great stepdad to Jasper, and we're buying a house in Sparks. So, why shouldn't we move forward and get married?"

"Been there, done that—twice—darlin', and it didn't work for me," Mike shot back. "You really need to think this through."

"You were probably never fully committed to either one of your marriages, were you?" Kit asked. "No wonder they failed. But Danny and I don't have that problem. Plus, he isn't a sexaholic like you."

There was a groan on Mike's end.

"That's ridiculous," he snapped. "I won't dignify that comment with a response."

"Whatever, Mike," Kit muttered. "So, will you be at the wedding, or not? I thought it would be nice for Jasper to see you and Danny in the same room together, getting along."

"Sounds delightful, Kit, but I have to decline. I don't approve of this marriage. And I'm not sure if it's the right thing for Jasper."

"Well, let me worry about Jasper," Kit retorted. "He's my responsibility, and I've handled things pretty well, so far. Stay in your lane, Mike."

"And what lane is that?" he bristled. "Baby daddy on the sidelines who sends the checks every month and keeps his mouth shut?"

"Um, well, yeah Mike," Kit came back. "But why complain? Isn't that the way you wanted it?"

There was an angry silence on Mike's end. Kit could just see his eyes rolling.

"So, will there be a honeymoon?" he asked, moving on.

"Yes, we're driving to San Francisco for a week, but then we have to get back for work," Kit replied. "Why do you ask?"

"Because I could take Jasper, if you want."

"No, thanks, Mike. We tried that once, and it was a disaster, remember? We're taking him with us. I don't want to leave him with anyone, including you."

"Still bitter that we didn't end up together, aren't you, Kit?"

After a short burst of laughter, she replied, "No, Mike, still bitter about the kidnapping that went down at your condo three years ago."

"I can't believe you're bringing that up again," he said, annoyed. "Look, I've got to go. I'm flying a couple of political types up to Carson City for a meeting with the governor this afternoon. We're leaving in a few minutes and I need to check some mechanical stuff. I hope this marriage-thing works out for you. Let me know if you need anything."

"Thanks, Mike, just the monthly checks," Kit doubled down.

His phone abruptly clicked off.

What a jerk, Kit thought. She was stung by the curtness, but there was no time to fret or over-analyze. Pre-wedding plans were barreling ahead, full throttle.

One week before the ceremony, Kit and Jasper checked into a room at the Silver Legacy. Kit, who was on a short personal leave from Sassy Sally's, thought it would be more traditional and romantic if she and Danny spent time apart before tying the knot.

After the ceremony and reception at the Antique Angel Wedding Chapel, the new family would make the four-hour drive to San Francisco. Kit couldn't wait to stroll around Fisherman's Wharf, ride the cable cars, and take Jasper on a cruise around San Francisco Bay. It would be his first time seeing the ocean, and she was looking forward to his reaction.

A few nights before their nuptials, Danny and Kit dined at dusky, romantic Mario's Ristorante, on Virginia Street, with Kit's BFF, Rainey, and her husband, Justin Pickett, who'd flown in from Kokomo for the big day.

Over glasses of Chablis and a to-die-for antipasto tray, the topic du jour was the wedding, of course. But Justin and Rainey also revealed poignant details of their ongoing struggles to have a baby. IVF was expensive, difficult, and hadn't worked, so they were now considering surrogacy, with Justin's mom as the carrier. As Kit and Danny listened sympathetically and wished their friends well, they both felt grateful and relieved for Jasper.

Over the next week, Justin and Rainey reveled in every moment of their stay in Reno. Their room at the Silver Legacy was on the same floor as Kit and Jasper's. But Justin was rarely around. The buff electrician spent all his spare time in the casino, bonding with the Legacy's legendary video poker terminals. That was cool with bride-to-be Kit and her matron of honor, Rainey, who preferred giggling in the spa's hot tub, or chatting intimately over Diet Cokes and BLTs in the hotel's quaint diner.

Over lunch one day, Kit leaned in and revealed the shocking details of how she and Danny had met. Rainey's jaw was on the floor.

"Danny was a porch pirate?" she asked incredulously.

"Yes, for years, all over Vegas and the suburbs around it. In the summer of 2017, we broke up over it, but then we got back together after Danny moved up here."

"Oh, my God! He stole the crib Justin and I sent the baby?"

"Yes, that's how we met," Kit replied. "UPS had just delivered it, and I was trying to stop him after he took it. I fell down some steps in front of my apartment, and my water broke. I was in a lot of pain, and really scared that the baby was hurt. He ended up driving me to the hospital. I was crammed in the back seat of his car with all these packages on both sides, and sparks were sort of flying."

"That's either the most twisted first meeting story I've ever heard, or the most romantic!" Rainey gushed. "Justin and I met cute, too. We were in the lunchroom at Taylor High, and he was staring my way. I thought he was crushing on me, but what he really wanted was my Jell-O salad. It had more marshmallows than his—something like that. So I traded him for his fries, and moved to his table. Then I waited six months for him to ask me out!

"After that, we dated steadily till dude dumped me in junior year and started seeing that slut from Beech Grove, Angela Dorsey. But it didn't last. Three years later, he drove out to Vegas with a diamond ring, found me, and begged me to marry him. It took me about 10 seconds to say, 'yes!'"

"That long?" Kit asked.

They both giggled.

"We had some rocky times," Rainey admitted, tossing her hands up, "but it was meant to be."

"The road to true love was filled with major speed bumps for both of us, wasn't it?" Kit mused. "Bottom line, we ended up marrying the dudes, and, hopefully, living happily ever after with them!"

Laughing and clinking their Diet Cokes, the besties drank to that.

CHAPTER TWENTY-TWO

A few days before their wedding, Danny and Kit had waltzed into the Washoe County clerk's office on 9th Street to purchase a marriage license. They had also lined up a local justice of the peace to preside over the ceremony, which would start at 11 AM, followed by a Hawaiian luau reception at noon.

On the big day, April 20, 2019, weather conditions were typical Reno in springtime: 60 degrees, mild and overcast.

After a quick room-service breakfast, Kit and Jasper got ready for the Antique Angel. Fifty guests were expected that morning at the quaint, pink-awninged wedding chapel on the banks of the roaring Truckee River.

Kit's bridal party color was lavender. Back in Kokomo, Rainey had splurged on a drop-dead-glam, long-sleeved lace and taffeta mermaid gown in this shade. Kit's two bridesmaids, both Kitty Kat Babes, would saunter down the aisle in similar frocks.

The bride, meanwhile, would be swathed, head-to-toe, in vintage ivory-lace from Reno's upscale White Dove Bridal Boutique. Kit's romantic gown featured a fancy, layered bustle, long sleeves, and a low-cut, sweetheart neckline.

At 9 AM, rangy, hazel-eyed Justin, in a dapper gray suit, and chestnut-haired chubette, Rainey, poured into her stunning gown, sashayed into Kit and Jasper's room. As Justin helped a fidgety Jasper with his shirt and tie, Rainey made a beeline for Kit.

"Did you get any sleep last night?" she asked, while hugging her.

"Not really," Kit confided, shaking her head. "Too nervous and excited. I've dreamt about this day all my life. This may sound weird, but I wish my parents were here. I can't help thinking about them. Grandma Rose always told me how awful and sad their two-year marriage was. I don't want to make a mistake with mine. This is a huge step. I want to get it right."

"Just relax," Rainey said softly, wrapping her arm around her friend.

"Your parents were in their teens and expecting a baby they didn't want. Oh, sorry, I didn't mean that the way it sounded," Rainey added quickly.

"I know," Kit told her. "But from everything I've heard over the years, it's pretty much the truth."

"Anyway," Rainey went on, "what I meant to say was, It was a classic shotgun wedding. My mom told me you were born just three weeks later. That's a lot of stress for two eighteen-year-olds to handle. This is nothing like that.

"You're just having pre-wedding jitters," Rainey assured Kit. "It's totally normal. You know, weddings are a lot like funerals, kind of scary and emotional. They bring up the past, good or bad. But your marriage won't be anything like your parents'. You and Danny have a special bond, and there's Jasper. The three of you are already a family. It's all good, girl!"

The besties hugged again, and Kit felt better. Nodding and smiling, she poured cups of room-service tea for two.

"Thank God you're here to talk me off the ledge!" Kit said, chuckling.

"Just doing my job," Rainey chirped. "I'm the matron of honor."

After Kit's short, but intense, bout of cold feet, she got a grip and the wedding juggernaut rolled on. Plopped on the bed in the middle of her room was everything she was taking to the Antique Angel, from hair-styling tools and make-up, to her lace gown and veil. Kit, who would change at the chapel, was in jeans and a pale-pink sweater.

Ring bearer Jasper wore a white suit that was preciousness on steroids. Kit had dressed the blue-eyed tyke, who was turning four that day, earlier, and Justin had knotted his tie just right. But with the way the two were now tumbling around the floor and rough-housing, Kit just hoped the suit would still be in one piece by the time the ceremony started.

The stoked groom would wear a traditional, charcoal-gray pin-striped tuxedo with tails over a lavender shirt and tie. Coordinating suits, worn by his best man and groomsmen, would feature the same hues. Danny planned to dress at his apartment and drive to Antique Angel around 10:30 to meet Kit, who would arrive at 9.

Speaking of Danny, he'd gotten tanked at his bachelor dinner the night before at the Brewer's Cabinet, a rowdy brew pub on Arlington Avenue. His best man, a family friend from Vegas, and his two younger brothers, who would be his groomsmen, had attended, along with a dozen pals from both his jobs. The raucous blowout had finally wound down around three AM.

On wedding morning, all was quiet at the Potter apartment on Nevada Street as the groom-to-be slept it off. But then, at 6 AM sharp, his phone rang. Not his personal cell, but the louder, more jarring emergency dispatch line from Reno Ambulance.

"Oh, shit!" Danny cursed when he realized his beeper was going off, too. What could it be? He had to pick up.

"Hey, Potter," the dispatch operator barked, "There's a standoff with hostages going down at the Golden Garter. You need to get over there fast. Three armed gunmen stormed the count room and tried to get out of the casino with sacks of cash and chips. Security chased them down and a brawl broke out. The cops showed up and the robbers took hostages. That was two hours ago. They're still holding them. Gunshots have been fired. There may be casualties. The mess is ongoing. Can you get over there right now and stand by?"

Still trying to wake up from a deep sleep and the throbbing effects of last night's booze, Danny blurted, "Today's my wedding day."

"What time's the ceremony?"

"Eleven o'clock."

"That's five hours from now, you should be out of there by then."

"Famous last words," Danny cracked. "Why are you calling me? Isn't Shanahan working this weekend?"

"His wife's water broke last night," dispatch shot back. "It's their first kid. He's at the hospital, and we can't get him out of there. She's still deep in labor, there may be complications. We already have Tony Sanders over at the Garter, but we need back-up."

"Okay, I'll get there as fast as I can," Danny muttered, glancing at the clock.

There was no time for coffee or a shower. Leaping off the bed, Danny threw on jeans, a gray tee, and the aqua-blue shirt he'd taken off a few hours before. Pulling his sneakers on, he grabbed his tux, dress shirt, and shoes, and ran out the door. Head pounding in the frantic rush, he dropped his cell in the parking lot of his apartment building. Unaware, he kept going.

Jumping in his car, Danny sped to the Reno Ambulance building. After parking in the lot, he hopped in a yellow RAC ambulance truck that was waiting for him. Strewn on the passenger seat beside him was his wedding stuff. Gunning it, he raced to the Golden Garter on the north end of Sierra Street, near Clydesdale Avenue. At 7 AM, with a white lab jacket thrown over his rumpled clothes that still reeked of booze and smoke, Danny rushed inside.

Camped in the middle of the casino were three toughs holding bulging sacks of cash. Each had taken a lone hostage at gun point.

The tension was palpable, as players, staffers, and onlookers darted around or paced, anxiously waiting to see what would happen next.

119

The cops were trying to negotiate, but the bandits weren't interested. They wanted to flee the Garter with the money and a guarantee that nobody would follow them. For insurance, they would take the hostages. The negotiators refused to consider these terms.

Minute by minute, the standoff dragged on for two more terror-filled hours. Danny couldn't leave the gambling hall, which annoyed him hugely because it was his wedding day, he needed a shower, and he was dealing with the hangover from hell. While the negotiators were trying to convince the goddamn robbers to let the hostages go, a flame-haired cocktail waitress in a near-topless, purple mini-dress toted Styrofoam cups of hot coffee to Danny and the other first responders. It helped.

With the anger and hostility ramping up on both sides, Danny worried about whether he would make the wedding on time. Borrowing a cell, he called Kit. There was no answer, so he left a rushed, jumbled message, telling her he was in a crisis situation at the Golden Garter, and to stay put till he got to the chapel.

Finally, around 9:30, with tensions mounting, the cops brought in an armed SWAT team of a dozen officers. In a Trojan horse convoy of four Plexiglass carts, they rolled into the casino and down the center aisle from opposite directions. Halting in front of a bank of Sex And The City mega slots, the leader of the team grabbed a megaphone and issued three terse commands.

"Let the hostages go. Drop your guns and the cash. Put your hands up."

The robbers were incensed that their earlier demands were still being ignored. In defiance, they suddenly started firing their handguns randomly—and the cops fired back.

With shells bursting everywhere, the hellacious gun fight quickly turned the gambling hall into a war zone. Bystanders rushed about in a panic, screaming, yelling, and crying, while others dove for cover under poker tables, or hid behind slots and keno machines.

Fifteen chaotic, terrifying minutes later, the robbers realized this was a gun battle they weren't going to win. They suddenly stopped firing and dropped their guns. By then, one of them had been wounded in the shoulder, another in the back, and a hostage had been shot in the leg. Slack-jawed onlookers gaped in horror, or shielded their eyes at the sight of bloody bodies sprawled around bullet-riddled slots and video poker terminals.

Screams, groans, and cries still echoed throughout the cavernous casino, but the standoff was more or less resolved. The SWAT team moved in fast to recover the sacks of cash, seize the robbers' guns, cuff the one bandit still standing, and hustle him out of the casino.

Meanwhile, a crew of EMTs, and more ambulances, had arrived. Medical assistance was quickly given to the three gunshot victims, who were all bleeding profusely, but still conscious. Also in need of medical help were the two unharmed hostages, who were badly shaken.

In the midst of all this bloody EMT, and bustling police, activity, Garter staffers in purple uniforms began scurrying about, removing yellow crime-scene tape. Rushing to the shot-up slots, eager gamers shoved in player's cards and waited for the ringing bells and flickering lights to come on. All systems were apparently go. Despite the war zone turbulence, the indestructible machines were still functioning.

Outside the Garter's sliding-glass doors, a pair of loud ambulances, with a lone robber in each, were racing down the long driveway. The wounded hostage and his wife were in a third truck, with Danny at the wheel driving like a madman—emergency lights flashing and sirens blaring.

The ER at Truckee Memorial Trauma Center was bedlam. Both unshot hostages had been brought in by the cops. One was ranting incoherently into a cell, the other screaming hysterically at a wide-eyed nurse backed against a wall.

After all three gun-shot victims were safely checked in, Danny looked at his watch. It was 11:00, wedding time at the

Antique Angel. His heart sank. He could just imagine his beautiful bride and the dozens of guests waiting anxiously for him. He thought of borrowing a phone to call Kit again, but instead begged his co-worker and buddy, Tony, for a ride.

Moments later they sped away, Indy-500-like, with lights flashing and sirens blaring at full tilt. Tony was at the wheel, Danny in the passenger seat. With the big, bulky ambulance truck rocking and rolling like a sailboat in choppy seas, the groom-to-be struggled to peel off his work clothes and squeeze into a snug gray tux, cummerbund, and all the trimmings. In the cramped cab, it was an exercise in dexterity that he pulled off, even borrowing Tony's comb at one point to groom his disheveled hair as they barreled through the streets of downtown Reno.

Tony was skilled enough to get them to the chapel by 11:30. Flashing and blaring, the long, yellow ambulance screeched to a halt in front of the red-brick wedding chapel. Under its pink awning, the guests, who had been monitoring the standoff on their I-phones, whooped and hollered.

In his classic gray tux and lavender shirt, Danny leapt out the passenger door, flashed a double thumbs-up, and acknowledged the cheers. Then the breathless groom exclaimed, "Sorry I'm late, there was a robbery-standoff with hostages at the Golden Garter. Everything's okay now. I hope my bride is still here!"

With a smiling Tony beside him, Danny scanned the crowd. Standing before him were his mom, brothers, and best man, along with Cruz's mom and sister. Justin, Rainey, Mrs. Brambles, a few Kitty Kat Babes, and assorted co-workers from both his jobs were also there.

Then Danny saw Kit, and the sun finally broke through the clouds. She had been inside, talking to the justice of the peace. Making a beeline for her, he hugged and kissed his pretty bride. She looked stunning—and stunned—in her ivory lace gown and cathedral veil.

"Mommy, Danny, Mommy, Danny, wedding!" a grinning Jasper yelped as he stood at their feet with his arms encircling their legs.

"Hey, little man!" Danny said, reaching down and scooping up the boy. Hugging him, he turned to Kit and said softly, "Sorry, babe, it was an emergency. I tried to get out of it, but couldn't. Hope you're okay. You look like a princess in a fairy tale."

"I'm fine," she murmured, with tears in her eyes as she clutched his arm. "Just glad you're here and everything can get started. I got your message. Thank God, the judge could wait."

"Cool, let's get married!" Danny whooped.

Still holding Jasper, he grabbed Kit's hand and led her up the steps and into the chapel. Trailing behind were the amped-up guests, who quickly re-claimed their seats.

At the altar, the justice was waiting. Everyone, including ring-bearer Jasper, got into position. The organ player keyed in the wedding march and Kit, a vision in ivory lace, strode down the aisle with a long veil covering her pale, luminous face. In her hands was a lush bouquet of lavender roses and white daisies.

At the altar, a beaming Danny, with a rose pinned to his gray satin lapel, stood poised. Everyone, including Tony in his grease-stained overalls, had tears in their eyes as the couple recited their vows and slid white-gold wedding bands onto each other's fingers.

At the festive, Hawaiian-luau reception afterwards, everyone feasted on Pacific crab cakes, Hawaiian meatballs with Big Kahuna pasta salad, and mango-chicken kebabs with fried rice. Then it was time to cut the pina-colada wedding cake, with rich layers of coconut-cream frosting, and swirls of lavender flowers embellishing all three tiers.

As the warm, festive lunch wound down, Danny toasted his glowing bride. Kit then stood up. Hoisting a glass of Kona Crystal champagne in his direction, she gushed, "To my husband, Danny, the porch pirate who stole my heart!"

Made in the USA
Monee, IL
20 November 2022

18220931R00074